SIXTH EDITION

INTERACTIONS 2
Listening/Speaking

- Dictations
- Games

TEACHER'S MANUAL WITH TESTS

Judith Tanka
Lida R. Baker

Teacher's Manual by
Ingrid Wisniewska

Interactions 2 Listening/Speaking, Teacher's Manual with Tests, Sixth Edition

Published by McGraw-Hill ESL/ELT, a business unit of The McGraw-Hill Companies, Inc. 1221 Avenue of the Americas, New York, NY 10020. Copyright © 2013 by The McGraw-Hill Companies, Inc. All rights reserved. Printed in the United States of America. Previous editions © 2007, 2001, and 1995. No part of this publication may be reproduced or distributed in any form or by any means, or stored in a database or retrieval system, without the prior written consent of The McGraw-Hill Companies, Inc., including, but not limited to, in any network or other electronic storage or transmission, or broadcast for distance learning.

Some ancillaries, including electronic and print components, may not be available to customers outside the United States.

This book is printed on acid-free paper.

1 2 3 4 5 6 7 8 9 0 TK/TK 1 0 9 8 7 6 5 4 3
ISBN: 978-1-10-792193-1
MHID: 1-25-907046-8

Senior Vice President, Products & Markets: Kurt L. Strand
Vice President, General Manager, Products & Markets: Michael J. Ryan
Vice President, Content Production & Technology Services: Kimberly Meriwether David
Director of Development: Valerie Kelemen
Marketing Manager: Cambridge University Press
Lead Project Manager: Rick Hecker
Senior Buyer: Michael R. McCormick
Designer: Page2, LLC
Cover/Interior Designer: Page2, LLC
Senior Content Licensing Specialist: Keri Johnson
Manager, Digital Production: Janean A. Utley
Compositor: Page2, LLC
Printer: Yurchak

Cover photo: Anna Omelchenko/Shutterstock.com

The Internet addresses listed in the text were accurate at the time of publication. The inclusion of a website does not indicate an endorsement by the authors or McGraw-Hill, and McGraw-Hill does not guarantee the accuracy of the information presented at these sites.

www.mhhe.com

www.elt.mcgraw-hill.com

Table of Contents

Introduction
Welcome to the Teacher's Manual — iv
The Interactions/Mosaic Program — v
Best Practices — vii

Student Book Teaching Notes and Answer Keys

CHAPTER 1	Education and Student Life	2
CHAPTER 2	City Life	20
CHAPTER 3	Business and Money	38
CHAPTER 4	Jobs and Professionals	58
CHAPTER 5	Lifestyles Around the World	78
CHAPTER 6	Global Connections	96
CHAPTER 7	Language and Communication	112
CHAPTER 8	Tastes and Preferences	130
CHAPTER 9	New Frontiers	146
CHAPTER 10	Ceremonies	164

Black Line Masters — BLM 1
Chapter Tests — T1
Chapter Test Answer Key and Audioscripts — T30
Placement Test — T41
Placement Test Answer Key and Audioscripts — T49

Welcome to the Teacher's Manual

The Teacher's Manual of *Interactions/Mosaic* provides support and flexibility to teachers using the *Interactions/Mosaic* 18-book academic skills series. The Teacher's Manual provides step-by-step guidance for implementing each activity in the Student Book. The Teacher's Manual also provides expansion activities with photocopiable masters of select expansion activities, identification of activities that support a Best Practice, valuable notes on content, answer keys, audioscripts, end-of-chapter tests, and placement tests. Each chapter in the Teacher's Manual begins with an overview of the content, vocabulary, and teaching goals in that chapter. Each chapter in the Student Book begins with an engaging photo and related discussion questions that strengthen the educational experience and connect students to the topic.

- **Procedural Notes**

  The procedural notes are useful for both experienced and new teachers. Experienced teachers can use the bulleted, step-by step procedural notes as a quick guide and refresher before class, while newer or substitute teachers can use the notes as a more extensive guide to assist them in the classroom. The procedural notes guide teachers through each strategy and activity; describe what materials teachers might need for an activity; and help teachers provide context for the activities.

- **Answer Keys**

  Answer keys are provided for all activities that have definite answers. For items that have multiple correct answers, various possible answers are provided. The answer key follows the procedural note for the relevant activity. Answer keys are also provided for the Chapter Tests and the Placement Tests.

- **Expansion Activities**

  A number of expansion activities with procedural notes are included in each chapter. These activities offer teachers creative ideas for reinforcing the chapter content while appealing to different learning styles. Activities include games, conversation practice, presentations, and projects. These expansion activities often allow students to practice integrated language skills, not just the skills that the student book focuses on. Some of the expansion activities include photocopiable black line masters included in the back of the book.

- **Content Notes**

  Where appropriate, content notes are included in the Teacher's Manual. These are notes that might illuminate or enhance a learning point in the activity and might help teachers answer student questions about the content. These notes are provided at the logical point of use, but teachers can decide if and when to use the information in class.

- **Chapter Tests**

  Each chapter includes a chapter test that was designed to test the vocabulary, reading, writing, grammar, and/or listening strategies taught in the chapter, depending on the language skill strand being used. Teachers can simply copy and distribute the tests, then use the answer keys found in the Teacher's Manual. The purpose of the chapter tests is not only to assess students' understanding of material covered in the chapter but also to give students an idea of how they are doing and what they need to work on. Each chapter test has four parts with items totaling 100 points. Item types include multiple choice, fill-in-the blank, and true/false. Audioscripts are provided when used.

- **Black Line Masters (Photocopiable Masters)**

  Each chapter includes a number of expansion activities with black line masters, or master worksheets, that teachers can copy and distribute. These activities and black line masters are optional. They can help reinforce and expand on chapter material in an engaging way. Activities include games; conversation practice; working with manipulatives such as sentence strips; projects; and presentations. Procedural notes and answer keys (when applicable) are provided in the Teacher's Manual.

- **Placement Tests**
Each of the four language skill strands has a placement test designed to help assess in which level the student belongs. Each test has been constructed to be given in under an hour. Be sure to go over the directions and answer any questions before the test begins. Students are instructed not to ask questions once the test begins. Following each placement test, you'll find a scoring placement key that suggests the appropriate book to be used based on the number of items answered correctly. Teachers should use judgment in placing students and selecting texts.

The Interactions/Mosaic Program

Interactions/Mosaic is a fully-integrated, 18-book academic skills series. Language proficiencies are articulated from the beginning through advance levels <u>within</u> each of the four language skill strands. Chapter themes articulate <u>across</u> the four skill strands to systematically recycle content, vocabulary, and grammar.

- **Reading Strand**
Reading skills and strategies are strategically presented and practiced through a variety of themes and reading genres in the five Reading books. Pre-reading, reading, and post-reading activities include strategies and activities that aid comprehension, build vocabulary, and prepare students for academic success. Each chapter includes at least two readings that center around the same theme, allowing students to deepen their understanding of a topic and command of vocabulary related to that topic. Readings include magazine articles, textbook passages, essays, letters, and website articles. They explore, and guide the student to explore, stimulating topics. Vocabulary is presented before each reading and is built on throughout the chapter. High-frequency words and words from the Academic Word List are focused on and pointed out with asterisks (*) in each chapter's Self-Assessment Log.

- **Listening/Speaking Strand**
A variety of listening input, including lectures, academic discussions, and conversations help students explore stimulating topics in the five Listening/Speaking books. Activities associated with the listening input, such as pre-listening tasks, systematically guide students through strategies and critical thinking skills that help prepare them for academic achievement. In the Interactions books, the activities are coupled with instructional photos featuring a cast of engaging, multi-ethnic students participating in North American college life. Across the strand, lectures and dialogues are broken down into manageable parts giving students an opportunity to predict, identify main ideas, and effectively manage lengthy input. Questions, guided discussion activities, and structured pair and group work stimulate interest and interaction among students, often culminating in organizing their information and ideas in a graphic organizer, writing, and/or making a presentation to the class. Pronunciation is highlighted in every chapter, an aid to improving both listening comprehension and speaking fluency. Enhanced focus on vocabulary building is developed throughout and a list of target words for each chapter is provided so students can interact meaningfully with the material. Finally, Online Learning Center features MP3 files from the Student Book audio program for students to download onto portable digital audio players.

- **Writing Strand**

  Activities in each of the four Writing books are systematically structured to culminate in a *Writing Product* task. Activities build on key elements of writing from sentence development to writing single paragraphs, articles, narratives, and essays of multiple lengths and genres. Connections between writing and grammar tie the writing skill in focus with the grammar structures needed to develop each writing skill. Academic themes, activities, writing topics, vocabulary development, and critical thinking strategies prepare students for university life. Instructional photos are used to strengthen engagement and the educational experience. Explicit pre-writing questions and discussions activate prior knowledge, help organize ideas and information, and create a foundation for the writing product. Each chapter includes a self-evaluation rubric which supports the learner as he or she builds confidence and autonomy in academic writing. Finally, the Writing Articulation Chart helps teachers see the progression of writing strategies both in terms of mechanics and writing genres.

- **Grammar Strand**

  Questions and topical quotes in the four Grammar books, coupled with instructional photos stimulate interest, activate prior knowledge, and launch the topic of each chapter. Engaging academic topics provide context for the grammar and stimulate interest in content as well as grammar. A variety of activity types, including individual, pair, and group work, allow students to build grammar skills and use the grammar they are learning in activities that cultivate critical thinking skills. Students can refer to grammar charts to review or learn the form and function of each grammar point. These charts are numbered sequentially, formatted consistently, and indexed systematically, providing lifelong reference value for students.

- **Focus on Testing for the TOEFL® iBT**

  The TOEFL® iBT *Focus on Testing* sections prepare students for success on the TOEFL® iBT by presenting and practicing specific strategies for each language skill area. The Focus on Testing sections are introduced in Interactions 1 and are included in all subsequent levels of the Reading, Listening/Speaking, and Writing strands. These strategies focus on what The Educational Testing Service (ETS) has identified as the target skills in each language skill area. For example, "reading for basic comprehension" (identifying the main idea, understanding pronoun reference) is a target reading skill and is presented and practiced in one or more *Focus on Testing* sections. In addition, this and other target skills are presented and practiced in chapter components outside the *Focus on Testing* sections and have special relevance to the TOEFL® iBT. For example, note-taking is an important testtaking strategy, particularly in the listening section of the TOEFL® iBT, and is included in activities within each of the Listening/Speaking books. All but two of the *Interactions/Mosaic* titles have a *Focus on Testing* section. Although *Interactions Access Reading* and *Interaction Access Listening/Speaking* don't include these sections because of their level, they do present and develop skills that will prepare students for the TOEFL® iBT.

- **Best Practices**

  In each chapter of this Teacher's Manual, you'll find Best Practices boxes that highlight a particular activity and show how this activity is tied to a particular Best Practice. The team of writers, editors, and teacher consultants has identified the following six interconnected Best Practices.

* TOEFL® is a registered trademark of Educational Testing Services (ETS). This product is not endorsed or approved by ETS.

Interactions/Mosaic Best Practices

Best Practices
Each chapter identifies at least six different activities that support six Best Practices, principles that contribute to excellent language teaching and learning. Identifying Best Practices helps teachers to see, and make explicit for students, how a particular activity will aid the learning process.

Making Use of Academic Content
Materials and tasks based on academic content and experiences give learning real purpose. Students explore real world issues, discuss academic topics, and study content-based and thematic materials.

Organizing Information
Students learn to organize thoughts and notes through a variety of graphic organizers that accommodate diverse learning and thinking styles.

Scaffolding Instruction
A scaffold is a physical structure that facilitates construction of a building. Similarly, scaffolding instruction is a tool used to facilitate language learning in the form of predictable and flexible tasks. Some examples include oral or written modeling by the teacher or students, placing information in a larger framework, and reinterpretation.

Activating Prior Knowledge
Students can better understand new spoken or written material when they connect to the content. Activating prior knowledge allows students to tap into what they already know, building on this knowledge, and stirring a curiosity for more knowledge.

Interacting with Others
Activities that promote human interaction in pair work, small group work, and whole class activities present opportunities for real world contact and real world use of language.

Critical Thinking
Strategies for critical thinking are taught explicitly. Students learn tools that promote critical thinking skills crucial to success in the academic world.

CHAPTER 1
Education and Student Life

In this CHAPTER

Students will read about different aspects of education and student life, such as having a conversation with another student, academic honesty, accepting and refusing invitations, and finding their way on campus. In Part 1, they will learn to recognize stressed and reduced forms and practice ways of asking for clarification. In Part 2, they will listen to a lecture about academic honesty in North America and discuss the issue of plagiarism. In Part 3, they will practice getting meaning from context and through intonation by listening to a variety of conversations. In Part 4, they will learn how to understand and describe locations. The topics in this chapter will encourage students to discuss various aspects of their student life.

Chapter Opener

- Have students look at the photo of the students graduating. Ask them the questions from the Connecting to the Topic section. Have students discuss as a class.
- Read and discuss the quotation by William Butler Yeats (1865–1939) on page 2. Ask students to explain the quotation in their own words. A possible interpretation is that a person's education does not end. It is like a fire that can continue to grow as long as it is fed. It is not like a bucket which can only hold a certain amount before it is full.

> "Education is not the filling of a bucket but the lighting of a fire."
>
> William Butler Yeats
> Irish poet and dramatist

Chapter Overview

Listening Skills and Strategies
Listening for main ideas and details

Getting meaning from intonation

Recognizing compass directions

Understanding expressions and statements of location

Using the prepositions *in*, *on*, and *at* in addresses and locations

Speaking Skills and Strategies
Asking for clarification

Discussing personal views on academic honesty and cheating in the U.S.

Talking about academic honesty in different countries' education systems

Using expressions of location

Describing map locations

Critical-Thinking Skills
Interpreting a photo

Using a lecture introduction to predict content

Taking effective lecture notes using indentation, keywords, and abbreviations and symbols

Using a Venn diagram to compare and contrast

Getting meaning from context

Vocabulary Building
Terms for academic life

Terms for writing papers and academic honesty

Expressions for making, accepting, and refusing invitations

Compass directions

Expressions of location

In, *on*, and *at* in addresses and locations

Pronunciation
Identifying and practicing stressed words

Identifying and practicing reduced pronunciation

Language Skills
Using context clues to guess information from conversations

Vocabulary

Nouns
- dormitory
- identification
- major
- penalty
- plagiarism
- quotation marks
- source
- syllabus
- term paper

Verbs
- avoid
- cite
- cut and paste
- expect
- fill out
- get caught
- give credit
- paraphrase
- quote
- rush
- summarize
- works out

Adjective
- unique

Expressions
- for short
- pretty good/ pretty well

TOEFL® is a registered trademark of Educational Testing Service (ETS). This product is not endorsed or approved by ETS.

PART 1   Conversation: On a College Campus   Student Book pages 4–5

Can You Guess?

- Ask students to discuss the questions below in groups and compare their answers with the correct answers.
- Discuss the issues raised by these questions: Do people think that an old university is better than a new one? Is this belief justified? What factors affect the numbers of international students? What factors affect the numbers of male and female graduates?

1. What is the oldest university in the world? **A.** *The University of Al-Karaouine in Morocco may be the oldest university in the world. It was founded in A.D. 859. Europe's oldest university was founded in the northern Italian city of Bologna in 1088.*

   (Source: http://collegestats.org/articles/2009/12/top-10-oldest-universities-in-the-world-ancient-colleges/)

2. What is the percentage of international students at U.S. universities? **A.** *International students make up about 8 percent of the total student enrollment at U.S. universities. The University of Southern California has the largest number of international students (8615 in 2010/2011).*

   (Source: http://www.iie.org/en/Research-and-Publications/Open-Doors/Data)

3. Are more U.S. university graduates men or women? **A.** *In 2010, 36 percent of women ages 25–29 held a bachelor's degree compared with only 28 percent of men.*

   (Source: http://www.pewsocialtrends.org/2011/08/17/)

Before You Listen

Best Practice

Activating Prior Knowledge

- The prelistening questions activate students' prior knowledge. This type of activity will help students relate their own experience of starting conversations with strangers to the new language in this chapter. When students activate their prior knowledge before learning new material, they are better able to map new language onto existing concepts, which aids understanding and retention.

① Prelistening Questions

- Ask a few volunteers from the class to describe the people and the location shown in the picture.
- Have students work in groups to read the questions and discuss them.
- Compare answers as a whole class.
- As a whole class, make a list of ways to start a conversation with a stranger. Organize the list under topic headings such as verbal, nonverbal, weather, sports, asking for help or information.

Culture Note

- Read the information in the box with the class.
- It may be of interest to students to discuss the university system in the U.S. and in other countries; for example, entry requirements, length and dates of semesters, credits, exams, fees, and funding.

② Previewing Vocabulary

- Play the recording and ask students to listen for the underlined words.
- Have students complete the vocabulary preview individually.
- Check answers as a whole class.

4   CHAPTER 1   Copyright © McGraw-Hill

Student Book page 5

- Ask students for examples for each item. For example:
  1. What forms of *identification* do you carry?
  2. Is anyone in this class called a name *for short*?
  3. What is or will be your *major*?
  4. Who *works out*? What do you do?
  5. What do the rooms in most *dormitories* look like?
  6. What is the last thing that you had to *fill out*?
  7. When is the last time that you were in a *rush*?
  8. What is the last movie that you saw that was *pretty good*?

ANSWER KEY
1. d 2. h 3. b 4. f 5. a 6. c 7. e 8. g

Listen

❸ Comprehension Questions

- Explain that these questions will help students focus on the main ideas in the listening. They do not need to understand every word to answer the questions.
- Read the questions aloud.
- Play the recording.
- Have students quickly write down the answer to each question and play the recording again for students to confirm their answers.
- Have students compare their answers in pairs.
- Check the answers as a class.

ANSWER KEY
1. Mari is in a building on a college campus. She is there to take an English placement test.
2. A woman who is checking students into the exam room asks her for identification.
3. Alex is another student who is taking the test. He is from Mexico.
4. Her grandmother is American.
5. Mari's major is business administration. Alex's is the same.
6. The gym is next to the Student Center, across from the grad dorms.
7. They will go to the gym.

AUDIOSCRIPT

Nancy: Good morning! Are you here for the English placement test?
Mari: Yes, I am.
Nancy: What's your name?
Mari: Mariko Honda.
Nancy: Could I see some identification?
Mari: Is my passport OK?
Nancy: Yes. All right... let me find your name on our list... OK Mariko, you can go in. The test will start in about ten minutes.
Mari: Thank you.
Mari: Excuse me, is this seat taken?
Alex: Pardon?
Mari: Is anyone sitting here?
Alex: Ah, no.
Mari: Thanks. I'm glad the test hasn't started yet. I thought I was going to be late.
Alex: Me too. I had to rush here to be on time. I'm Alex, by the way.
Mari: Oh, nice to meet you. My name is Mariko. Or just Mari, for short.
Alex: Nice to meet you, Mari.
Mari: Where are you from?
Alex: Mexico. And you?
Mari: Japan.
Alex: Really? Your English accent is really good.

PART 1

Mari:	Oh, that's because my grandmother is American. We always spoke English when I was little, so I can speak pretty well, but my reading and writing are really weak.
Alex:	I see. So, um, are you planning to go to college here?
Mari:	Yes, exactly.
Alex:	What's your major?
Mari:	Business administration. How about you?
Alex:	The same!
Mari:	Cool! How long have you been studying here?
Alex:	You mean in the English program?
Mari:	Yeah.
Alex:	This is my second semester.
Mari:	Oh, so you know the campus pretty well?
Alex:	Oh, yeah.
Mari:	Could you tell me how to get to the gym? I want to go work out after the test.
Alex:	The gym? Yeah, it's next to the Student Center, across from the grad dorms.
Mari:	Sorry... the what?
Alex:	The grad dorms. Um, the dormitories for graduate students. Here, I can show you on the campus map...
Mari:	That's OK, I know.
Alex:	I'm actually planning to go there, too. Want to go together?
Mari:	Sounds great.
Announcement:	Good morning everyone. The test is going to start in about five minutes. Please put away your cell phones, iPads, all electronic devices. Start filling out the green information sheet and raise your hand if you have any questions. I or one of the other teachers will be happy to help you.
Alex:	The green paper... here it is. Well, good luck on the test.
Mari:	Thanks, you too.

Stress

Focus

- Read aloud the instruction notes and practice the example sentence.
- Play the recording and ask students to listen and repeat the sentence they hear.
- Write these sentences on the board. Say them aloud and ask students to identify the stressed words.

What's your **name**?
Where are you **from**?
I'm a **student**?
Nice to **meet** you.

4 Listening for Stressed Words

- Tell students that they will listen to part of the conversation from Activity 3 again and fill in the missing stressed words. Tell students to read the conversation first and notice the words that are missing.
- Listen to the recording as students follow along in their books.
- Pauses on the recording will allow time for students to repeat and write the missing words.
- After listening, have students check their answers with the audioscript on page 263 in their books.
- Have students read the conversation with a partner, paying attention to stressed words in their pronunciation.

pp. 6-7

AUDIOSCRIPT and ANSWER KEY

Mari:	<u>Excuse</u> me, is <u>this</u> seat taken?
Alex:	Pardon?
Mari:	Is anyone <u>sitting</u> here?
Alex:	Ah, no.
Mari:	Thanks. I'm <u>glad</u> the test hasn't <u>started</u> yet. I thought I was going to be <u>late</u>.

Student Book pages 5–8

Alex:	Me too. I had to _rush_ here to be on _time_. I'm Alex, by the way.
Mari:	Oh, _nice_ to _meet_ you. _My_ name is Mariko. Or just Mari, for _short_.
Alex:	Nice to meet you, Mari.
Mari:	_Where_ are _you_ from?
Alex:	Mexico. And _you_?
Mari:	Japan.
Alex:	Really? Your English _accent_ is really good.
Mari:	Oh, _that's_ because my _grandmother_ is American. We _always_ spoke English when I was _little_, so I can _speak_ pretty well, but my _reading_ and writing are really _weak_.
Alex:	I see. So, um, are you planning to go to _college_ here?
Mari:	Yes, _exactly_.
Alex:	What's your _major_?
Mari:	_Business_ administration. How about _you_?
Alex:	The _same_!
Mari:	Cool! How long have you been _studying_ here?
Alex:	You mean in the _English_ program?
Mari:	Yeah.
Alex:	This is my _second_ semester.
Mari:	Oh, so you know the _campus_ pretty well?
Alex:	Oh, yeah.
Mari:	Could you _tell_ me how to _get_ to the _gym_? I want to go work _out_ after the _test_.
Alex:	The _gym_? Yeah, it's next to the _Student_ Center, _across_ from the grad dorms.
Mari:	Sorry… the _what_?
Alex:	The grad dorms. Um, the _dormitories_ for graduate students. Here, I can show you on the campus map…
Mari:	That's OK, I _know_.
Alex:	I'm actually planning to go there, _too_. Want to go _together_?
Mari:	Sounds _great_.

 A good icebreaker for 2nd lesson

Expansion Activity

- The purpose of this activity is for students to get to know each other, to establish shared goals for the class, and to practice starting conversations and ways of showing interest.
- Please see Black Line Master "Class Survey" on page BLM 1 of this Teacher's Manual. Photocopy and cut it into strips.
- Give one strip to each student. There are ten different questions. If you have more than ten students, have students work in pairs or threes.
- Ask two or three students the first question, _Excuse me. Why do you want to study English?_ and model taking notes of the answers.
- Explain that the aim is for each student to ask everyone in the class.
- Have students walk around the room (with their notebooks and pens with them) and ask other students their question, taking notes on the answers.
- At the end of the activity, they will report to the class on the information they have collected. For example, _I found out that most students want to…_

Reductions

FOCUS

Reductions

- Read aloud the instruction note.
- Play the recording and ask students to repeat the reduced forms.

PART 1

Student Book pages 8–9

Content Note

Some students may think of reduced forms as incorrect. Emphasize that these forms are commonly used in spoken English and it is important to be able to understand them. It is not essential for communication to use them, but if they do not use reduced forms, their English may sound too formal.

5 Comparing Unreduced and Reduced Pronunciation

- Play the recording and have students listen and read the sentences.
- Play the recording again and have students repeat the sentences.
- Listen carefully and correct pronunciation as a group.
- You can also have students volunteer to repeat the sentences individually.

6 Listening for Reductions

- Have students read through the conversation and try to guess the missing reduced words.
- Play the recording and have students write their answers.
- After listening, have students check their answers with the audioscript on page 264 in their books. Check the answers as a whole class.
- Have students practice the conversation in pairs, paying attention to reduced forms in their pronunciation.

pp. 8-9

AUDIOSCRIPT and ANSWER KEY

1.
Student: Hi. I'm here _to_ take the English placement test.
Teacher: OK. _What is your_ name?
Student: Phailin Montri.
Teacher: _Could you_ spell that for me, please?

2.
Paul: I _have to_ leave early tomorrow. This morning I _had to_ rush to catch the bus and I was almost late _to_ work.
Marine: What time are you _going to_ leave?
Paul: Around 7:30.

3.
Lara: Ann, this is my friend Richard.
Richard: Nice _to meet you_. Where are you from?
Ann: Toronto.
Richard: Oh, _you mean_ you're Canadian?
Ann: Right.

After You Listen

7 Reviewing Vocabulary

- Have students ask and answer the questions in pairs.
- Ask pairs to report to the class on their partner's answers. Make sure that they include the underlined vocabulary words in their answers.

Using Language Functions

FOCUS

Asking for Clarification

- Read the instruction note. Then read aloud each expression, modeling appropriate rising intonation on each.
- Say something to a few students that is difficult to hear. Have them respond with one of the expressions. Correct their pronunciation and intonation as necessary.
- Point out that the expressions *What?* and *Huh?* are very informal and should only be used among friends and informal company. These would be inappropriate when speaking to a teacher or employer.

Student Book pages 9–10

Content Note

Point out that when asking for clarification, English speakers often use non-verbal language. For example, they might step closer to the speaker, cock their head in that person's direction, or look questioningly at the speaker. Ask students to mime the non-verbal language that they use in their culture when asking for clarification. Explain that non-verbal language, like verbal language, has to be learned and used appropriately in different cultures.

Best Practice

Interacting with Others

The Focus activity is an example of collaborative learning to encourage fluency and confidence. In this activity, designed to practice verbal and non-verbal ways of asking for clarification, communication is more important than grammar. Students can practice these strategies in pairs and then improve their performance by switching roles or partners. By providing feedback to each other, they learn skills of self-evaluation.

8 Asking for Clarification

- Read the instructions aloud. Divide the class into groups of three or four.
- In each group, one student will talk about a topic of their choice for two minutes while the other students listen and ask for clarification as necessary and for practice. Then students rotate roles so that each student in the group practices speaking and listening.
- Make sure students understand the task and their roles by asking one or two students to repeat the instructions back to you.
- Set a time limit of 20 minutes.
- Monitor the groups as they are doing the activity and make notes of errors.
- At the end of the activity, ask a representative from each group to report back on ways of asking for clarification. Which ones were used the most? Which ones were used the least?

PART 2 Lecture: Academic Honesty

Student Book pages 10–12

Before You Listen

- Read aloud the information above the photo.
- Ask for some suggestions about what kind of information a professor might give about academic honesty.
- Ask students to look at the picture and describe what the man and the woman are doing. Ask students what they think about cheating.

Culture Note

Honor Code

- Read aloud the information in the Culture Note box.
- Explain that cheating and receiving help on papers and examinations is viewed differently in different cultures. In the U.S., it is considered dishonest and students can be punished for it. How is this viewed in the students' cultures? Do universities in their countries have similar honor codes?

Best Practice

Making Use of Academic Content

The prelistening discussion helps to stimulate students' ideas about the topic. Thinking about and discussing their existing notions will help students prepare to understand new ideas and opinions about a topic.

1 Prelistening Discussion

- Read aloud the instructions and the situations as a class. Check for comprehension of the situations and explain any new words.
- Have students decide individually if each action is okay to do and write a "+" or a "–" next to it. Then have students form groups of three or four to discuss their opinions.
- Review students' opinions as a class. Take a poll to see how many students believe that each situation is acceptable.

2 Previewing Vocabulary

- Play the recording and ask students to listen to the words.
- Have students check any words that they don't know. Then have students compare answers with a partner and explain words to each other if they can. Tell them that they will work out the meaning of the new words by listening to the lecture and doing the activities that follow.

Listen

Strategy

Using the Introduction to Predict Lecture Content

- Read aloud the information in the Strategy box. Explain that a lecture is organized in the same way as an essay. Elicit from students the format they follow when writing an essay. Tell them to imagine that a lecture is simply an essay that is being read aloud. One difference, however, as explained by the Note is that sometimes the lecturer will include bits of extra information that are not part of the lecture. Students must listen and be able to tell the difference.
- Answer any questions. Tell students that they will practice using a lecture introduction to predict content in the next activity.

3 Taking Notes on the Introduction

- Call students' attention to the photo at the bottom of the page. Ask students what is happening in the picture. Explain that this is a college classroom and the students are listening to a lecture. Ask if this is what college classrooms look like in the students' countries.

- Read aloud the instructions. Explain that students will listen to the introduction of a lecture and practice listening and taking notes. Point out the note paper on the page and tell students that they will be listening for the general topic of the lecture and the main ideas that the speaker will talk about.
- Ask students to close their books and listen to the lecture. Then have students open their books and take notes on the lecture as you play the recording a second time.
- Ask students to compare their notes with a classmate. Then go over the answers as a class.

> **ANSWER KEY**
>
> **General topic of the lecture:** academic honesty
>
> **Main ideas that the speaker will talk about:** types of cheating, how to avoid it, and what can happen if you get caught

AUDIOSCRIPT

Teacher: Good morning. Welcome to English 4. How's everyone doing? Did everyone get a chance to look at the course syllabus online? No? OK, well since this is our first meeting, I'd like to go over a couple of things quickly. First, if you looked at the syllabus, then you saw that we're going to do a lot of writing in this course—at least four essays and a term paper. And you probably saw that I said something about academic honesty also. Did you get that? Actually, I'd like to spend a little time on that topic right now, just to be sure. I mean, everyone knows that cheating is not okay, but I want to go over the specific types of cheating that students are sometimes confused about—especially international students who come from different cultures, with different customs. So let's talk about types of cheating, how to avoid it and finally, about what can happen if you get caught.

> ## Strategy
>
>
>
> **Three Keys to Writing Effective Lecture Notes**
>
> - Read the information in the Strategy box.
> - Give examples for each point (see below).
> - Ask students to explain each key in their own words.
>
> Indentation (example):
>
> Academic Honesty
>   1. Types of cheating
>   2. How to avoid it
>   3. What can happen if you get caught
>
> Key words (example)
> *plagiarism, source, penalty*
>
> Abbreviations and symbols (example):
>   & = and; @ = at (for other abbreviations, see page 262 in the Student Book.)

4 Taking Effective Lecture Notes (Part 1)

- Read aloud the instructions.
- Play the recording. Have students take notes in the space provided, using keywords, abbreviations, and indentation.

AUDIOSCRIPT

Teacher: To start, who can give me some examples of cheating?

Student A: Um, copying test answers from another student…

Teacher: Yes, obviously…

Student B: Using notes during an exam.

Teacher: Yeah, what else?

Student C: Copying homework from a classmate?

Teacher: Right. What else?

Student: Texting the answers to someone.

Teacher: Yes. That's why I don't allow students to use phones in my class. Anything else?

PART 2

Student Book pages 13–15

Teacher: What about plagiarism? It's right here at the bottom of my syllabus: P-L-A-G-I-A-R-I-S-M. This is especially important in a writing class. Plagiarism means using other people's paragraphs, sentences or unique ideas as your own writing. In other words, it's borrowing other peoples' writing or ideas and not using quotation marks or saying where you found them. So now let me ask you: Are these things considered plagiarism? One: cutting and pasting information from a website.

Class: Yes.

Teacher: Right. OK, two: copying information from a book, magazine, newspaper or any other published source.

Class: Yes/No.

Teacher: The answer is yes. I'll explain why in a minute. OK, next: buying an essay or term paper online, you know, from places like easyessays.com and services like that.

Class: Yes.

Teacher: Good. In addition, asking your friend or cousin to write your essay or term paper is also plagiarism. And this includes asking them to write several sentences or paragraphs for you, even if it's not the whole paper. Now, I want to mention that people in different cultures think of cheating, of plagiarism, in different ways. In some traditional cultures in Asia and the Middle East, teachers expect students to use words and ideas of famous, well-respected people. And they're not expected to change those words or even mention the source. That's because the teachers already should know where the words came from. But in Western cultures, we believe that words and original ideas belong to their owners. You know, like this computer on my desk here belongs to me. The same with my ideas. If you repeat my ideas, you need to give me credit. You need to mention my name, that you got it from me. And that's what I want to talk about next. How to give credit, how to mention the source so that you can avoid plagiarism.

5 Identifying the Three Keys to Taking Effective Lecture Notes

- Look at the notes on page 14 as a class. Explain that the notes are written by two different students, listening to the same lecture. The notes contain the same information, but one is easier to read. Elicit that Student A's notes are better because they use indentation, keywords, and abbreviations. Ask students to find examples of each key in Student A's notes.

- Have students work with a partner to compare their own notes with their partner's and also with the notes of Student A and Student B in their book. Tell them to identify good things in their notes, but also how they could be improved.

6 Taking Effective Lecture Notes (Part 2)

- Read aloud the instructions. Look at the outline on page 15 as a class. Explain that this outline shows how to organize their notes. Tell students that they will listen to the second part of the lecture and fill in the outline.

- Play the recording. Have students listen and fill in the outline.

- Play the recording again. Pause the recording after each main point to allow students time to write.

- Have students compare their outlines with a partner. Go over the answers with the whole class. Sample answers are below.

ANSWER KEY

I. How to avoid plagiarism
   A. Show <u>sent. & ideas not yours</u>
      1. <u>quote = use exact words</u>
      2. <u>use quotation marks</u>
   B. Summarize / Paraphrase
      1. This means <u>you present orig. info in own words</u>
      2. <u>change vocab & grammar</u>
      3. <u>don't change meaning</u>
   C. Remember to cite sources
      1. <u>who said orig. words</u>

Student Book pages 14–16

2. where you found them
   a. website: web address & date visited
   b. article: newspaper, writer, date, page, etc.

AUDIOSCRIPT

Teacher: OK, so let's talk about how to avoid plagiarism.

To show clearly that sentences or ideas are not yours, there are two things you can do. One, you can quote them. Quote means repeating a speaker's exact words. If you do this, you have to put quotation marks at the beginning and at the end of the text you're quoting. Like these.

The second thing you can do is paraphrase or summarize the original text. Basically this means presenting the original information but in your own way, using your own words. So you can change the original vocabulary, the original grammar, but you can't change the original meaning. And you can't add your opinion to it. For example, if I say "We're going to have a test two weeks from today," the paraphrase would be "The teacher is going to give an exam the week after next." See how I changed the sentence but not the meaning? This was a simple example, but paraphrasing and summarizing are not easy to do. I'll teach you some specific ways later this semester.

And finally—and this is really important—whether you use an exact quote or paraphrase or summarize, always remember to cite sources. By cite, I mean give information about who said the original words and where you found them. If the information came from a website, give the web address and the date you visited the website. If it's from a newspaper article, of course you'll need to cite the name of the newspaper, the name of the writer, the date, the page, etcetera. Don't worry; later in this course, I'll teach you exactly how to do this as well, you know, how to cite sources in the right way.

OK, I think you all got my point. I want you to produce original work in my class. I don't expect perfect writing, just honest, original work. If you don't, if you cheat, I'll have to follow university rules. And I'm sorry to say, the rules, the penalties, are very strict. Let's talk about those next.

After You Listen

7 Reviewing Vocabulary

- Look back at the vocabulary list in the Student Book, Activity 2 on page 11.
- Have students work in small groups to ask each other questions about the new vocabulary. Tell them to find the words in the lecture and study the context to guess the meanings.

Example:

Student A: What is plagiarism?
Student B: Using other people's paragraphs, sentences or unique ideas as your own writing.
Student C: That's right.

Strategy

Graphic Organizer: Venn Diagram
- Read the information in the Strategy box about Venn diagrams.
- You may want to draw an example on the board, using a different topic such as subjects studied at school and university.

8 Discussing the Lecture

- Read aloud the instructions. Tell students that they will create a Venn diagram to compare their country's rules and customs related to academic honesty with the rules in the lecture.
- Read through the list of topics to discuss. Assign one or two topics to each group (depending on how many groups are in the class). Tell the groups to discuss their topic(s) and create a Venn diagram for each.
- Move around the room and monitor students' work.
- Have a volunteer from each group draw their Venn diagrams on the board and explain them to the class.

PART 2

Student Book page 16

On the Spot!

9 What Would You Do?

- Explain to students that when you're "on the spot," you have to make a difficult decision. In the On the Spot! activities in this book, students will work with classmates to solve difficult problems or discuss difficult situations.
- Read the situation with the class, or ask students to read it silently.
- Give students ten minutes to read the questions in groups and discuss their answers.
- Groups can decide who will report on each of the questions. (Try to make sure every student gets a chance to speak.)
- Brainstorm a list of different possible reactions to this situation and write them on the board.

Best Practice

Cultivating Critical Thinking

This is an example of a collaborative team activity. This type of activity requires students to process the information they have learned and apply it to a situation that could happen in real life. It involves reinterpretation, synthesis, and application of concepts. The process of comparing different viewpoints on the topic of plagiarism, trying to reach agreement, and listing alternative courses of action will help develop critical thinking skills.

Content Note

The definition of plagiarism varies in different cultures. Students may understand this concept differently, or the issue may have different ethical implications for them. It is important not to assume that all plagiarism is intentional. On the other hand, students should be aware that plagiarism in homework or on tests is treated very seriously at North American colleges and can have serious consequences.

Expansion Activity

- The aim of this activity is to help students understand the concept and definition of plagiarism within a North American cultural context and its possible consequences.
- See Black Line Master "What is Plagiarism?" on page BLM 2 of this Teacher's Manual. Photocopy and distribute one to each student.
- Divide students into groups of four and have each person in the group choose one question.
- Students can use a search engine, typing in keywords such as *plagiarism* or *What is plagiarism?* or use the websites below. Please check these websites before giving them to students.

  http://www.plagiarism.org/

  http://owl.english.purdue.edu/owl/resource/589/01/

  http://www.indiana.edu/~wts/pamphlets/plagiarism.shtml

- Students will individually research their chosen question on the web. This can be done in a computer lab class or assigned for homework.
- Then students reform their groups to complete the worksheet.
- Ask for volunteers to share the information from Part 2 with the class.

PART 3 Strategies for Better Listening and Speaking

Getting Meaning from Context

FOCUS ON TESTING — TOEFL iBT

- Give examples for each point in the Focus box.
  - words = What words show the main idea?
  - synonyms and paraphrases = Are any unfamiliar words explained by words with the same meaning?
  - transitions = Are there any signpost words, e.g., *on the other hand, finally*?
  - stressed words = Which words are louder and clearer?
  - intonation = Which words are higher?
  - a speaker's tone of voice = Is the message friendly? helpful? angry?
  - your knowledge of the culture, speakers, or situation = What type of communication usually takes place in this type of context?

Using Context Clues

- Play each conversation. Pause after the question to allow students to fill in their answers and write the clues. Remind students to fill in the circles completely.
- Play the final sentence, which gives the correct answer.

ANSWER KEY
1. B; posted, coming out, C
2. A: hate, economics, switch, graduate
3. C: appointment, academic affairs office
4. D: essay, originality, plagiarized

AUDIOSCRIPT

Conversation 1
A: Are they posted yet?
B: No, they're coming out on Friday.
A: I think I'm gonna get a C.
B: Oh, come on, you always say that.

Question 1: *What are the women talking about?*
B: Don't worry. I'm sure you'll get a good grade. You always do.

Conversation 2
Man: … I hate economics.
Woman: You've been saying that all semester. Why don't you switch?
Man: It's too late! I'm already in my third year. I'm supposed to graduate next year.
Woman: Why did you choose it if you hate it so much?
Man: I didn't. My parents wanted me to study it, and I didn't want to disappoint them.

Question 2: *Why is the man unhappy?*
Man: Economics is the wrong major for me, but now I have to finish it.

Conversation 3
A: Do you have time to go get some coffee?
B: No, I have an appointment with Dr. Brown in the academic affairs office.
A: About what?
B: About studying abroad next year. I'm spending next semester in Brazil, remember? Dr. Brown is gonna help me select my classes.
A: Well, good luck. I've heard he's really helpful.

Question 3: *Who is Dr. Brown?*
B: Yeah, I'm lucky to have him as my advisor.

Conversation 4
Student: Professor Cates?
Professor: Oh, hello Darla, come in.
Student: You said you wanted to talk to me about my essay?
Professor: Yes. Well, I checked the originality of your paper on the Internet. According to the website I used, only 25 percent of your essay is original.
Student: Uh… really? Only 25 percent? But I was really careful to use my own words.

Question 4: *What is the professor probably thinking?*
Professor: You need to be more careful about plagiarism, Darla. I'm going to let you rewrite your paper this time, but if it happens again, you will receive an F.

PART 3

Focused Listening

FOCUS

Getting Meaning from Intonation

- Read the instruction note.
- Play the recording. Check the answers as a class.

ANSWER KEY
1. happy   2. neutral   3. sad

AUDIOSCRIPT
How much financial aid did you get?
Eight hundred dollars.

1 Listening for Intonation Clues

- This recording includes two conversations that are repeated. Each conversation is spoken in two ways. There is a question at the end of each conversation.
- Play each conversation. Pause after the question.
- Then play the final sentence of the conversation, which gives the correct answer.

ANSWER KEY
1a. A   1b. B   2a. A   2b. B

AUDIOSCRIPT

Conversation 1A *Happy*
Sarah: Hello?
Mark: Hi Sarah. How's it going?
Sarah: Pretty good, thanks. How are you?
Mark: Good. Listen, I finished work early and I was wondering if you'd like to go to a movie with me.
Sarah: When—tonight?
Mark: Yeah.

Sarah: When—tonight? *Sick*
Mark: Yeah.
Sarah: Oh Mark, I would really love to go with you, but I can't. I have to take care of some things here at my apartment.
Mark: Oh yeah? What's going on?
Sarah: You remember my roommate, Janna?
Mark: Yeah, sure. You're always talking about her. What about her?
Sarah: Well, she's moving out.
Question 1A: *How does the woman sound?*
Mark: That's great! Maybe now you can find a nice new roommate.

Conversation 1B *Sad*
Sarah: Hello?
Mark: Hi Sarah. How's it going?
Sarah: Pretty good, thanks. How are you?
Mark: Good. Listen, I finished work early and I was wondering if you'd like to go to a movie with me.
Sarah: When—tonight?
Mark: Yeah.
Sarah: Oh Mark, thanks for asking, but I can't. I have to take care of some things here at my apartment.
Mark: Oh yeah? What's going on?
Sarah: You remember my roommate, Janna?
Mark: Yeah, sure. You're always talking about her. What about her?
Sarah: Well, she's moving out.
Question 1B: *How does the woman sound?*
Mark: That's too bad. I know how much you enjoyed living with her.

Conversation 2A *annoyed*
Robby: Hi Mom.
Mom: Hi honey.
Robby: What's up?
Mom: I'm just calling to remind you it's grandma's birthday…
Robby: I know…

Student Book pages 18–21

Mom: ... so you don't forget to call her this time.

Robby: I won't forget, Mom.

Mom: Because last year you forgot, and she was upset.

Robby: I know Mom. It won't happen again.

Mom: Yeah, well, that's what you said about Dad's birthday, and you forgot that, too.

Robby: I know. I had a big test that day.

Mom: So call Grandma, OK?

Robby: OK, I will!

Question 2A: *How does Robby sound?*

Robby: You know, Mom, it's really annoying when you keep telling me the same thing over and over again.

Conversation 2B

Robby: Hi Mom.

Mom: Hi honey.

Robby: What's up?

Mom: I'm just calling to remind you it's grandma's birthday...

Robby: I know...

Mom: ... so you don't forget to call her this time.

Robby: I won't forget, Mom.

Mom: Because last year you forgot, and she was upset.

Robby: I know Mom. It won't happen again.

Mom: Yeah, well, that's what you said about Dad's birthday, and you forgot that, too.

Robby: I know. I had a big test that day.

Mom: So call Grandma, OK?

Robby: OK, I will.

Question 2B: *How does Robby sound?*

Robby: Tell you what, I'll do it right now so that I don't forget.

2 Using Intonation To Express Feelings

- Read aloud the steps of the activity.
- You can set a time limit of five minutes for students to practice in pairs.

Using Language Functions

FOCUS

Making, Accepting, and Refusing Invitations

- Read the instructions.
- Ask for volunteers to play the roles of Mark and Sarah and read the phone conversation aloud.

ANSWER KEY

Mark says, "I was wondering..."
Sarah says, "Thanks for asking, but I can't."

3 Making, Accepting, and Refusing Invitations

- Read the instructions with the class. Together, fill in the expressions used in the conversation in the Focus activity on page 19.
- Read the information in the Language Tip box.
- Have students work in pairs to complete the chart, using expressions that they already know.

4 Role-Play: Making, Accepting, and Refusing Invitations

- Read the instructions and the situations.
- Have students work with a partner and choose one situation to role-play.

REPRODUCIBLE | **Expansion Activity**

- The aim of this activity is to practice the functions of making, accepting, and refusing invitations.
- See Black Line Master "Would You Like to...? on page BLM 3 of this Teacher's Manual. Photocopy and distribute one to each student.
- Explain that students will choose four activities.
- Select one student and ask: *Would you like to go to a movie on Thursday at 4:00?* Mime *yes* by nodding so that the student will accept. Then write the student's name on your calendar.

Copyright © McGraw-Hill — Interactions 2 Listening/Speaking 17

PART 4 — Real-World Task: Reading a Map

Student Book pages 21–23

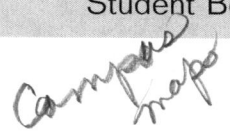

Before You Listen

1 Reviewing Compass Points

- If possible, bring a compass to class and pass it around the class.
- Have students look at the compass in the book, or draw the points of the compass on the board
- Practice the pronunciation of each direction.
- Establish the direction of north in the classroom.
- Call out one direction and have students stand and face the correct direction.

Listen

2 Expressions of Location

- Have students read through the list of expressions.
- Play the recording and ask students to repeat each expression.
- Have students work individually to write the numbers from the map next to the correct expression.
- Play the recording again. Check the answers as a whole class.

ANSWER KEY

a. 8   b. 2   c. 4   d. 1   e. 5   f. 6   g. 7
h. 3   i. 9

Language Tip

- Read aloud the information about prepositions.
- Have students read the sentences aloud.
- Ask for volunteers to give their personal information about their street, address, city, and state, using the prepositions *in*, *on*, and *at*.

3 Expressions of Location in Context

- Give students one or two minutes to study the map of the college campus.
- Play the recording and give students time to write their answers.
- Check the answers as a class.

ANSWER KEY

1. T   2. F   3. F   4. T
5. F   6. F   7. F   8. F

AUDIOSCRIPT

1. The library is across the quad from the Language Arts building.
2. There's a student parking lot at the intersection of Lass Avenue and Dale Ave.
3. The Information Technology building is between the stadium and the gymnasium.
4. The Fine Arts building is next to the sculpture garden.
5. There are parking lots on both sides of Dale Ave.
6. The bookstore is opposite the student center.
7. The Computer Science building is beside the Fine Arts building.
8. The Language Arts building is beside the Cafeteria.

Student Book pages 24–25

After You Listen

4 Using Expressions of Location

- Give students time to write five of their own true or false sentences.
- Have students read their sentences to a group of three or four students. The students try to answer correctly. Allow time for each student to read his or her sentences to the group.
- Ask for volunteers to read their sentences to the class. The class answers *true* or *false*.

5 Describing Map Locations

- Call students' attention to the pictures and questions at the bottom of the page. Discuss as a class how students find their way to a new place when they are driving or walking.
- Have students work in pairs. Student A should look at the map on page 244. Student B should look at the map on page 252.
- Remind students not to show their page to their partner. Set a time limit of ten minutes.
- Move around the room to monitor correct use of expressions of location and take notes on errors. At the end of the activity, discuss common errors as a whole class.

Expansion Activity

- The aim of this activity is to practice real language for describing locations and apply it to real contexts.
- Have students work in pairs to create a map of your college campus or of the local neighborhood. The maps should show the locations of eight to ten buildings.
- Buildings can be shown as squares and numbered.
- Below the map, students should list descriptions of the locations of each building.
- Pairs will then exchange maps and identify the buildings and their numbers.
- At the end of the activity, you may want to collect the maps for display in the classroom.

Best Practice

Scaffolding Instruction
The learning log develops skills of evaluating one's own progress in learning. By completing the log at the end of each chapter, learners will review what they have learned, identify the language functions and study skills they have practiced, and evaluate how well they have understood the chapter.

Self-Assessment Log

- The Self-Assessment Log at the end of each chapter helps students track their own strengths and weaknesses and also encourages them to take ownership of their own learning.
- Explain to students that thinking about their learning can help them decide what to focus on in their lessons and homework and help them chart their progress.
- Read the directions aloud and have students check the vocabulary they learned in the chapter and are prepared to use. Have students check the strategies they practiced in the chapter and the degree to which they learned them. Have students work individually to complete the sentences at the bottom of the page.
- Put students in small groups. Ask students to find the information or an activity related to each strategy in the chapter.
- Tell students to find definitions in the chapter for any words they did not check.
- If possible, meet privately with each student on a regular basis and review his or her assessment log. This provides an opportunity for the student to ask key questions and for you to see where additional help may be needed and to offer one-on-one encouragement.

CHAPTER 2: City Life

In this CHAPTER

Students will read about different aspects of city life, such as looking for accommodations, neighborhood crime prevention, housing repairs, and giving directions. In Part 1, they will learn to recognize stressed and reduced forms and practice ways to open and close a phone conversation. In Part 2, they will listen to a talk about the neighborhood watch. They will also discuss the issue of gun safety. In Part 3, they will practice different forms of address between people. In Part 4, they will learn how to request and give directions using a map.

> "I love cities. I love neighborhoods and the ways in which they interact with each other... I love the long gradual shifts in culture they contain. I love the fact that they work at all."
>
> Jason Sutter
> U.S. blogger

Chapter Opener

- Discuss the questions from the Connecting to the Topic section as a class.

- Read and discuss the quote. Ask other questions, such as: What is a neighborhood? What kind of neighborhood do you think the writer lives in? Is it like your neighborhood? What kind of "identity" does your neighborhood have?

- Brainstorm adjectives to describe life in a city and life in the country or in the suburbs, for example, *safe/dangerous, expensive/cheap, stressful/relaxing, noisy/peaceful.*

Chapter Overview

Listening Skills and Strategies
Listening for main ideas and details
Making inferences
Listening for clues to relationships between people
Following directions

Speaking Skills and Strategies
Using the phrase *by the way*
Opening and closing phone conversations
Talking about crime
Expressing frustration
Learning names of professions
Requesting and giving directions
Saying you don't understand

Critical-Thinking Skills
Predicting questions speakers will ask
Getting meaning from context
Speculating about hypothetical situations

Taking notes on statistics
Using transitions as cues for note-taking
Taking notes on an informal talk

Vocabulary Building
Expressions for opening and closing conversations
Terms for expressing frustration
Expressions for requesting and giving directions
Names of professions
Terms for expressing lack of understanding
Using the phrase *by the way*

Pronunciation
Identifying and practicing stressed words
Identifying and practicing reduced pronunciation

Language Skills
Using context clues to identify a speaker

Vocabulary

Nouns	Verbs	Adjective	Expressions
alarm	break into	violent	can't miss
break-in	bug		get into the habit
deadbolt	come by		(can/can't) make it
decal	prevent		never lift a finger
device			
front/back (of)			
license			
right			
slob			
(car) theft			
timer			
valuables			

PART 1   Conversation: Finding a Place to Live

Student Book pages 28–29

Can You Guess?

- Ask students to discuss the questions below in groups and compare their answers with the correct answers.
- Discuss the issues raised by these questions: Why is it difficult to determine the answers to these questions? Why is it difficult to measure the population of a city? What factors are measured to determine safety? What are the different ways of measuring the size of a department store? What are the differences between living in an old city and a newly built city?

1. Which three world cities have the largest populations? **A.** *Tokyo, Japan; Delhi, India: Sao Paolo, Brazil. (Per 2010 UN survey)*
2. What is the world's safest city? **A.** *"Luxembourg ranks as the world's top city for personal safety and security, according to a quality of life survey by Mercer Human Resource Consulting."*
3. What and where is the world's largest department store? **A.** *Shinsegae Centum City in Busan, Korea covers an area of 5.49 million square feet (509,810 square meters).*
4. What is the world's oldest continuously inhabited capital city? **A.** *Damascus, Syria.*

Before You Listen

1 Prelistening Questions

- Have the students look at the photo on page 28, read the questions on page 29, and discuss them in small groups.
- Compare answers as a whole class.
- As a whole class, make a list of questions a roommate might ask Mari and write them on the board.

2 Previewing Vocabulary

- Play the recording and have students listen for the underlined words.
- Have students complete the vocabulary preview individually.
- Compare their answers as a whole class and write the correct answers on the board.
- Practice the pronunciation of new words or phrases.

ANSWER KEY
1. b   2. e   3. d   4. f   5. a   6. c

Listen

3 Comprehension Questions

(The audioscript follows Activity 4.)

- Explain that these questions will help students focus on the main ideas in the listening. They do not need to understand every word to answer the questions.
- You may want to write the questions on the board.
- Read the questions aloud.
- Play the recording.
- After listening, have students compare their answers in pairs.
- Check the answers as a class.

22   CHAPTER 2   Copyright © McGraw-Hill

Student Book pages 29–31

ANSWER KEY
1. Nancy and Mari.
2. Mari is calling about a room for rent.
3. Mari is living in a house with some other students, but it's really noisy, and it's not very clean.
4. The other people in the house are Nancy's husband, Andrew, and her cousin, Jeff.
5. The neighborhood is safe, and she can walk to school.
6. Mari will come by to see the house at 5:00 P.M.

Stress

4 Listening for Stressed Words

- Review the meaning of stressed words from the previous unit.
- Listen to the recording again, this time with books open.
- The recording has pauses to allow time for students to repeat and write the missing words.

After listening, have students check their answers with a partner, looking at the audioscript in their books.

Have students read the conversation with a partner, paying attention to stressed words in their pronunciation and intonation.

AUDIOSCRIPT and ANSWER KEY

Nancy: Hello?
Mari: May I speak to Nancy, please?
Nancy: _Speaking_.
Mari: Uh hi, uh, my name is Mari, and I'm calling about the _room_ for rent. I saw your _ad_ at the campus _housing_ office.
Nancy: Oh, right. OK, uh, are you a _student_?
Mari: Well, right now, I'm just studying _English_, but I'm planning to start _college_ full-time in _March_.
Nancy: I see. _Where_ are you living _now_?
Mari: I've been living in a _house_ with some other students, but I _don't like_ it there.
Nancy: Why? What's the _problem_?
Mari: Well, _first_ of all, it's really _noisy_, and it's not very clean. The other people in the house are real _slobs_. I mean they never lift a _finger_ to clean _up_ after themselves. It really _bugs_ me! I need a place that's cleaner and more _private_.
Nancy: Well, it's really _quiet_ here. We're not _home_ very much.
Mari: What do you _do_?
Nancy: I teach _English_ at the college.
Mari: _Wait_ a minute! Didn't we meet yesterday at the _placement_ exam?
Nancy: Oh… _you're_ the girl from _Japan_! What was your name again?
Mari: Mari.
Nancy: Right. What a _small world_!
Mari: It really is. By the way, who _else_ lives in the house? The ad said there are _three_ people.
Nancy: Well besides me there's my _husband_, Andrew, and my _cousin_, Jeff. He's a musician and a part-time _student_. Uh, are you OK with having _male_ roommates?
Mari: Sure, as long as they're clean and not too _noisy_.
Nancy: _Don't_ worry. They're both _easy_ to live with.
Mari: OK. Um, is the _neighborhood_ safe?
Nancy: Oh sure. We haven't had _any_ problems, and you can _walk_ to school from here.
Mari: Well, it sounds really _nice_. When can I come by and _see_ it?
Nancy: Can you make it this _evening_ around _five_? Then you can meet the _guys_, too.
Mari: Yeah, five o'clock is _good_. What's the _address_?

PART 1

Student Book pages 31–33

Nancy:	It's 3475 Hayworth Avenue. Do you know where *that* is?
Mari:	No, I don't.
Nancy:	OK. From University Village you go seven blocks *east* on Olympic Avenue. At the intersection of Olympic and Alfred there's a *stoplight*. Turn *left*, and go *up* one and a half blocks. Our house is in the *middle* of the block on the *left*.
Mari:	That sounds *easy*.
Nancy:	Yeah, you *can't miss* it. Listen, I've got to go. Someone's at the door. See you this *evening*.
Mari:	OK, see you *later*. Bye.
Nancy:	Bye-bye.

Language Tip

- Point out that *by the way* is not used to introduce a main or an important idea.
- Read aloud the information in the box.
- Ask two students to read the short conversation.

Expansion Activity (REPRODUCIBLE)

- The purpose of this activity is to practice opening and closing phone conversations on the topic of looking for housing.
- Please see Black Line Master "Looking for a Place to Live" on page BLM 4 of this Teacher's Manual. Photocopy and cut it into strips.
- Give one strip to each student. There are ten different strips. If you have more than ten students, have students work in pairs or threes.
- Explain that some people are looking for accommodations, and some are offering accommodations.

- Students walk around the room and try to find their partner. Ask them not to show their paper to the other students. They must "phone" each person they meet until they find a partner.
- When they have found a partner, they can sit down and practice their conversation again.

Reductions

5 Comparing Unreduced and Reduced Pronunciation

- Read the directions aloud.
- Play the recording and have students listen and read the sentences.
- Play the recording again. This time, pause the audio to allow time for students to repeat

6 Listening for Reductions

- Before listening to the conversation, you can first have students read through the conversation and try to guess the missing words.
- Play the recording, pausing after each conversation to allow time for students to write their answers.
- After listening, have students check their answers with the audioscript in their books.
- Have students practice the conversation in pairs, paying attention to reduced forms in their pronunciation.

AUDIOSCRIPT

Conversation 1

Mari: Hey Jeff, _where_ _are_ _you_ going?

Jeff: I _want_ _to_ get a present for Nancy. It's her birthday, _you_ know.

Mari: Yeah, I know. _What_ _do_ _you_ think I should get her?

Jeff: Well, she likes music. _How about_ a CD?

Conversation 2

Nancy: _How_ _do_ _you_ like my new haircut, Mari?

Mari: It's great! Who's your hairstylist?

Nancy: His name's José.

Mari: _Can_ _you_ give me his phone number?

Nancy: Sure, but he's always very busy. _You_ _can_ try calling him, but he might not be able _to_ see _you_ until next month.

Conversation 3

Andrew: _What_ _do_ _you_ _want_ _to_ do tonight, Nancy?

Nancy: Nothing special. I've _got_ _to_ stay home _and_ correct my students' compositions.

After You Listen

7 Reviewing Vocabulary

- Review the vocabulary items in the box.
- Model the conversation with a student.
- Ask students to suggest one or two ways of continuing the conversation.
- Have students practice the conversation in pairs. Remind them to include vocabulary from the box.
- Ask for volunteers to perform the conversation for the class.

Using Language Functions

FOCUS

Starting a Phone Conversation

- Read the instruction note.
- Ask students to repeat the expressions using their own or imaginary names.

FOCUS

Ending a Phone Conversation

- Read the instruction note.
- Have students reread the conversation between Mari and Nancy to see a typical closing of a phone conversation.

Best Practice

Interacting with Others

This type of activity is an example of collaborative learning to encourage fluency and confidence. This is an information gap activity designed to practice ways of opening and closing phone conversations. It is similar to real-life situations because students have to share information to complete the task. In this activity, communication is more important than grammar. Students can practice phone strategies in pairs and then improve their performance by switching roles or partners. By providing feedback to each other, they learn skills of self-evaluation.

8 Role-Play

- Have students work in pairs. Student A should look at page 245. Student B should look at page 253.
- Remind students not to show their page to their partner.
- Ask for two volunteers to read the example conversation.
- Set a time limit of ten minutes.

PART 1

- Move around the room to monitor use of appropriate phone language and take notes of errors.
- Ask for volunteers to perform conversations for the class.

Best Practice

Scaffolding Instruction

This type of activity mirrors the authentic experience of using language on the telephone. By practicing fixed phrases that can be used in many different situations, students will learn to predict the kinds of language they will come across in telephone conversations. They will later learn to vary these phrases more freely according to their own individual needs.

9 Telephone Game

- This game is homework for students to practice their phone language using real phones.
- Before the class, make a numbered list of "secret" messages to give to various groups in your class. You will need one message for each group. The messages may be complex, but in simple language.

Examples:

The concert will begin at 8:00 on Friday night, but I can't go because it is my sister's birthday and we're having a party.

The time of the reading exam tomorrow has been changed from 9:30 A.M. to 10:30 A.M.

- Read the instructions for the game.
- Help students form groups and exchange phone numbers.
- Make sure they each know who will call first in the group.
- At the beginning of the next class, ask the first person and the last person in each group to read out their messages to see if they are the same.

Note: If you do not want to ask students to exchange phone numbers because of privacy issues, have students role-play this activity in class using made-up phone numbers.

PART 2 — Lecture: Neighborhood Watch Meeting

Student Book pages 36–38

Before You Listen

- Read the information that introduces the next listening.
- Look at the signs about Neighborhood Crime Watch. These will be discussed in the next activity.
- Read the *Culture Note*. Explain that a Neighborhood Watch is a type of citizens' organization (not police) that tries to prevent crime and vandalism in its neighborhood by watching out for suspicious activity.

1 Prelistening Discussion

- Read through the list of questions.
- Have students work in groups to answer the questions.
- Review the responses as a class.

2 Previewing Vocabulary

- Play the recording and ask students to listen for the words.
- Have students check the words they know. Then discuss their meanings with a partner.
- Explain that they will work out the meaning of the new words by listening to the talk. As they learn new words, they should come back to this list and check them.

Listen

Strategy

Taking Notes on Statistics
- Read the information in the Strategy box.
- Tell the students that they will fill in the blanks when they do the next activity.

3 Abbreviating Statistics

- Review the meaning of *abbreviation*, and give some examples.
- Have students work individually to write the abbreviations for the terms in the box.
- Check the answers as a class.
- Emphasize that students may use their own symbols as long as they are clear and easy to read.

ANSWER KEY

Nouns:

% percent

\# number

½ half

⅓ third

¼ quarter

Verbs:

↑ increase, go up, rise

↓ decrease, decline, go down

X2 double

Other phrases:

< less than

> more than

= equal to or the same as

---

4 Taking Notes on Statistics

- Explain that students will hear three sentences.
- They will take notes using their abbreviations from Activity 3.
- Have students work in pairs to recreate the sentences.
- Invite volunteers to write the sentences on the board.

PART 2

Student Book pages 38–40

ANSWER KEY

1. last yr 48 burglaries ↑ 60 this yr
2. # car thefts x2
3. ½ (50%) burglaries unlocked doors or windows

AUDIOSCRIPT

1. A year ago, there were 48 burglaries in your area; this year it's gone up to 60 so far.
2. The number of car thefts has almost doubled.
3. Did you know that in half of all burglaries, 50 percent, the burglars enter through unlocked doors or windows?

Strategy

Transitions (Connecting Words)
Read the information in the Strategy box. Ask if students can think of any other examples, e.g., *first, the main thing, finally*.

Best Practice

Scaffolding Instruction
The transition outline helps students to organize the lecture into main and secondary ideas. By providing students with the transitions as a support, they can see how the transitions help the listener to structure the content of the talk. This guided activity prepares them for the skill of identifying main and secondary ideas without the help of an outline.

⑤ Listening for Transitions

- Read the directions and then give students a couple of minutes to read the transition word outline.

- Play the recording. The recording is in two sections. You may want to pause between the two sections to check answers.
- Have students write their answers individually and then compare their answers in pairs.
- Read the questions in part 2.
- Play the recording again.
- Compare answers as a class.
- Note that students will be introduced to numbering conventions used in outlines in the next chapter. At this stage, they should focus only on transitions.
- Next, have students answer the three questions on page 40 of the Student Book.

ANSWER KEY

Part 1

First of all, <u>outside lights</u>.

Next, <u>lights inside the house</u>.

All right then. The next topic I want to discuss is <u>locks</u>.

    First of all, <u>cheap locks are not safe</u>.

    Also, <u>there are special locks for windows</u>.

Part 2

OK, now let's move on and talk about <u>how to prevent car theft</u>.

    First, <u>put car in garage</u>.

    The most important thing is <u>put valuables in the trunk</u>.

Now my last point is <u>neighbors can help each other</u>.

    The main thing is <u>when you go on vacation, ask someone to watch your house</u>.

    Also, <u>if you see something unusual, call the police</u>.

    And one more thing: <u>put Neighborhood Watch decal in window</u>.

Student Book pages 39–40

> **ANSWER KEY**
>
> 1. Five main ideas
>   Transitions: First of all; The next topic; Next, let's talk about; Now let's move on; Now, my last point is
> 2. They are subheadings under the main heading.
> 3. No, they don't contain essential information.

AUDIOSCRIPT
Part 1

Police Officer: Good evening. My name is Officer Jenkins. Thanks for inviting me tonight. OK, so, as you know, there have been a number of break-ins recently in your neighborhood, and even though it's true that there's been very little *violent* crime, um, especially compared to other parts of the city, burglary and car theft are both up in this area. Let me give you some statistics. OK, a year ago there were... 48 burglaries in your area; this year, it's gone up to 60 so far, and the number of car thefts has almost doubled, too. Now, I'm not here to try to scare you. What I want to do tonight is to give you some simple suggestions that will make your homes and automobiles safer. OK?

So, first of all, let's talk about lights outside the house. If you live in a house, you need to have lights both in the front of your house and in the back, and be sure to turn on those lights at night. In my opinion, this is the most important thing you can do to prevent burglaries. Next, let's talk about lights inside the house. It's...

Woman in Audience: Excuse me, what about apartments? I mean, I live in an apartment building...

Police Officer: Yeah, good question. If you live in an apartment building, you want to have good, bright lighting in the garage, the hallways, and by the door to your apartment. If a light is broken, don't ignore it. Report it to your manager immediately. And whether you live in a house or an apartment, it's a good idea to put automatic timers on your lights. You know what a timer is, right? It's like a lock that turns on your lights automatically, so it looks like someone is home even if you're out. Are you with me on that?

All right, then... the next topic I want to discuss is locks. First of all, forget cheap locks 'cause they're not safe. Every door in your place should have a deadbolt... um, a deadbolt at least one inch thick. Also, there are special locks you can buy for your windows. By the way, did you know that in half of all burglaries, 50 percent, the burglars enter through unlocked doors or windows? I'm telling you, even in a peaceful neighborhood like this, where you know all your neighbors, you have to get into the habit of keeping your windows and doors locked.

Part 2

OK, now let's move on and talk about how you can prevent car theft. First, if you have a garage, use it for your car, not for your ping-pong table! [Laughter] But seriously, the most important thing is—and I hope this is obvious—if you've got valuables in the car, hide them in the trunk. Don't leave them out on the seat, not even for five minutes! Last week, we got a report from a guy who left his laptop on the car seat while he ran in to buy a cup of coffee. When he came back, it was gone. The thief just broke the car window and reached in and took it. And also...

Man in Audience: What about a car alarm?

Police Officer: Well, most research shows that noisy alarms don't do anything to prevent car theft. It's better to have the kind of device thieves can see, like a lock on your steering wheel. But the best thing of all is just to lock your car and keep valuables out of sight.

All right. Now my last point is what you, as neighbors, can do to help each other. The main thing is that when you go on vacation, ask someone to watch your house for you, to collect your mail, take in your newspaper, stuff like that. Also, If you see something unusual, like a strange van or truck in your neighbor's driveway, or people carrying furniture out, *don't* go out there and try to stop it. Just call the police! And one more thing. Each of you should put this Neighborhood Watch decal —this picture right here of the man in a coat looking over his shoulder—in your front window. This tells criminals that this area has a Neighborhood Watch and that someone might be watching them. OK, are there any questions?

Man in Audience: Yeah, there's something I want to know... Do you think it's a good idea to keep a gun in the house?

Police Officer: Well now, that is a very complicated question. I think that it's a bad idea to have a gun in your house, especially if you have kids. Thousands of people die in gun accidents each year in this country. So, in my opinion, it's just not safe to have a gun in your house. But of course it *is* legal to have a gun, if that's what you want. Just make sure you get the proper license and that you take a course in gun safety, OK? All right. Anything else?

Best Practice

Organizing Information

This type of activity uses an outline to categorize information. Using an outline encourages students to process and organize information while they are listening and also provides a record for them to refer to when reviewing their notes. This type of graphic organizer emphasizes listing and categorizing skills. It also helps them practice using abbreviations and symbols to take notes. Other types of graphic organizers are used throughout this book.

---

6 Taking Notes

(See audioscript in the previous activity.)

- Point out the use of underlining, indenting, and numbering in the outline.

Student Book pages 40–42

- Ask students to identify which type of words are underlined, indented, and numbered.
- Have students complete the outline, using their notes from Activities 4 and 5. Remind them to use abbreviations.
- Play the recording again so they can check their answers.

ANSWER KEY

Date:

Ways to Prevent Crime

Part 1

Intro:

Very little violent crime in neighbor-hd. But:

Burglaries ↑:

    Last yr: *48*

    This yr: *60*

Car theft ↑: *2x*

How to keep home & auto safe:

1. House lights
   - need lights in front and *back*
   - turn on *at night*
2. *Lights inside the house*
   - bright lights in garage, hallway, apt. door
   - fix broken lights
   - house or apt: use automatic *timers*
3. *Locks*
   - —*Cheap locks are* not safe
   - —every door needs *a deadbolt*
   - —get special locks for *windows*
     - —50% *enter through unlocked doors and windows*

Part 2

4. *How to prevent car theft*
   - —use *your garage*
   - —put *valuables in the trunk*
   - —alarms don't *work*
   - —better to have *a steering wheel lock*
5. *Neighbors can help each other*
   - —Go on vacation, *ask someone to watch your house*
   - —See someth. unusual, *call the police*
   - —Put *Neighborhood Watch decal in window*

After You Listen

Best Practice

Activating Prior Knowledge

This is an example of an activity that encourages students to make text-to-self connections. The discussion questions ask students to relate the content of the lecture on crime prevention to their own lives. This aids understanding and retention of new material.

7 Discussing the Lecture

- Have students discuss the questions in groups.
- Encourage students to use the new vocabulary in their discussion.
- Ask for representatives from each group to report back on the discussion.

8 Reviewing Vocabulary

- Look back at the vocabulary list in Activity 2 on page 37 in the Student Book.

Have students work in small groups to ask each other questions about the new vocabulary.

PART 2

Student Book pages 42–43

On the Spot!

Best Practice

Making Use of Academic Content

This is an example of a group discussion on a real-world issue. This type of activity requires students to agree and disagree and give reasons for their opinions. They will also have to utilize skills for interrupting, holding the floor, and taking their turn in the discussion. Active participation in discussion is a course requirement in many academic courses.

9 What Would You Do?

- Read the situation with the class, or ask students to read it silently.
- Give students 10–15 minutes to read the questions in groups and discuss their answers.
- Choose one person from each group to report to the class.
- Write a list of arguments for and against owning guns on the board.

Content Note

This topic is one that may be very sensitive for students who have been victims of violence. You may wish to advise students to maintain a balanced discussion on general issues of crime prevention and the law and avoid discussing personal experiences.

REPRODUCIBLE — Expansion Activity

- The purpose of this activity is to help students be aware of safety issues and develop skills for using the Internet to get advice.
- Students can use a search engine typing in keywords such as *campus safety* or *campus crime prevention*.
- The research part of this activity can be done in a computer lab class or assigned for homework.
- Please see Black Line Master "Safety on Campus" on page BLM 5 of this Teacher's Manual. Photocopy and distribute one to each student.
- Divide the students into groups of four and have each person in the group choose one issue.
- Students will research their chosen issue on the web and write the safety tips in the appropriate circle in the mind map, a type of graphic organizer.
- Then re-form their groups to complete the worksheet. As students listen to their group members' reports, have them write the information they hear in the mind map.
- Display the worksheets on the classroom wall.

PART 3 — Strategies for Better Listening and Speaking

Student Book pages 44–45

Getting Meaning from Context

FOCUS ON TESTING — TOEFL® iBT

Using Context Clues

- Remind students of strategies for using context clues. (See Chapter 1, Part 3, page 17.)
- Read the instructions.
- This recording has five sections. There is a question at the end of each section. Play each section of the recording.
- Pause after the question to allow students to circle their answers and write the clues.
- Then play the final part of each section which gives the correct answer.

ANSWER KEY

Answer	Clue
Questions 1 through 3 are based on a conversation between a man and a women.	
1. B the apartment manager	check for you, fifth of the month, Mr. Bradley
2. C an exterminator	cockroaches, spray, kill those bugs
3. B It's in bad condition.	said you'd fix, hole in the…, still haven't done that
Questions 4 and 5 are based on a conversation between two neighbors.	
4. D He is happy to help Donna.	pleasant tone of voice
5. C He is annoyed with Donna.	annoyed tone of voice

AUDIOSCRIPT

Conversation 1

Manager: Yes? Who is it?

Tenant: It's Donna from 206. I've got a check for you.

Manager: Oh, it's you. Do you know it's the fifth of the month?

Tenant: Yes, Mr. Bradley. I'm sorry. I know it was due on the first, but my grandma got sick, and I had to go out of town suddenly.

Question 1: *Who is the man?*

Manager: Look, my job as manager here is to collect the rent on the first. If you're late again next month, you'll have to look for another place to live.

Conversation 2

Tenant: OK, Mr. Bradley. But look, while I'm here, I need to talk to you about a couple of things.

Manager: Yeah?

Tenant: First, about the cockroaches. They're all over the kitchen again. I'm sick of them!

Manager: Have you used the spray I gave you?

Tenant: It's no good. I need something stronger to kill those horrible bugs once and for all.

Question 2: *Who will the manager probably need to call?*

Manager: OK, I'll call the exterminator next week.

Conversation 3

Tenant: Next week?! Last week you said you'd fix the hole in the ceiling, and you still haven't done that! I'm fed

PART 3

Student Book pages 45–46

up waiting for you to fix things around here!

Question 3: *What can you guess about Donna's apartment?*

Tenant: Why should I pay so much rent for a place in such bad condition?

Manager: Well, you're not the only tenant in this building. If you don't like it, why don't you move out?

Conversation 4

John: Hi, Donna. What do you need this time?

Donna: Hello, John. A couple of eggs. Do you mind?

John: No, come on in.

Question 4: *How does John feel about Donna's request?*

Donna: Thanks so much, John!

John: You're welcome!

Conversation 5

John: Hi, Donna. What do you need this time?

Donna: Hello, John. A couple of eggs. Do you mind?

John: No, come on in.

Question 5: *How does John feel about Donna's request?*

Donna: Thanks, John.

John: OK, but next time go ask somebody else, all right?

Focused Listening

FOCUS

Guessing Relationships Between People

- Read the information note about guessing relationships between people.
- Ask students for examples of how they address people they know.

1 Listening for Clues to Relationships Between People

- Have students read the directions for Activity 1.
- Have them work in groups of four, divided into two pairs. One person will look at page 245. The other person will look at page 253.
- Set a time limit of ten minutes for this activity
- Invite volunteers to perform the conversations for the class.

Content Note

Formality and politeness vary in different cultures. In some cultures, it is impolite to be too informal with one's teacher. Therefore, it may be difficult for some students to address the teacher by his or her first name.

Using Language Functions

FOCUS

Expressing Frustration

- Read the instruction note.
- Review use of intonation to express feelings.
- Ask them to give some situations that make people frustrated.

2 Role-Play

- Have students work in pairs. One student will look at page 246. The other student will look at page 254.
- Set a time limit of ten minutes for students to practice their conversations.
- Monitor the groups as they are doing the activity and make notes of errors.
- Invite volunteers to perform their conversation for the class.

Student Book page 46

3 **Follow-up Discussion**

- Review the vocabulary in the chart and practice the pronunciation as needed.
- Have students work in groups to discuss the questions.
- Ask representatives from each group to report to the class.

Expansion Activity

- The aim of this activity is to practice language of building repairs and repair workers.
- Have students work in small groups.
- Please see Black Line Master "Can You Fix It?" on page BLM 6 of this Teacher's Manual. Photocopy and distribute one to each group of students.
- Explain that they will discuss the problems with their group and write the problems in the correct places on the chart.
- Check the answers as a class.
- Students who finish early can go on to part 2.
- Invite representatives from one or two groups to perform their conversations for the class.

ANSWER KEY

Answers for this Expansion Activity will vary depending on the skills in the group. Mice and cockroaches, for example, could be dealt with by buying commercial products from a hardware store.

Possible answers:

Plumber	Electrician
Dripping faucet	Microwave doesn't work
Broken toilet	Lights don't work
Leaking water pipe	No electricity
Shower doesn't work	Refrigerator doesn't work
Carpenter	**Extermination**
Broken window	Mice
Broken front door	Cockroaches
Broken closet door	
Fix it yourself	
Broken shower curtain	
Bugs in the food	

Copyright © McGraw-Hill

Interactions 2 Listening/Speaking

PART 4 Real-World Task: Following Directions

Student Book pages 47–48

Before You Listen

2 Prelistening Questions

- Ask students to make a list of all the expressions they know for requesting and giving directions.
- Practice requesting and giving directions using the map.
- Then read the information in the box about language for requesting and giving directions.

ANSWER KEY

Answers will vary. Possible answers:

1. How do I get to the Chinese restaurant? / Could you tell me how to get to the Chinese restaurant?
2. Go straight for two blocks. Turn right on Main Street. Walk for two blocks. It's on your right.

Listen

FOCUS

Requesting and Giving Directions

- Review expressions for giving directions from Chapter 1, Part 4, pages 21 and 22 of the Student Book.
- Read the information in the Requesting and Giving Directions note.
- Practice the expressions using places that are well known to the students.

2 Following Directions

- Give students some time to study the map.
- Check comprehension of any new vocabulary.
- The recording has four sections. Each section will be heard twice. There is a question at the end of each section.
- Play each section of the recording.
- Pause after the question to allow students to write their answers.
- Play the recording again. Check the answers as a whole class.

ANSWER KEY

1. department store
2. public library
3. supermarket
4. bookstore

AUDIOSCRIPT

1. You are at the X. Go two blocks west on 2nd Avenue. Turn left and go down one block. What's on your left?
2. You are at the intersection of Main Street and 3rd Avenue. Go one block south on Main. Turn left. Go straight for half a block. What's on your left?
3. You have just eaten dinner at the French restaurant at the intersection of 4th and Pine. Go south on Pine Street to 2nd Avenue. Turn right. Go one block west on 2nd. Turn left. Go down Main Street for half a block. What's on your right?
4. You work in the office building at the intersection of 3rd and Main. After work you decide to go shopping. Go one block east on 3rd. Turn left and go one block up Pine Street. Turn right. Go one block east until you reach Oak Street. What's on your right?

After You Listen

FOCUS

Saying You Don't Understand

- Read the instruction note about language for saying you don't understand.
- Have students practice saying these expressions with the correct pronunciation and intonation.

36 CHAPTER 2

Copyright © McGraw-Hill

Best Practice

Cultivating Critical Thinking

This is an example of a problem-solving activity where students have to share information. In this activity, students first have to read and interpret maps. Then they have to give and understand directions in order to complete the task. This requires applying language to new contexts, checking understanding, and synthesizing written and verbal information.

3 Requesting and Giving Directions

- Have students work in pairs. One student will look at the map on page 246. The other student will look at the map on page 254.
- Set a time limit of ten minutes for students to practice their conversations.
- Monitor the groups as they are doing the activity and make notes of errors.
- Invite volunteers to perform their conversation for the class.

Expansion Activity

- The aim of this activity is to practice language for requesting and giving directions using real locations.
- Have students work in pairs and write questions asking for directions to a place somewhere near your school.
- Have pairs of students exchange questions and write the answers.
- (If students finish early, have them exchange with another pair.)
- Move around the room and monitor their work, taking notes of any errors.
- Have students read out their directions. The other students in the class will try to guess where they are going.

Self-Assessment Log

- The purpose of the log is to help the students reflect on their learning.
- Read the directions aloud and have students check vocabulary that they learned in the chapter and are prepared to use.
- Have students check the strategies they understand.
- Put students in small groups. Ask students to find the information or an activity related to each strategy in the chapter.
- Tell students to find definitions in the chapter for any words they did not check, or they can look in their dictionaries.

CHAPTER 3
Business and Money

In this CHAPTER

Students will read about different aspects of business and money, such as borrowing money, how to start a business, how to use banking services, and finally, how to balance a checkbook. In Part 1, they will learn to recognize stressed and reduced forms and practice ways of requesting and giving advice. In Part 2, they will listen to a lecture about the process of starting your own company. In Part 3, they will listen to advertisements for different banking services. At the end of the chapter, they will learn about how to balance a checkbook. These topics will encourage students to think about ways of spending and saving money and the function of money in our economy.

> "If you work just for money, you'll never make it, but if you love what you're doing and you always put the customer first, success will be yours."
>
> Ray Kroc
> American businessman, founder of McDonald's Corp., 1902–1984

Chapter Opener

- Have students look at the photo. Ask them the questions from the Connecting to the Topic section. Have students discuss as a class.

- Read and discuss the quote. Discuss the meaning of *you'll never make it* (meaning *you'll never be successful*) and *always put the customer first* (meaning *always consider, or think about, what the customer wants*). What values are represented by the quote? Are these values typical of businesses today?

- Brainstorm different ways to save and invest money. Write a list of useful words on the board, e.g., *bonds, stocks, pensions, investment account, savings account*.

Chapter Overview

Listening Skills and Strategies
Listening for main ideas and details

Making inferences

Distinguishing between *can* and *can't*

Distinguishing between teens and tens

Recognizing expressions of advice

Speaking Skills and Strategies
Talking about managing money

Talking about entrepreneurs

Talking about abilities

Using the words *borrow* and *lend*

Asking for, giving, and refusing advice

Critical-Thinking Skills
Outlining a lecture

Getting meaning from context

Taking notes on a process

Vocabulary Building
Terms for talking about money

Borrow vs. *lend*

Expressions for asking for, giving, accepting, and rejecting advice

Terms for talking about entrepreneurs and the entrepreneurial process

Terms related to banking

Pronunciation
Identifying and practicing stressed words

Identifying and practicing reduced pronunciation

Pronouncing *can* and *can't*

Pronouncing teens and tens

Language Skills
Using context clues to identify banking services

Vocabulary

Nouns
- balance
- brilliant idea
- budget
- income
- interest
- quality
- solution
- team
- tightwad
- vision

Verbs
- balance a checkbook
- earn
- enter
- found
- have (something) in common
- hire
- identify
- pay off
- raise capital
- solve
- surf the Internet
- take risks

Adjective
- broke

Expressions
- an arm and a leg
- make ends meet

PART 1 — Conversation: Borrowing Money
Student Book pages 52–53

Can You Guess?

- Ask students to discuss the questions below in groups and compare their answers with the correct answers.
- Brainstorm different types of taxes, e.g., federal, state, income, sales, property, etc. How are they collected? What are they used for?

1. What is the average yearly salary in the United States? **A.** *About $47,000.*
2. Which of the following countries have no income tax: Sweden, Kuwait, Switzerland, the Bahamas, Venezuela, Taiwan? **A.** *Kuwait and Bahamas.*
3. In which of the following countries do people save the largest percentage of their salaries: Switzerland, Korea, Sweden, United States, China, Germany, Japan? **A.** *China: 30 percent; Germany: 11 percent; Sweden: 11 percent; Korea: 10 percent; Switzerland: 10 percent; Japan: 5 percent; United States: 1 percent.*

Before You Listen

Best Practice

Activating Prior Knowledge

The prelistening questions activate students' prior knowledge. This type of activity will help students relate their own experience of saving and spending money to the new language in this chapter. When students activate their prior knowledge before learning new material, they are better able to map new language onto existing concepts, which aids understanding and retention.

1 Prelistening Questions

- Have students look at the photos and try to guess what the people are talking about.
- Have the students read the questions and discuss them in small groups.
- Compare answers as a whole class.
- As a whole class, make a list of ways to borrow money or tips for managing your budget.

2 Previewing Vocabulary

- Play the recording and have students listen for the underlined words.
- Have students complete the vocabulary preview individually.
- Compare their answers as a whole class and write the correct answers on the board.
- Ask students for additional paraphrases (or examples) for each item, e.g., 1. very expensive, 2. spends more than she earns, 3. stingy, 4. short of money, 5. carefully planned amount of spending money, 6. earnings / salary, 7. make money.
- Practice the pronunciation of new words and phrases.

ANSWER KEY

1. a 2. d 3. c 4. b 5. f 6. e

Content Note

In some cultures, it is not acceptable to discuss one's financial situation. In the U.S., students would normally feel comfortable telling who was paying for their college education and how much an item of clothing costs. However, other financial information, such as how much a person makes is considered personal information.

Listen

3 Comprehension Questions

(The audioscript follows Activity 4.)

Student Book pages 53–55

- Explain that these questions will help students focus on the main ideas in the listening. They do not need to understand every word to answer the questions.
- You may want to write the questions on the board.
- Read the questions aloud.
- Play the recording.
- After listening, have students compare their answers in pairs.

ANSWER KEY

1. He's broke.
2. Make a budget; Don't spend more than you earn; Work more hours at the computer store.
3. He won't have time to study if he works any more hours.
4. He's angry.

Stress

4 Listening for Stressed Words

- Listen to the recording again.
- There will be a pause on the recording at the end of each sentence to allow time for students to repeat and write the missing words.
- After listening, have students check their answers with the audioscript in their books.
- Have students read the conversation with a partner, paying attention to stressed words in their pronunciation and intonation.

AUDIOSCRIPT and ANSWER KEY

Dad: Hello?

Jeff: Hi, Dad.

Dad: Jeff! How _are_ you?

Jeff: I'm fine, Dad. How's Mom? Did she get over her _cold_?

Dad: Yes, she's _fine_ now. She went back to _work_ yesterday.

Jeff: That's good. Um, Dad, I need to _ask_ you something.

Dad: Sure, son, what _is_ it?

Jeff: Well, uh, the truth is, I'm _broke_ again. Could you _lend_ me $200 just till the end of the month?

Dad: Broke again? Jeff, when you moved _in_ with Nancy and Andrew, you said you could _make_ ends _meet_. But this is the _third_ time you've asked me for help!

Jeff: I know, I know, I'm sorry. But, see, my old guitar broke, and I had to buy a _new_ one. I _can't play_ on a broken guitar, right?

Dad: Look Jeff, if you want to play in a _band_, that's OK with me. But you _can't_ keep asking _me_ to pay for it!

Jeff: OK, OK, you're right. But what do you think I ought to _do_? Everything costs an _arm_ and a _leg_ around here.

Dad: Well, first of all, I think you'd better go on a _budget_. Make a list of all your _income_ and all your expenses. And then it's simple. Don't _spend_ more than you _earn_.

Jeff: But that's _exactly_ the problem! My expenses are _always_ larger than my income. That's why I need to borrow money from _you_.

Dad: Then maybe you should work more hours at the _computer_ store.

Jeff: Dad! I _already_ work 15 hours a week! How can I _study_ and _work_ and find time to play with my band?

Dad: Come _on_, Jeff, when _I_ was your age…

Jeff: I know, I know. When _you_ were my age you were already _married_ and working and going to school…

Dad: That's right. And if I could do it, why can't _you_?

Jeff: Because _I'm_ not _you_, Dad, that's why!

Dad: All right, Jeff, calm down. I don't _expect_ you to be like me. But I _can't lend_ you any more money. Your mother and I are on a budget _too_, you know.

PART 1

Student Book pages 55–56

Jeff: Maybe I should just drop _out_ of school, _work_ full-time, and play in the band in the evenings. I can go back to school _later_.

Dad: I wouldn't do that if I were you.

Jeff: Yeah, but you're _not_ me, remember? It's my life!

Dad: All right, Jeff. Let's not _argue_. Why don't you _think_ about this very carefully and call me _back_ in a few days. And in the meantime, you'd _better_ find a way to _pay_ for that new guitar.

Jeff: Yes, Dad.

Dad: All right. Good-bye, son.

Jeff: Bye.

Language Tip

- The difference between _lend_ and _borrow_ can be confusing because some languages use the same word for both actions. The action is the same, but it is seen from two different points of view: _borrow_ is from the point of view of the person receiving the money; _lend_ is from the point of view of the person giving the money. You may find this easier to illustrate by drawing a diagram.

- Check comprehension by saying, for example, "I'm going to _give you_ $10. I'm going to _____ you $10." (class should respond _lend_) or "You're going to _give me_ $10. I'm going to _____ $10." (class should respond _borrow_). Practice with individual students, or have students practice in pairs.

Expansion Activity

- Please see Black Line Master "Lend or Borrow?" on page BLM 7 of this Teacher's Manual. Photocopy and distribute one copy to each student.

- Model the activity. Choose a student who doesn't have a cell phone and say: _I really need to phone my sister. Can you lend me your cell phone?_ The student should answer _I'm sorry, I don't have a cell phone._ Then choose a student who has a cell phone and say: _I really need to phone my sister. Can you lend me your cell phone?_ The student should answer _Yes, of course. Here you are._ Write the student's name on your list.

- Divide the class in half. One half is part of group A. They will look at Table A and ask to borrow things. The other half is part of group B. They will look at Table B. They have things to lend.

- Have students walk around the room and ask each other questions until they write someone's name next to each item. Point out that they can use a classmate's name only once. They can start with any item on the list. (The items to be lent or borrowed are imaginary. They do not have to physically lend or borrow these items.)

- When students have completed the worksheet, they can sit down.

- Then have them switch roles.

Reductions

5 Comparing Unreduced and Reduced Pronunciation

- Play the recording and have students listen and read the sentences.

- Play the recording again. This time, ask students to repeat.

6 Listening for Reductions

- If you wish, and if you have time, have students read through the text first and try to guess the missing words.

- Play the recording and have students write their answers.

Student Book pages 56–57

- After listening, have students check their answers with the audioscript in their books. You can check answers in the audioscript below.
- Have students practice the conversation in pairs, paying attention to reduced forms in their pronunciation and intonation.

AUDIOSCRIPT

Customer: Hi, my name is Chang Lee.
Teller: How _can_ I help you?
Customer: I _want to_ check my balance.
Teller: OK. _Can_ I have your account number, please?
Customer: 381335.
Teller: Your balance is $201.
Customer: OK. _And_ I _asked_ my father _to_ wire me some money. I'd like _to_ know if it's arrived.
Teller: I'm sorry, your account doesn't show any deposits.
Customer: Oh, no. I need _to_ pay my rent tomorrow. _What do you_ think I _ought to_ do?
Teller: Well, we're having some computer problems today. So, uh, why _don't you_ call us later to check again? Or _you can_ come back. We're open till 5:00.
Customer: OK, thanks.
Teller: You're welcome.

After You Listen

7 Using Vocabulary

- Review the vocabulary items in this activity. Check that students know which ones are verbs and nouns.
- Brainstorm a few example questions with the class. Remind students they should not ask personal questions.

Example questions:

When did you last borrow something? (What did you borrow?)

When did you last lend something to somebody? (What did you lend?)

How much does a (name of a job) or (name of a movie / sports star) earn in a year?

What percentage of your income do you save (or would you like to save) every month?

How much do you spend on gas every month?

- After they write their questions, have students work in pairs. Student A will look at page 247 in the Student Book. Student B will look at page 255.
- Explain that they have different sets of sentences that they will have to read and answer appropriately. They should not show each other their books.
- Have students read their sections and ask if there are any questions.
- Model the pair work activity with one pair of students.
- Set a time limit of five minutes.
- Check the answers as a class.
- If there is time, have students choose one pair of sentences and continue the conversation.

ANSWER KEY

1. **A:** You look worried. What's wrong?
   B: I'm broke again. I can't pay my rent.
2. **A:** I can't make ends meet on $600 a month. I need more income!
   B: Maybe you should get a part-time job.
3. **A:** What's the secret to living on a budget?
   B: Don't spend more than you earn.
4. **A:** Why didn't you go to the concert?
   B: Because the tickets cost an arm and a leg.

PART 1

Student Book pages 57–58

Pronunciation

FOCUS

Can versus Can't

- Read the instruction note and practice the examples.

Pronunciation Note

- Students sometimes have difficulty distinguishing *can* from *can't* because they listen for the final *t* in *can't* which often disappears in rapid speech, especially if the following word starts with a *t* or a *d*, e.g., *I can't dance*.
- The main differences are in the sound of the vowel /ə/ in *can* and /æ/ in *can't* and in the stress pattern. *Can* is usually unstressed (unless indicating emphasis or contrast). *Can't* is usually stressed.

8 Pronouncing *Can* and *Can't*

- Read the directions for the activity.
- Play the recording. There will be a pause after each sentence to allow time for students to repeat and write an accent mark over the stressed words.

ANSWER KEY

Affirmative	Negative
1. Jeff **can pláy** on a broken guitar.	1. Jeff **cán't pláy** on a broken guitar.
2. Jeff's father **can páy** for his new guitar.	2. Jeff's father **cán't páy** for his new guitar.
3. Jeff **can wórk** more hours at the computer store.	3. Jeff **cán't wórk** more hours at the computer store.
4. I **can lénd** you more money.	4. I **cán't lénd** you more money.
5. Jeff **can gó** back to school later.	5. Jeff **cán't gó** back to school later.

9 Distinguishing Between *Can* and *Can't*

- Play the recording and have students circle the correct answers.
- Have students compare answers in pairs. Then play the recording again.
- Write (or ask a student to write) the correct answers on the board.

ANSWER KEY

1. can   2. can't   3. can't   4. can   5. can't
6. can't   7. can   8. can't   9. can   10. can

AUDIOSCRIPT

1. Sue can pay her bills by herself.
2. Jeff can't work and study at the same time.
3. I can't find my wallet.
4. You can pay with a credit card here.
5. You can't open an account without identification.
6. Anna can't work in the United States.
7. I can lend you five dollars.
8. We can't make ends meet.
9. You can apply for a loan at the bank across the street.
10. Jeff can play the guitar very well.

Student Book pages 58–60

10 Talking About Abilities

- Read the directions and model the example. Add a further example with *can't*.
- Go through the list, saying what you can and can't do, and have students raise their hands to identify *can* or *can't* (left hand for *can*, right hand for *can't*).
- Check comprehension of any new vocabulary.
- Divide students into pairs and have them complete the activity, telling their partners what they can and can't do. Monitor pronunciation of *can* and *can't* while walking around the classroom.
- When all or most students have completed the activity, have students tell the class three things that their partner can and can't do.

Using Language Functions

11 Recognizing Expressions of Advice

- Explain that you are looking for different expressions for asking for and giving advice. Ask students to come up with their own ideas orally.
- Direct students to pages 271–272 in the Student Book to look at the audioscript and fill out the chart.

ANSWER KEY

Asking for advice	Giving advice
Jeff:	Jeff's father:
What do you think I should do?	1. You'd better go on a budget.
	2. Don't spend more than you earn.
	3. Maybe you should work more hours at the computer store.
	4. I wouldn't do that if I were you.
	5. Why don't you think about this very carefully and call me back in a few days?

Best Practice

Interacting with Others

This type of activity is an example of collaborative learning to encourage fluency and confidence. In these role-plays, based around the topic of financial advice, communication is more important than grammar. Students can practice the role-plays in pairs and then improve their performance by switching roles or partners. By the time they perform the role-play for the class, they should feel more confident in the use of the new language.

12 Role-Play

- Read through the expressions in the chart. Model some short dialogs with two or three students by asking for advice. Respond using expressions from the chart.

Example problems:

I don't have enough money for a new car; My credit card payments are very high; I lost my ATM card; I want to save more money every month; I think there's a mistake on my pay check.

- Read through the four situations with the class. Ask each pair to choose a situation that interests them. Have students practice in pairs, switching roles and partners if there is time. Remind them to use expressions from the chart.
- Ask volunteers to perform one of their role-plays for the class. Make notes of significant errors.
- After everyone has finished, comment on general errors without mentioning students by name.

PART 2 Lecture: Entrepreneurs

Student Book pages 60–62

Before You Listen

- Read the information that introduces the next listening.

> **Best Practice**
>
> **Making Use of Academic Content**
> The prelistening discussion is an example of an activity that encourages students to practice impromptu speaking skills. When participating in discussions in class, students may be asked to give their opinion without being given a lot of preparation time. This activity provides an opportunity to practice that skill.

1 Prelistening Discussion

Question 1

- Have students answer these questions in small groups.
- You may want to write the word *entrepreneur* on the board. Ask students what they know about the word: its meaning, the contexts in which it is used, its grammatical form.

Question 2

- Brainstorm qualities that make a businessperson successful and write them on the board. Examples: creativity / creative, imagination / imaginative, confidence / confident, determination / determined, adventurous, brave, ruthless, tenacious, risk-taking.

  Alternatively, write a list of adjectives on the board and have students rank them in order of importance.

Question 3

- Invite students to talk about friends or family who have started their own businesses. Relate their stories to the vocabulary in part 2.

Question 4

- Encourage students to think about their own strengths and skills in relation to this topic.

2 Previewing Vocabulary

- Play the recording and have students listen to the words.
- Have students check the words they know, then compare answers with a partner. Explain that they will work out the meaning of the new words by listening to the lecture and doing activities that follow the lecture.

Listen

3 Taking Notes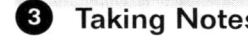

(The audioscript follows Activity 4.)

- Explain that students will listen to a lecture and practice listening and taking notes. The lecture is in two parts and they will hear each part twice. The first time, they should try to answer the main idea questions and take notes of any other important points. The second time, they will practice outlining.
- Play part 1 of the recording and check the answers to the questions.

> **ANSWER KEY**
>
> 1. An entrepreneur is a person who starts a completely new business or industry.
> 2. Characteristics of successful entrepreneurs are: They have vision; They are not afraid to take risks.

> **Best Practice**
>
> **Organizing Information**
> Activity 4 uses an outline to categorize information. Using an outline encourages students to process and organize information while they are listening and also provides a record for them to refer to when reviewing their notes. This type of graphic organizer emphasizes listing and categorizing skills. Other types of graphic organizers are used throughout this book.

Student Book pages 62–63

Strategy

Outlining

- Go over the outline pattern in the Strategy box. Point out the use of Roman numerals and the visual and spatial relationship between the three sets of letters and numbers and the different columns.

- Have students look at the photos. Ask them what they know about each person and each company.

4 Outlining the Lecture

- Go over the sample outline for the lecture. Have students use their notes to fill in the information. Check the answers and write them (or have a student write them) on the board.

Content Note

- Amazon.com is an online bookstore where you can search for and order from a choice of millions of new and used books, which are mailed directly to your home. It now also sells many other items, such as video games, electronics, and clothing.

- FedEx (Federal Express) is the name of a company that transports packages and mail by air and ground using a system of planes and trucks that operate across the United States. You can send mail with guaranteed overnight delivery.

- Anita Roddick was the founder of The Body Shop, a chain of stores selling cosmetics made from natural ingredients not tested on animals. The chain has associated its name with environmental issues. Customers can return product containers to the store to be refilled for a 15 percent discount.

ANSWER KEY

Topic: Entrepreneurs

I. Intro
  A. Example: Jeff Bezos
  B. Def. of entrep: starts new business / industry

II. Characteristics (similar)
  A. vision—see opportunities
    1. Ex. Jeff Bezos' idea to sell products on the Internet
  B. risk takers
    1. Ex. Frederick Smith / FedEx

III. Background (diff.)
  A. well educated / not well educated
    1. Ex. Jeff Bezos graduated Princeton
    2. Ex. Bill Gates didn't graduate college
  B. rich and poor
    1. Ex. Frederick Smith (founder of FedEx) from wealthy family
  C. Many ent. are immigrants or children of immigrants
    1. Ex. Jerry Yang from Taiwan, founder of Yahoo!
  D. young and age 40 or older
  E. men and women
    1. Ex. Anita Roddick of The Body Shop

AUDIOSCRIPT

Part 1

How many of you know the name Jeff Bezos? OK, how about Amazon.com? Have you heard of that? Well, Amazon is the world's first and largest Internet bookstore. And Jeff Bezos is the man who started Amazon back in 1995. Five years later, Amazon was serving millions of customers in 120 different countries. Amazing, right? And this is the reason why, in 1999, Jeff Bezos was selected as *Time* Magazine's Person of the Year, a very great honor.

Now, Jeff Bezos is actually not the topic of my lecture today, but he is a perfect example of my topic, which is entrepreneurs. That's *entrepreneurs*, spelled E-N-T-R-E-P-R-E-N-E-U-R-S. *Entrepreneur* is a French word meaning a person who starts a completely new business or industry; um, someone who does something no one else has done before; or who does it in a completely new way, like Jeff Bezos. Entrepreneurs like Jeff Bezos are very highly respected in American society and, I think, in many other countries too. So, in today's lecture I want to talk about three things. First, the characteristics of entrepreneurs—I mean, what kind of people they are. Second, the kind of background they come from. And third, the entrepreneurial process, that is, the steps entrepreneurs follow when they create a new business.

OK, let's begin by looking at the characteristics or, um, the qualities, of entrepreneurs. There are two qualities that I think all entrepreneurs have in common. First, entrepreneurs have vision. I mean that they have the ability to see opportunities that other people simply do not see. Let's look again at the example of Jeff Bezos. One day in 1994, he was surfing the Internet when suddenly he had a brilliant idea: why not use the Internet to sell products? Remember, at that time, no one was using the Internet in that way. After doing some research, Bezos decided that the product he wanted to sell was books. That's how Amazon got its start.

The other quality that I think all entrepreneurs have is that they're not afraid to take risks. I mean they're not afraid to fail. As an example, let me tell you about Frederick Smith. He founded FedEx, the company that delivers packages overnight. Smith first suggested the idea for his company in a college term paper. Do you know what grade he got on it? A C! Clearly, his professor didn't like the idea, but this didn't stop him. Today FedEx is worth more than 20 billion dollars and employs more than 130,000 people.

OK, we've just seen that all entrepreneurs have at least two important qualities in common. But now let's take a look at some differences. We'll see that their backgrounds can be very different. First of all, some entrepreneurs are well educated, like Jeff Bezos, who graduated from Princeton University. But others, like Bill Gates, the founder of Microsoft, never even finished college. Next, some entrepreneurs come from rich families, like Frederick Smith, the founder of FedEx. In contrast, other entrepreneurs come from poor families, and many are immigrants or the children of immigrants. A great example is Jerry Yang, one of the men who started Yahoo.com. He was born in Taiwan and came to America as a young boy in the 1970s.

OK, the third difference is that although many entrepreneurs start their businesses at a young age, lots of others don't start until age 40 or later. And finally, I think it's important to remind you that entrepreneurs are not always men. A famous woman entrepreneur, for example, is Anita Roddick. She founded The Body Shop. You can find her natural cosmetics shops all over the world. So, to conclude this section, you can see that entrepreneurs come from many different backgrounds.

5 **Taking Notes on a Process**

- Explain that students will listen to the second part of the lecture on the steps in the entrepreneurial process. They will listen and try to fill in the outline.
- Play the recording of part 2 of the lecture.

> **ANSWER KEY**
> IV. Entrepreneurial Process
>   A. Identify a problem
>   B. Think of solution
>   C. Prepare business plan

Student Book page 64

D. Hire team (finding the right people to work in the new business)
E. Test marketing
F. Raise capital (money)

AUDIOSCRIPT
Part 2

I want to move on now and take a look at the entrepreneurial process. There are six basic steps that most entrepreneurs follow when they start their businesses. In the first step, they identify a problem; in other words, they see a need or a problem that no one else sees. Then in the second step, they think of a solution, what needs to be done to solve the problem or meet the need. I think we've already seen several examples today of people who saw a need or an opportunity and then came up with a creative solution.

Step three is to prepare a business plan. This means looking at things like equipment, location, financing, marketing, and so on. There are thousands of details to think about when you start a new business; as a result, this stage can take months or even years.

The next step, the fourth step, is putting together a team—in other words, hiring the right people to work with the entrepreneur in the new business. After that, the fifth step is something called *test marketing*. That's test marketing. This involves making and selling a small amount of the product or service just to try it out and see if customers like it. And if they do, then, finally, entrepreneurs go to the sixth step, which is raising capital. *Capital* is another word for "money." The entrepreneur has to raise a lot of money, you know, from the bank, or friends, or family, in order to produce and sell the product or service in large quantities.

I want to say, in conclusion, that entrepreneurs like Jeff Bezos are among the most respected people in the United States. They are cultural heroes, like movie stars or sports heroes. Why? Because, starting with a dream and working very hard, these people created companies that solved serious, important problems. They provided jobs for millions of people, and in general, their companies made life easier and more pleasant for all of us. If you ever order a book from Amazon, or use natural make-up from The Body Shop, say thanks to the remarkable people who created these companies.

After You Listen

6 Discussing the Lecture

- Have students work in pairs to complete and discuss questions 1–6 of this activity.
- Compare answers as a class.

ANSWER KEY

1. 1. e 2. a 3. d 4. c 5. b
2. They have vision and they take risks.
3. They can be well educated or not; they can be rich or poor; they can be immigrants; they can be men or women.
4. The six steps are: a. Identify a problem b. Think of a solution c. Prepare a business plan d. Hire a team e. Test the market f. Raise capital (money)
5. Entrepreneurs are cultural heroes because they started with a dream and worked very hard to create companies that make our lives better and provide jobs for millions of people.
6. Answers will vary.

7 Reviewing Vocabulary

- Refer students to Activity 2 on page 61 of the Student Book. Review any new items and have students check the meaning in a dictionary if necessary.

PART 2

Student Book page 65

Talk It Over

Best Practice

Cultivating Critical Thinking

This is an example of a collaborative team activity resulting in a final product. This type of activity requires students to process the information they have learned and apply it to a new situation. This involves reinterpretation, synthesis, and application of concepts. The process of manipulating language and concepts in this way will create deeper processing of new material, which will allow students to evaluate whether they have understood the new material and help them remember it better.

8 Become an Entrepreneur!

- Read the instructions with the class.
- Brainstorm possible ideas for new products and services and write them on the board.
- Divide the class into groups and have each group develop an idea by following steps 1 and 2. (They can choose one from the list, provided another group has not chosen it, or they can come up with their own idea.)
- Set a time limit of 15 minutes for groups to follow the steps in part 3.
- If there is time in class, have students present their business plan to the class. Or you may assign preparation for this as homework and ask students for their presentation in the next class.

Expansion Activity

- The aim of this activity is for students to use the Internet as a resource to obtain information about famous entrepreneurs. They will then process the information by discussing and making notes about it in their groups.
- Students can use a search engine entering *entrepreneurs* or the name of the websites below. Check these websites before passing them on to students.
www.entrepreneurs.about.com/od/famousentrepreneurs/
www.financial-inspiration.com/famous-entrepreneurs.html/
- The research part of this activity can be done in a computer lab class or assigned for homework.
- Please see Black Line Master "Famous Entrepreneurs" on page BLM 8 of this Teacher's Manual. Photocopy and distribute one to each group.
- Divide the students into small groups and have each person in the group choose one famous entrepreneur from the list.
- Students will research their chosen entrepreneur on the web. Then re-form their groups to complete the worksheet.
- If students need more room to write, they can write on the back of the page, making 4 new boxes.
- Note that if there is an entrepreneur you would like to include, or who is famous in your area, feel free to include that person (or those persons) in the list of options.
- Finally, ask for volunteers to share the information from part 2 with the class.

PART 3 — Strategies for Better Listening and Speaking

Student Book pages 65–66

Getting Meaning from Context

1 Prelistening Questions

- Point to the picture and ask students to describe it. Where is it? What is the person doing? Why is she waiting? Answers: She is waiting at an ATM (automated teller machine). She might be waiting to get cash, make a deposit, or check her balance.
- Question 1 can be approached by either first looking at the lettered list of banking services in Activity 2 or by first brainstorming a list of services offered by banks in the U.S. and comparing it with the list in Activity 2. Check that students understand all these items.
- Discuss Questions 2 and 3 as a class.

Best Practice

Scaffolding Instruction

This is an example of an activity that raises metacognitive awareness of learning strategies. In real life, we use surrounding context clues to work out the meanings of unfamiliar words. This activity asks students to use the surrounding verbal clues in each advertisement to work out the main topic. By writing the clues, students are guided through the steps of developing this skill.

ANSWER KEY

Topic	Clues (These answers may vary.)
1. a. a safe deposit box	valuable possessions, protect, safe place, lock up
2. c. a home improvement loan	lend you money, remodeling, old house, new one, heating, roof, bank, finance
3. d. an automated banking machine (an ATM machine)	Insta (like *instant*), bank, money, easy, get cash, bank is closed
4. b. a savings account	earn interest, money, deposit, investor

Content Note

In the U.S., Europe, and many other countries, you can pay for store-bought items with a credit card or with a debit card. If you use a credit card, it means that you borrow money and may have to pay interest. If you use a debit card, it means that the money is taken directly from your account, so there is no interest, although there is sometimes a small store fee.

FOCUS ON TESTING — TOEFL iBT

Using Context Clues

- This recording has four advertisements. Play each advertisement, pausing after the question at the end of the advertisement to allow students to circle their answers and write the clues.
- Then play the final part of each section, which gives the correct answer.

PART 3

Student Book pages 66–67

AUDIOSCRIPT

Advertisement 1

Every person has valuable possessions that are difficult or impossible to replace, for example, family photographs, jewelry, a passport, old coins, or insurance policies. You should protect these priceless valuables by putting them in a safe place. Lock up your treasures in International Bank, and you'll never have to worry about losing your valuables again.

Question 1: *The speaker is talking about...*

The International Bank Safe Deposit Box—safety and protection the easy way!

Advertisement 2

Right now International Bank can lend you money for dozens of projects. For instance, remodeling a kitchen or a bathroom can change an old house into an exciting new one. Thinking about solar heating? Need a new roof? International Bank can help you finance them.

Question 2: *The speaker is talking about...*

For any home improvement loan, talk to International Bank first.

Advertisement 3

With an Insta-Teller Card from International Bank, you're close to your money night or day. The Insta-Tellers operate 24 hours a day, seven days a week, 365 days a year. It's an easy way to get cash, pay your bills, make a deposit, or check your balance even when your bank is closed.

Question 3: *The speaker is talking about...*

Insta-Teller automated banking machines—any transaction, any time.

Advertisement 4

How would you like to earn 4.5 percent interest and still be able to take out money any time you need it? You can do both! Just deposit $5,000 and keep a minimum average balance of $500. Come in and ask about our investor's plan.

Question 4: *The speaker is talking about...*

International Bank Investor's Plan—a savings account and more!

Pronunciation

FOCUS

Teens and Tens

- Read the information about the pronunciation of *teens* and *tens*.
- Model some examples of each number. Have students raise their hands to identify if it is a *teen* or a *ten* (left hand for *teen* and right hand for *ten*).

2 Pronouncing *Teens* and *Tens*

- Read the directions for Activity 2.
- There will be a pause on the recording after each pair of words to allow time for students to repeat.

3 Distinguishing Between *Teens* and *Tens*

- Play the recording.
- Have students compare answers in pairs.
- Play the recording again and check the answers as a class.

Student Book pages 67–68

ANSWER KEY

1. $40.10
2. $16.99
3. 18
4. 90
5. 230
6. 260
7. 14.5
8. $2,215
9. 1764
10. 1890

AUDIOSCRIPT

1. He paid $40.10 for the bottle of wine.
2. *Woman*: How much does this dictionary cost?
   Man: $16.99.
3. Most credit card companies charge 18 percent interest per month on your outstanding balance.
4. We drove at a speed of 90 miles per hour.
5. I bought my coat in Paris for 230 euros.
6. The plane from Buenos Aires carried 260 passengers.
7. My dog weighs 14 and a half kilos.
8. The rent on this apartment is $2,215 a month.
9. My aunt lives at 1764 Wilson Avenue.
10. International Bank is located at 1890 West Second Street.

4 Pair Practice with Teens and Tens

- Have students work in pairs. Student A will look at page 247 in the Student Book. Student B will look at page 255.
- Students will take turns reading the sentences and circling the numbers they hear.
- Monitor the activity while walking around the classroom.
- Select a few students to model the pronunciation for the whole class.

On the Spot!

5 What Would You Do?

- Read the directions and the four situations.
- Ask students to decide what they would do in each situation and to write their answers.

6 Discussing the Situations

- Divide students into small groups of three or four. Give them five minutes to discuss questions 1–3.
- Ask a leader from each group to report the results of their discussion to the class.

Copyright © McGraw-Hill
Interactions 2 Listening/Speaking

PART 3

Expansion Activity

- The aim of this activity is to practice vocabulary connected with the theme of banking services and to encourage students to express personal opinions about why they do or not use each of these services.
- Please see Black Line Master "Group Survey" on page BLM 9 of this Teacher's Manual.
- Photocopy and cut the page into strips. You will need one strip for each student in your class. If there are more than ten students in your class, photocopy more than one page. (This activity can be done as a whole class walk-around activity, which will take longer, or in smaller groups.)
- Distribute strips to the students.
- Explain that they will have to ask a *yes/no* question based on their sentence in order to find out whether their sentence is true or false *about their class or group*.
- Model the activity with one student. Select one student and ask: *Do you have a credit card?* If they say *yes* mark one check in the *Yes* section.
- Remind students they should keep a note of which students they have asked, so as not to ask the same student twice!
- At the end of the activity, have students report their findings to the class. Tell whether their statement is true or false, based on the number of *yes/no* answers.

  For example, Student A might say: *My sentence was* Everyone in this group has a credit card. *I found that my sentence is true because I asked everyone in this class, and they all have a credit card. It's the most convenient way to pay for things in the store.*

PART 4 — Real-World Task: Balancing a Checkbook

Student Book pages 69–70

- Have students read the information about a checking account. Answer any questions they might have.
- Explain (or ask students to explain) the difference between checking and savings accounts.
- If possible, bring in examples of bank brochures for different types of accounts (in English or in the students' own languages) and an example of a checkbook record.

Before You Listen

1 Prelistening Questions

- Put the students in small groups.
- Have them read and discuss questions 1–4.

2 Previewing Vocabulary

- Play the recording and have students listen to the words and phrases.
- Explain that the words in the left-hand column will appear in the recording.
- Have students work individually to match each phrase with a definition from the right-hand column. Then compare answers as a class.

> **ANSWER KEY**
> 1. c 2. e 3. d 4. a 5. b

Listen

3 Balancing a Checkbook

- Ask students to look at the checkbook record. Check comprehension by asking questions. For example:

  What's the account number? (132-98804)

  What's in the first column? (check number)

  When did they pay the Electric Company? (October 27)

  How much did they pay to Compu-Tech on November 1? ($125)

  How much was in their account on November 8? ($525.18)

- Read the directions.
- Check that students understand which items are missing. (12 items)
- Play the recording.
- Have students compare their answers in pairs. Encourage them to use math to check the amounts.
- Play the recording again.
- Check the answers as a whole class.

ANSWER KEY

No	Date	Description	Payment	Deposit	Balance
200	10/25	ABC market	30.21		490.31
201	10/27	Electric company	57.82		432.49
202	10/27	Time magazine	35		397.49
203	10/30	Birthday present	70		327.49
204	11/1	Compu-Tech	125.00		202.49
205	11/1	Dr. Painless	40		162.49
	11/1	Deposit		1234.69	1397.18
206	11/2	House payment	412		985.18
207	11/4	Visa payment	155.00		830.18
208	11/8	Auto insurance	305.00		525.18
209	11/10	Traffic ticket	68		457.18

PART 4

Student Book pages 70–71

Content Note

It used to be traditional in the United States for married couples to have a joint checking account. It is now more common for husbands and wives to have separate checking accounts and sometimes a joint account for household expenses.

AUDIOSCRIPT

George: Let's see here. Check number 200. October 25th. Did you write this check?

Martha: $30.21. Oh, yes. That was last Thursday. ABC Market.

George: OK, so that leaves a balance of $490.31. Next: number 201. Electric bill. $57.82. So now we have $432.49. Next: October 27th. *Time* magazine. I forgot to enter the amount.

Martha: I remember that. It was $35.00.

George: OK. So that leaves $397.49. Now what's this $70?

Martha: That was for your sister's birthday present.

George: Oh, yes. OK... And here's check 205. When did we pay the dentist?

Martha: The same day I deposited my paycheck. November first.

George: Fine. So after the deposit, the balance was $1,397.18. And then I made the house payment, check number 206. That's $412, and the VISA payment—that's $155, so now our balance is $830.18.

Martha: You know, George, we should really pay off our credit card balance. The interest is 18 percent a year.

George: You're right. But we can't afford it right now. Look at this car insurance bill! $305 to Auto Insurance of America. And that's just for four months. And here's another traffic ticket!

Martha: Last month it was you, this month it was me.

George: Oh, man... How much was it this time?

Martha: $68. What's the balance now?

George: $457.18. I guess we're OK for the rest of the month as long as we don't get any more traffic tickets.

After You Listen

4 Discussion

- Have students form small groups to discuss Questions 1–3.
- Set a time limit of five minutes.
- Ask group leaders to report to the class on the results of the discussion.

5 Find Someone Who...

- Read the instructions with the class.
- Explain that students must turn each statement into a question, e.g., *Are you carrying any money today? Do you or have you ever worked in a bank?*
- Model example dialogs with two or three students. Use the question openers from the *Language Tip* box on page 71 of the Student Book.
- Set a time limit of ten minutes. Have students walk around the class to complete the activity.
- Monitor the activity by walking around the classroom.
- At the end of ten minutes, have students sit down and compare how many names they collected.

Student Book pages 72–73

Talk It Over

6) Interview

- Assign this task for homework. Suggest that students interview someone who is not from their own cultural background. Remind them to use the question openers from the *Language Tip* box on page 71 of the Student Book.
- During the next class, have students share their information in groups.
- Have group leaders present a summary to the class at the end.

Expansion Activity (REPRODUCIBLE)

- The aim of this activity is to practice the math and language skills associated with balancing a checkbook. It also reviews pronunciation of *teens* and *tens*.
- Have students work in pairs.
- Please see Black Line Master "Balancing Your Checkbook" on page BLM 10 of this Teacher's Manual.
- Photocopy the Black Line Master, one copy for each pair of students. Cut each page in half, one half for each student in a pair.
- Remind students they must not look at their partner's paper.
- Explain that they will have to ask questions to complete the missing information in their "checkbook." Their partner has the answers.
- Model the activity with one student. Select a Student A and ask: *How much was the auto payment on May 23?* Student A will answer: $160.00.
- At the end of the activity, have students check their answers by comparing papers.

ANSWER KEY

No	Date	Description	Payment	Deposit	Balance
					598.12
150	5/21	(B) Phone	(A) 118.06		480.06
151	5/21	(A) Gas	60.17		(B) 419.89
152	5/23	Auto payment	(B) 160.00		(A) 259.89
153	5/26	(B) Groceries	(A) 180.14		79.75
	5/30	Deposit		(B) 625.00	(B) 704.75
154	6/02	(A) House insurance	(B) 219.45		(A) 485.30
155	6/03	(B) Credit card payment	(A) 415.00		(B) 70.30
	6/05	Deposit		(A) 316.00	386.30
156	6/08	Groceries	(A) 150.17		236.13
157	6/09	(A) Doctor	(B) 15.00		(A/B) 221.13

Self-Assessment Log

- The purpose of the log is to help the students reflect on their learning.
- Read the directions aloud and have students check vocabulary that they learned in the chapter and are prepared to use.
- Have students check the strategies they understand.
- Put students in small groups. Ask students to find the information or an activity related to each strategy in the chapter.
- Tell students to find definitions in the chapter for any words they did not check, or they can look in their dictionaries.

CHAPTER 4
Jobs and Professions

In this CHAPTER

Students will read about various topics related to jobs and professions, such as looking for a job, interviewing, and comparing jobs. In Part 1, they will learn to recognize stressed and reduced forms and practice ways to apologize and reconcile. In Part 2, they will listen to a talk about changes in the U.S. job market. They will also practice a job interview. In Part 3, they will practice listening to conversations and guessing people's jobs. In Part 4, they will practice sequencing events in the typical day of a househusband.

> "Work and play are words used to describe the same thing under differing conditions."
>
> Mark Twain
> American author and humorist,
> 1835–1910

Chapter Opener

- Have students look at the photo and describe what they see. Ask them the questions from the Connecting to the Topic section. Have students discuss as a class.
- Read and discuss the quote. What makes work seem like play? When do you enjoy working? What aspects of your job do you (or would you) enjoy most?

Chapter Overview

Listening Skills and Strategies
Listening for main ideas and details
Making inferences
Recognizing the intonation of tag questions
Recognizing a sequence of events
Taking notes on causes and effects
Creating abbreviations
Taking notes on statistics

Speaking Skills and Strategies
Talking about jobs and careers
Apologizing and reconciling
Role-playing a job interview
Learning idioms related to housework
Talking about "men's" and "women's" jobs
Interviewing a person about his/her job
Giving a short oral report

Critical-Thinking Skills
Interpreting information in a table
Getting meaning from context

Speculating about hypothetical situations
Taking notes on a lecture
Predicting the order of a set of pictures
Using a matrix diagram to organize ideas

Vocabulary Building
Terms related to jobs and careers
Expressions for apologizing and reconciling
Idioms related to housework
Terms signaling cause and effect

Pronunciation
Identifying and practicing stressed words
Identifying and practicing reduced pronunciation
Asking and answering negative tag questions

Language Skills
Using context clues to guess people's jobs

Vocabulary

Nouns
- automation
- bottom line
- categories
- competition
- economy
- health care
- illness
- job market
- labor costs
- manufacturing
- rank
- salary
- service
- trend

Verbs
- complain
- grow by X%
- spend time
- support

Expressions
- in the mood
- the worst

PART 1 — Conversation: Finding a Job

Can You Guess?

- Ask students to discuss the questions below in groups and compare their answers with the correct answers.
- Discuss the issues raised by these questions: Why do people decide to change jobs? What factors make a person want to stay in his or her job? What makes a job stressful? What kinds of jobs have disappeared? What new jobs are becoming popular?

1. How many times does the average American change jobs in his or her lifetime? A. *U.S. Department of Labor Statistics shows that the average person makes four to six career changes and 12 to 15 job changes in his or her lifetime.*

2. Which of the following jobs is the most stressful, according to research? Why?
   A. Computer programmer. B. Mail carrier. C. Teacher. D. Veterinarian. E. Carpenter.
   A. *Teacher. According to research done in Great Britain, the most stressful jobs involve direct contact with the public in emotionally intense situations. Such jobs included teachers, paramedics, police officers, and social workers.*

3. Name three occupations that will be in high demand in the United States between now and the year 2012. A. *The following occupations will be in the highest demand in the United States through 2012:*
   1. *Teachers (K-12)*
   2. *Registered nurses*
   3. *College instructors*
   4. *Customer service representatives*
   5. *Computer support staff*

Before You Listen

- Read the text that introduces the next listening. Students will discuss the photo in the next activity.

1 Prelistening Questions

- Have the students read the questions and discuss them in pairs.
- Compare answers as a whole class.
- As a whole class, make a list of places you could go to find a job. These might include: Classified ads in the newspaper, employment websites or company websites on the Internet, job center, employment agency, community notice board.

2 Previewing Vocabulary

- Play the recording and have students listen for the underlined words and phrases.
- Have students complete the vocabulary preview individually.
- Compare their answers as a whole class and write the correct answers on the board.

ANSWER KEY

1. d   2. c   3. e   4. b   5. a

Listen

3 Comprehension Questions

(The audioscript follows Activity 4.)

- Explain that these questions will help students focus on the main ideas in the listening. They do not need to understand every word to answer the questions.
- You may want to write the questions on the board.
- Read the questions aloud.
- Play the recording.
- After listening, have students discuss their answers in pairs.
- Check the answers as a class.

Student Book pages 77–79

ANSWER KEY

1. He wants a full-time job;   2. In a record store;   3. In a fast-food restaurant;   4. It was boring;   5. It's very tiring, and the classes are too large;   6. Because she is an international student (which means that she probably doesn't have a work permit);   7. that they all go out for dinner

Stress

4 Listening for Stressed Words

- Play the recording again, this time with books open.
- There will be a pause at the end of each sentence to allow time for students to repeat and write the missing words.
- After listening, have students check their answers with the audioscript in their books.
- Have students read the conversation with a partner, paying attention to stressed words in their pronunciation.

AUDIOSCRIPT and ANSWER KEY

Mari: Hey, Jeff, what's going _on_?

Jeff: Oh, I'm looking at the _classified_ ads. It looks like I have to get a _job_.

Mari: I thought you _had_ a job, at a computer store or something?

Jeff: Yeah, but that's _part_-time. I need something _full_-time.

Mari: Really? But what about _school_? What about your _band_? How can you work full-time?

Jeff: Well, to tell you the _truth_, I'm probably going to drop _out_ of school for a while. I'm just not in the _mood_ for _studying_ these days. I'd rather spend my time _playing_ with my band. But my father won't _support_ me if I'm not in school.

Mari: I see… Well, what kind of job do you want to _get_?

Jeff: Well ideally, something involving _music_, like in a record store. But if _that's_ not possible… I don't know, but whatever I do, it'll be better than my _first_ job.

Mari: Oh yeah? What was _that_?

Jeff: Believe it or not, the summer after I finished _high_ school I worked at Burger Ranch.

Mari: You? In a _fast_-food place? What did you _do_ there?

Jeff: I was a _burger_ flipper. You know, I made hamburgers all day long.

Mari: That sounds like a pretty _boring_ job!

Jeff: It was the _worst_. And I haven't gone inside a Burger Ranch since I _quit_ that job.

Nancy: Hi, what's so _funny_?

Jeff: Do you remember my _job_ at the Burger Ranch?

Nancy: Oh yeah. That was pretty _awful_. But actually, it doesn't sound so bad to me right now.

Mari: Why, Nancy? What's _wrong_?

Nancy: Oh, I'm just really, really _tired_. I'm teaching four different _classes_ this term, and _two_ of them are really _large_. Sometimes I think I've been _teaching_ too long.

Mari: How long have you been _teaching_?

Nancy: Twelve years. Maybe it's time to try something _else_.

Mari: Like _what_?

Nancy: Well, I've always wanted to be a _writer_. I could work at home…

Jeff: Oh, _don't_ listen to her, Mari. She _always_ talks this way when she's had a bad day at school. At least you _have_ a good _job_, Nancy. Look at me: I'm _broke_, and Dad won't _lend_ me any more money…

Interactions 2 Listening/Speaking **61**

PART 1

Student Book pages 79–80

Nancy:	Oh, stop _complaining_. if you're so poor, why don't you go _back_ to the Burger Ranch?
Mari:	Listen you two, stop _arguing_. Look at me! I _can't_ work at _all_ because I'm an international student.
Jeff:	OK, OK I'm _sorry_, Nancy. Tell you what. Let's go out to _dinner_. _I'll_ pay.
Nancy:	But you're _broke_!
Jeff:	All right, _you_ pay!

Reductions

5 **Comparing Unreduced and Reduced Pronunciation**

- Review the meaning of reduced forms.
- Play the recording and have students listen and read the sentences.
- Play the recording again. This time, ask students to repeat.

6 **Listening for Reductions**

- Explain that students will hear a conversation between a manager and a job applicant.
- You may want to have students read through the conversation and try to guess the missing words.
- There will be a pause on the recording after each speaker to allow students time to write their answers. (Students should write the long forms.)
- Check the answers to Activity 6 with the audioscript.
- Have students practice the conversation in pairs, paying attention to reduced forms in their pronunciation. You may want to try asking students to read the line silently, then look up and say the line to their partner. This will help them to focus on pronunciation, not reading.
- Move around the room to monitor pronunciation and provide help if needed.

AUDIOSCRIPT

Manager:	I'm _going to_ ask you some questions, O.K.? What _kind of_ jobs have you had?
Applicant:	Mostly factory jobs. The last five years I worked in a plastics factory.
Manager:	_What did you_ do there?
Applicant:	I _used to_ cut sheets of plastic.
Manager:	_What do you want to_ do here?
Applicant:	I _don't know_. I'll do anything. I'm good with my hands, and I'm a hard worker.
Manager:	Why _don't you_ fill out an application in the office. It looks like we're _going to_ have an opening next week. I'll call you.
Applicant:	Thanks.

After You Listen

7 **Reviewing Vocabulary**

- Have students work in pairs. One student will look at page 248 in the Student Book. The other student will look at page 256.
- Have students read their section and ask if there are any questions.
- Set a time limit of five minutes.
- Check the answers as a class.
- If there is time, have students choose one pair of sentences and continue the conversation.

Student Book pages 80–81

ANSWER KEY

1. **A:** How was your trip to New York last December?
   B: It was the worst. It snowed for five days straight.
2. **A:** Did you do anything about the broken elevator in your building?
   B: Yeah. I complained about it to my apartment manager.
3. **A:** Do you want to go to the beach this afternoon?
   B: No, thanks. I'm not in the mood.
4. **A:** I heard your mother got a full-time job.
   B: Yeah. She's supporting me while I finish my B.A.
5. **A:** What's your brother doing these days?
   B: He spends all his time studying. I almost never see him.

Using Language Functions

FOCUS

Apologizing and Reconciling

- Read the information note.
- Ask two students to read the dialog using the appropriate intonation.
- Read the information in the *Culture Note*. Ask students for more examples of each one, for example, invite someone for dinner, buy some flowers, next time I'll be more careful.

Best Practice

Interacting with Others

Activity 8 is an example of collaborative learning to encourage fluency and confidence. In this activity, communication is more important than grammar. Students can practice apologizing and reconciling in pairs. They can improve their confidence by switching roles or partners and practicing the same situations again. By providing feedback to each other, they learn skills of self-evaluation.

8 Role-Play

- Read the situations and check comprehension of any new vocabulary.
- Have students work in pairs to practice the role-plays.
- Set a time limit of five minutes.
- Move around the room to monitor and provide feedback. Take notes of errors.
- Comment on common errors, without mentioning who made them.
- Ask for volunteers to perform conversations for the class.

9 Discussion

- Ask students to read through the situations and questions silently and ask about any unfamiliar vocabulary.
- Have students work in groups of three or four to discuss the questions.
- Set a time limit of ten minutes.
- Move around the room to monitor and provide feedback.
- At the end, ask for volunteers to summarize their group's discussion.

PART 1

Expansion Activity

- The purpose of this activity is to practice appropriate responses to situations where you need to apologize.
- Put the students in small groups of three or four.
- Please see Black Line Master "Saying You're Sorry" on page BLM 11 of this Teacher's Manual. Photocopy one copy for each group.
- Cut each copy into strips and distribute one set of strips to each group of students.
- Students will place the strips face down in the center of the group.
- Each student in turn will pick up a strip, read the situation, and apologize.
- The other students in the group will advise the student on an appropriate way to reconcile (each suggestion must be different).
- The person with the best suggestion gets a point (chosen by the person who picked and read the situation).
- Demonstrate the activity with one group.
- Set a time limit of ten minutes.
- Monitor groups and provide feedback.
- At the end of the activity, ask for examples of the most interesting or most creative ways of reconciling.

PART 2 — Lecture: Changes in the U.S. Job Market

Student Book pages 82–85

Before You Listen

- Read the text that introduces the next listening.

1 Prelistening Discussion

- Have students look at the table.
- Ask students to explain the title in their own words.
- Before reading, ask students to try and predict what kinds of occupations they think will be the "fastest growing."
- Read the list of occupations and check comprehension of any new words.
- Have students work in pairs to answer the questions below the table.
- Review the responses as a class.

ANSWER KEY

1. Information about which professions are increasing most rapidly.
2. The table covers the years 2002–2012.
3. The four columns give information about a) The types of jobs that will grow fastest b) The percentage increase in the number of people in these jobs c) The salary for that job in relation to other jobs.
4. Answers will vary.
5. All jobs require a college education except numbers 1, 4, 7, 10, and 12.
6. The jobs with the highest salaries in this table are mainly computer- or health-related, and all require a college degree.

2 Previewing Vocabulary

- Play the recording and have students listen to the words.
- Have students check the words they know and then compare answers with a partner.
- Explain that they will work out the meaning of the new words by listening to the lecture.

Listen

Strategy

Taking Notes on Causes and Effects

- Read the information in the Strategy box.
- Review the difference in meaning between *cause* and *effect*.
- Point out the use of punctuation with these different expressions.

3 Taking Notes on Cause-and-Effect Statements

- Read the directions and have students work individually to take notes from the sentences in the box.
- Remind them to write key words, use abbreviations, and use symbols for cause and effect. (= or • or ↓)

ANSWER KEY

Note: In this answer key, the cause is followed by the effect to avoid confusion.

1. robots → factory jobs ↓
2. robots less $ than humans → factory robots ↑
3. humans ≠ 24 hrs → robots ↑
4. labor cost in Asia less $ → U.S. factories to Asia
5. robots → no fact. jobs ↓
6. robots less $ → robots ↑, humans ↓
7. automation → 1st cause of unempl.

4 Creating Abbreviations

- Have students read the words in the table.
- Use dictionaries to check the meanings if necessary.

PART 2

Student Book page 85

- For each word, students should come up with a symbol or abbreviation that they will find easy to remember and use.

ANSWER KEY
Possible answers:

Words	Abbreviations
economy	econ
manufacturing	manf
service	svce
technology	tech
approximately	approx
million	m
medical	med
computer	comp
percent	%
bachelor of arts	BA

5 Listening and Taking Notes on Causes and Effects

- Play the recording and have students take notes using their symbols.
- Have students listen to each statement twice before taking notes. Otherwise, they won't benefit from the repetition because they'll be starting to write already.

ANSWER KEY
1. tech → manf w/ machine, not people
2. tech → ↓ manf jobs
3. people live longer → ↑ med services
4. med tech → people live longer
5. working wmn → growth

AUDIOSCRIPT
1. Because of technology, we're able to manufacture goods by using machines instead of human workers.
2. As a result, thousands of manufacturing jobs don't exist anymore.
3. We're going to need more medical services because people are living longer and longer.
4. Also, because of developments in medical technology, people with serious illnesses are able to live much longer than they could in the past.
5. The main reason for the huge growth in this category is that most married women now work outside the home.

6 Taking Notes on Statistics

- Review the box on page 38 in the Student Book about taking notes on statistics.
- Play the recording and have students take notes using their symbols.
- They will hear each statement twice.
- Have students compare notes with a partner and try to reconstruct the sentences on the recording.
- Compare answers as a class. Write the sentences on the board.

ANSWER KEY
1. 2.5m manf jobs ↓ since 2001
2. svce jobs ↑ 20m nxt 10 yrs
3. ½ jobs in hlth
4. hlth jobs ↑ 3m nxt 10 yrs
5. # comp. jobs ↑ 30% nxt 10 yrs

Student Book pages 85–87

AUDIOSCRIPT

1. According to the United States government, approximately 2.5 million manufacturing jobs have disappeared just since the year 2001.
2. At the same time that the number of manufacturing jobs is decreasing, the number of service jobs is probably going to grow more than 20 million just in the next ten years!
3. Almost half of the jobs on the list are in the field of health care.
4. According to the United States Department of Labor, the number of health care jobs will increase by almost three million in the next ten years.
5. The number of jobs in the computer industry is expected to grow by almost 30 percent in the next ten years.

❼ Taking Notes

(The audioscript follows Activity 8.)

- Read the questions and have students focus on them as they listen and take notes the first time.
- Play the recording.
- Check the answers as a class.

ANSWER KEY
Part 1
1. from a manufacturing economy to a service economy
2. because of technology and foreign competition

Part 2
3. health care, computers, and personal care and services
4. get a degree

Best Practice
Scaffolding Instruction
The outline helps students to organize the lecture into main and secondary ideas. By providing students with the outline as a support, they can see how outlining can help the listener to structure the content of the talk. This guided activity prepares them for the skill of identifying main and secondary ideas without the help of an outline.

❽ Outlining the Lecture

- Ask student to use their notes to complete the outline.
- Play the recording again.
- Have students fill in any missing information.
- Check the answers as a class.

ANSWER KEY
The Changing U.S. Job Market

Part 1
I. 2 questions this lec. will answer:
  A. _best jobs_?
  B. _how to prepare_?
II. History: Last 100 yrs., change in U.S. labor market: from _manf_ to _service_ economy
  A. Definitions
    1. _manf = make things_
       e.g.: _cars, furniture, clothes_
    2. _service = do things_
       e.g.: _cut hair, fix shoes, sell computers_
III. Reasons for ↓ in manf jobs
  A. _tech_
  B. _for. comp._
    1. stat: 2.5m. ↓ since 2001
    2. _trend to continue in 21st cent_.
IV. ↑ _in service jobs_
  A. Stat: ↑ _20m nxt 10 yrs_.

Interactions 2 Listening/Speaking

Part 2

V. Fastest growing service jobs

   A. _health care_

      1. e.g.: _medical assts, phys therapy, dent hygienists_

      2. Reasons

         -we live longer
         -tech ↓ ill people live longer

   B. computers

      1. e.g.: _engineers, database admin._

      2. Stat: _↑ 30% next 10 yrs_

   C. _personal care services_

      1. e.g.: _caterers, home health workers, and day care providers_

      2. Reason: _↑ women workers_

VI. Educ. requirement for good jobs: _college degree_

AUDIOSCRIPT

Part 1

Lecturer: If you'll be graduating from high school or college in the next year or two, then I'm sure you're very concerned about finding a job. There are two questions that young people like you always ask me. First, what are the best jobs going to be? And second, how can I prepare myself to get one of those good jobs? Well in the next few minutes, I want to try to answer these questions for you, and I hope this information will help you make the right choices about your future career.

Let's start with a little history. In the last 100 years, there's been a big change in the U.S. job market, from a manufacturing economy to a service economy. What does that mean? Well, in a manufacturing economy people _make_ things, like cars or furniture or clothes. In a service economy, people _do_ things. Uh, they cut your hair, they fix your shoes, they sell you a computer. Uh, airline pilots, doctors, restaurant workers—all of these are examples of service workers. OK? So again, my point is that the number of manufacturing jobs has been going down for quite a long time. Now why do you think that is? What's the cause?

Student 1: I think automation, you know, robots, computers...

Lecturer: That's one reason, yes. Because of technology, we're able to manufacture goods by using machines instead of human workers. As a result, thousands of manufacturing jobs don't exist anymore. OK, can you think of another reason?

Student 2: Foreign competition. I mean... most manufacturing is done outside of the U.S. now, in countries where the labor costs are cheaper.

Lecturer: Yes, that's right. According to the U.S. government, approximately 2.5 million manufacturing jobs have disappeared just since 2001. And that trend is definitely going to continue as we move further into the 21st century.

But now let's talk about service jobs. Here the trend is exactly the opposite. At the same time that the number of manufacturing jobs is decreasing, the number of service jobs is probably going to grow by more than 20 million just in the next ten years! Now, would everybody please look at the handout I gave you, which shows a list of the occupations that will grow the fastest between the years 2002 and 2012. If you study the list carefully, you'll see that most of the jobs on the list are in three categories: health care, computers,

Student Book pages 86–87

Part 2

and personal care and services. Let me say a few words about each of these categories

First, health care. Almost half of the jobs on the list are in the field of health care. Uh, medical assistants, physician assistants, physical therapy aides, dental hygienists—these are just a few examples. According to the U.S. Department of Labor, the number of health care jobs will increase by almost three million in the next ten years. And why is that? Simple. We're going to need more medical services because people are living longer and longer. Also, because of developments in medical technology, people with serious illnesses are able to live much longer than they could in the past. And many of them need a lot of special care and medical help.

All right, now, getting back to the list, you can see that there will be many new jobs related to computers. We're going to need people who can design and build computers, like engineers, but in addition, there will be lots of jobs for people who manage and operate computers, like database administrations. As you know, computers are used in everything these days from rockets to coffee machines, so it's no surprise that the number of jobs in the computer industry is expected to grow by almost 30 percent in the next ten years.

Now let me explain the third category, personal-care services. Some examples of jobs in this group are caterers, home-health workers, and day care providers. One reason for the huge growth in this category is that most women now work outside the home. So a lot of the work that women used to do in the home, like cooking and taking care of small children, is now done by service workers.

OK, now while we're looking at the list, there's one more thing I'd like you to notice. Look at all the jobs that have a salary rank of 1. OK? And what do you notice about the educational requirements for those jobs? That's right. They all require at least a Bachelor of Arts degree.

So in conclusion, let me go back to the two questions I mentioned at the beginning of this talk. First, where will the good jobs be?

We've seen today that the areas of greatest growth will be in the fields of computers, health care, and personal services. If you still haven't decided which career you want to follow, you should think about getting a job in one of these fields. However, it's important to remember that many service jobs don't pay very well. The best jobs all require a college education. So the answer to the second question—how you can prepare yourself to get a good job—the answer is simple. Go to college and get a degree. That's the bottom line.

PART 2

Student Book pages 87–89

After You Listen

> **Best Practice**
>
> **Activating Prior Knowledge**
> This is an example of an activity that encourages students to make text-to-self connections. The discussion questions ask students to relate the content of the lecture on changes in the job market to their own lives. This aids understanding and retention of new material.

9 Discussing the Lecture

- Have students discuss the questions in groups.
- Encourage students to use the new vocabulary in their discussions.
- Ask for representatives from each group to report back on the discussions.

10 Reviewing Vocabulary

- Ask students to complete this activity individually.
- Review the answers together in class.

> **ANSWER KEY**
> 1. manufacturing; 2. service; 3. trend;
> 4. economy; 5. automation; 6. competition;
> 7. labor costs; 8. categories; 9. health care;
> 10. salary; 11. bottom line

On the Spot!

> **Best Practice**
>
> **Making Use of Academic Content**
> This is an example of collaborative problem-solving. Interviewing skills are important at many different stages of students' academic experience. This type of activity requires students to process information and practice their interviewing skills. They will also practice self-evaluating and evaluating each other.

11 What Would You Do?

- Read the situation with the class, or ask students to read it silently.
- Give students time to read the instructions.
- You can ask students to explain the instructions in their own words.
- Help students to form groups. Include one interviewer and three applicants in each group.
- Note on page 260 that there are four positions available. For each position, there are descriptions of three applicants. Assign the four interviewers the positions they'll be interviewing for—manager, checker, stock clerk or butcher.
- Assign each interviewee the role of one of the applicants.
- As a group member is being interviewed, have the others in that group go somewhere so they don't hear their group members' interviews.
- Set a time limit of 20 minutes.
- Move around the room to provide encouragement and feedback.
- At the end, invite a representative from each group to report on their decision.

Content Note

In some cultures, it is not advisable to praise oneself and one's abilities at a job interview. Modesty and politeness are more important than showing confidence. You may want to mention some of the cultural assumptions involved in job interviews in the U.S. Identify some of the qualities, such as confidence or initiative, that are considered positive.

Expansion Activity

- The purpose of this activity is to help students become aware of the kind of information on the Internet that can help them when choosing a career.
- Students can use a search engine, typing in keywords like *jobs* or *careers* and the name of their chosen job.
- The research part of this activity can be done in a computer lab class or assigned for homework.
- Please see Black Line Master "Researching Your Career" on page BLM 12 of this Teacher's Manual. Photocopy and distribute one copy to each student.
- Divide the students into groups of four and have each person in the group choose one job (preferably jobs that they are interested in).
- Students will research their chosen job on the web. Then re-form their groups to report what they found and have students complete the worksheet. Remind them to write on the back of their piece of paper if they need more room.
- Display the worksheets on the classroom wall.

You may wish to suggest some of the following websites, but please check them before doing this activity.

www.careers.org
www.quintcareers.com
www.nycareerzone.org

PART 3 — Strategies for Better Listening and Speaking

Student Book pages 90–91

Getting Meaning from Context

1 Prelistening Questions

- Ask students to look at the photos on page 90 and answer the questions on page 91.
- Discuss the answers as a class. If any students have had experience with these jobs, have them share their experiences with the class.

FOCUS ON TESTING — TOEFL iBT

Using Context Clues

- There are five conversations on this recording. There is a question at the end of each one.
- Play each section of the recording.
- There will be a pause after the question to allow students to write their answers.
- Then play the final sentence, which gives the correct answer.

ANSWER KEY

Questions	Clues
_f_ 1. What's the woman's job?	driver's license, ran a red light
_h_ 2. What's the woman's job?	check-up, insurance, dentist
_d_ 3. What's the man's job?	reservation, inside or out, coffee
_a_ 4. What's the woman's job?	taxes, lost money, inherited, professional
_i_ 5. What's the man's job?	sleeves, longer, how much

AUDIOSCRIPT

Conversation 1
Woman: May I see your driver's license, please?
Man: What did I do?
Woman: You ran a red light.
Man: But I'm sure it was yellow.
Question 1: *What's the woman's job?*
Woman: Are you trying to argue with a police officer?

Conversation 2
Woman: Is this your first visit?
Man: No, I come in every six months for a check-up.
Woman: Oh, I see. Did you bring your insurance form with you?
Man: Here it is.
Woman: OK. Take a seat, and the dentist will be with you shortly.
Question 2: *What is the woman's job?*
Man: You're new here, aren't you? What happened to the other receptionist?

Conversation 3
Man: Do you have a reservation?
Woman: Yes, Jackson, party of four.
Man: Inside or out on the patio?
Woman: Outside. And could you bring us some coffee right away?
Question 3: *What's the man's job?*
Man: I'm the host. I'll ask the waiter to bring you some coffee right away.

Conversation 4
A: Hi, Jim. It's Carl. It looks like I'm going to need your professional services this year.
B: I thought you always did your taxes by yourself.

72 CHAPTER 4

A:	Yeah, but this year things are too complicated. I lost money in the stock market, and then I inherited my uncle's house, remember?
B:	Hmm. You need professional help, for sure.
Question 4:	***What is Jim's job?***
B:	But you know, it's not a good idea to use your best friend as your accountant. I think you should find someone else.

Conversation 5

Man:	May I help you?
Woman:	The sleeves on this jacket are too short. How much will it cost for you to make them longer?
Man:	Let me look at it… I can do it for 30 dollars.
Woman:	That much?
Question 5:	***What's the man's job?***
Man:	Well, that's what any tailor would charge.

2 Game: Twenty Questions

- Read the instructions and model an example with one or two students.
- Have students work in groups to play the game.
- Set a time limit of ten minutes.

Focused Listening

FOCUS

Understanding the Intonation of Tag Questions

- Read the instruction note.
- Review the formation of tag questions (see the Expansion Activity on page 74 of this Teacher's Manual for extra practice).
- Read the examples in the box and ask students to identify the intonation.

3 Recognizing the Intonation of Tag Questions

- Have the students read the directions.
- Play the recording.
- There will be a pause after each item to allow students to write their answers.
- Check the answers as a class.

ANSWER KEY

Real questions: 1, 4, 5, 7, 10
Expecting agreement: 2, 3, 6, 8, 9

AUDIOSCRIPT

1. We're having a staff meeting tomorrow, aren't we? [rising]
2. You're the programmer from Turkey, aren't you? [falling]
3. This exercise is easy, isn't it? [falling]
4. The supervisor is married, isn't she? [rising]
5. Smoking is forbidden here, isn't it? [rising]
6. That test was really hard, wasn't it? [falling]
7. The secretary speaks Arabic, doesn't he? [rising]
8. That training video was really boring, wasn't it? [falling]
9. The marketing director speaks beautiful Japanese, doesn't she? [falling]
10. We need to sign our names on these reports, don't we? [rising]

PART 3

Using Language Functions

FOCUS

Answering Negative Tag Questions

- Read aloud the instruction note.
- Have students practice the three dialogues.
- Tag questions are sometimes difficult to answer. Does the answer agree with the verb in the tag, or not? The answer is that both are possible. Sometimes negative tags get negative answers and sometimes they get positive answers. The answer will be negative or positive depending on the fact given in the answer. For example, *You're 21, aren't you?* can be answered *Yes, I am* (if you are 21) or *No, I'm not* (if you aren't 21). You might also answer with a question, *Am I?*
- A possible student error is to say *yes* when agreeing with the speaker, and *no* when disagreeing with the speaker, for example, *No, I am* or *Yes, I'm not*.

4 Asking and Answering Negative Tag Questions

- Have students work in pairs. One student will look at page 248 in the Student Book. The other student will look at page 256.
- Students will take turns asking each other questions.
- Set a time limit of five minutes.
- Move around the room to provide feedback on intonation and grammar as needed. Take notes of errors.
- Invite volunteers to demonstrate their conversations to the class.

Expansion Activity (REPRODUCIBLE)

- The aim of this activity is to practice the language of negative tag questions.
- Please see Black Line Master "Tag Questions" on page BLM 13 of this Teacher's Manual. Photocopy and distribute one copy to each student.
- Explain that they will first complete the questions with the appropriate tag.
- Then they will go over their answers with a partner.
- Have each pair choose one question and make up a dialog using that question.
- Set a time limit of five minutes.
- Walk around the room to monitor and provide feedback.
- Invite students to perform their dialogs for the class. Check for appropriate intonation.

ANSWER KEY

1. isnt' it; 2. aren't they; 3. aren't we; 4. don't you; 5. doesn't he; 6. weren't you; 7. didn't she (or he); 8. didn't she; 9. won't you; 10. won't we; 11. didn't I; 12. don't you; 13. don't they; 14. aren't you; 15. isn't he (or she); 16. don't you; 17. doesn't she; 18. don't we

PART 4   Real-World Task: A Homemaker's Typical Day

Student Book pages 94–95

Before You Listen

1. Prelistening Discussion

- Read the questions with the class.
- Ask students to suggest answers for each question.
- Write the answers to Question 3 on the board.

2. Previewing Vocabulary

- Play the recording and have students listen to the idioms.
- Ask students to complete the chart individually. They may use dictionaries to check the meanings.
- Review the answers all together.

ANSWER KEY

Possible answers:
Cook food; wash dishes; prepare the beds for sleeping; keep a record of family income or expenses; wash the clothes; put water on the grass; buy food for the family

3. Predicting

- Have students work in pairs to describe each picture using idioms from Activity 2.
- Then ask students to discuss the probable order of the pictures. They will check their answers when they listen to the recording.

Listen

4. Sequencing Events

- Play the recording.
- Have students number the pictures in the correct order and compare answers with a partner.
- Play the recording again if necessary.
- Review the answers as a class.

ANSWER KEY

3, 7, 5, 1, 8, 4, 6, 2, 10, 9

AUDIOSCRIPT

Do you want to know what I do on a typical day? Well, I'll tell you what I did yesterday as an example. I woke up before my wife and son, and the first thing I did was to come into the kitchen and make the coffee. Then I made my son's lunch, you know, to take to school, and after that I started cooking breakfast. I made eggs, oatmeal, and toast because I always want my family to start the day with a full stomach. Then my wife and son came into the kitchen and sat down to eat. While they were eating, I threw a basket of laundry into the washing machine, and then I also sat down to eat.

After breakfast, I walked my son to the bus stop, and I waited with him until the bus came. I kissed him good-bye and walked home. As soon as I entered the house, the phone rang. It was my mother-in-law. She wanted to know if my wife was still there, but I told her she had just left. So I talked with her for a few more minutes, about the weather and her garden, and then I got off the phone. After that, uh, let's see, I spent three hours cleaning the house, and after lunch, I went shopping for groceries. By then it was three o'clock, and it was already time to pick up my son at the bus stop. I helped him with his homework, and then my wife came home. Normally she gets home at about 6:00 P.M., but yesterday she was a few minutes early. I was so busy all day that I hadn't had time to water the garden, so I did it while my wife made dinner. Finally, after dinner, I washed the dishes while my wife put our son to bed. And then both of us just collapsed in front of the TV.

And that was my day. Nothing glamorous—just really busy!

PART 4

Student Book pages 96–98

After You Listen

5 Discussion

- Have students work in small groups to discuss the questions.
- Set a time limit of five minutes.
- Compare answers as a class.

Best Practice

Organizing Information

Activity 6 will teach students to organize information using a graphic organizer called a matrix diagram. This allows students to better assimilate and recall information at a later date, a valuable study tool. In this case, students use the diagram to identify differences between their own opinions and traditional opinions in their culture.

Best Practice

Cultivating Critical Thinking

In Activity 6, students are asked to examine their own preconceptions about "men's" and "women's" jobs and reflect on them from a critical perspective. They are asked to take a critical stance toward traditional assumptions in their culture and to distinguish this from their own personal opinion. This means that they will have to reinterpret and synthesize their existing mental frameworks in the light of discussion and reflection.

Content Note

Notions of '"traditional" jobs for men and women vary across cultures and may also be closely tied to religious beliefs. In the U.S., it is seen as a sign of progress that *traditional* views of men's and women's jobs are changing, and the word *traditional* has a somewhat negative connotation, but this is not the case in all other cultures. It may be difficult or impossible for some students to separate their own beliefs from those that are widely held in their culture. In such cases, you may wish to ask students to reflect on changing attitudes to men's and women's jobs in the U.S.

Strategy

Graphic Organizer: Matrix Diagram

- Read the information about a graphic organizer called a matrix diagram.
- Point out that they can see (and will use) the matrix diagram on pages 96–97 of the Student Book.

6 Talking About "Men's" and "Women's" Jobs

- Have students complete the chart individually.
- Then have students form groups to discuss the questions under the chart.
- Set a time limit of ten minutes.

7 Interview

- Ask students to complete this activity for homework.
- Invite students to suggest some additional questions.
- Encourage them to interview a native speaker of English if possible.
- Have the students prepare a short oral report. Read the sample report, which students can use as a model.

Student Book page 99

Expansion Activity

- The aim of this activity is to practice language for talking about jobs and to practice making a matrix diagram.
- Have students work in pairs to choose a job that they are familiar with.
- Have students draw a matrix diagram similar to the one in Activity 6 on pages 96–97 of the Student Book.
- Make a list of activities involved in carrying out this job.
- For each activity, students should mark if it is interesting, difficult, or both.
- Give an example using the job of teacher.

Job: Teacher	Interesting	Difficult	Both
meet people	✓		
give grades		✓	
every lesson/class is different			✓

- Have students complete the charts in pairs.
- Invite volunteers to read out some of their activities. Other students will try to guess what job it is.

Self-Assessment Log

- The purpose of the log is to help the students reflect on their learning.
- Read the directions aloud and have students check vocabulary that they learned in the chapter and are prepared to use.
- Have students check the strategies they understand.
- Put students in small groups. Ask students to find the information or an activity related to each strategy in the chapter.
- Tell students to find definitions in the chapter for any words they did not check, or they can look in their dictionaries.

CHAPTER 5

Lifestyles Around the World

In this CHAPTER

Students will read about different lifestyle issues in the U.S., such as single parents, working mothers, looking after children, and caring for older people. In Part 1, they will learn to recognize stressed and reduced forms and practice ways of asking for favors. In Part 2, they will listen to a lecture about changes in American families. In Part 3, they will listen to conversations people talking about aspects of their home and family life. At the end of the chapter, they will learn about how to record and interpret statistics using charts and line graphs.

Chapter Opener

- Have students look at the photo and describe the scene. Then ask students the three questions in the Connecting to the Topic section.

- Brainstorm different definitions of the word *lifestyle*. These may include: types of family and work, food, housing, ways of spending money, and ways of spending free time. Have students make a list of the most important things in their lives.

- Read and discuss the quote.

“It takes a village to raise a child.”

African proverb

Chapter Overview

Listening Skills and Strategies
Listening for main ideas and details

Making inferences

Recognizing stress in two- and three-word verbs

Speaking Skills and Strategies
Talking about single parents

Talking about changes in the American family

Asking for help and favors

Talking about numbers and percentages

Comparing lifestyles in different countries

Critical-Thinking Skills
Interpreting information in a line graph

Taking notes on a lecture

Getting meaning from context

Vocabulary Building
Two- and three-word verbs used in a conversation between neighbors

Expressions used to ask for help or a favor

Terms used to talk about changes in the American family

Expressions used to signal examples

Terms used for discussing lifestyles

Pronunciation
Identifying and practicing stressed words

Identifying and practicing the dropped *h* in unstressed words

Pronouncing linked phrases

Language Skills
Using context clues to guess people's lifestyles

Vocabulary

Nouns
- cost of living
- daycare center
- flexibility
- homemaker
- maternity leave
- opportunity
- policy

Verbs
- benefit
- can/can't afford
- check up on
- look into
- run out
- take off
- transfer
- volunteer

Adjectives
- flexible
- old-fashioned

PART 1 — Conversation: A Single Mother

Student Book pages 102–103

Can You Guess?

- Ask students to discuss the questions below in groups and compare their answers with the correct answers.
- Brainstorm reasons for and against getting married earlier or later; reasons why mothers decide to work or stay at home; reasons for and against paying mothers and homemakers for the work they do.

1. At what age does the average American get married? **A.** *Men: 29 Women: 27*
   Some other countries:
   Japan: Men: 31 Women: 29
   Korea: Men: 32 Women: 29
   Canada: Men: 31 Women: 28
   England: Men: 31 Women: 29
   France: Men: 32 Women: 30

2. What percentage of single Americans in their mid-20s live with their parents? **A.** *Fifteen percent in the United States.*

3. Which country requires husbands to pay their wives for the housework they do? **A.** *Taiwan. The law, passed in June, 2003, says that a working spouse must pay a sum to a home-maker for the housework he or she does, the sum to be agreed on between the two spouses.*

Before You Listen

Content Note

In some cultures, it is not acceptable to have children outside of marriage. This topic may be distressing for students who have experienced discrimination because of this issue. There are many cultures where it is unusual for children to be raised by a single parent. If this does happen, it is usually the result of a divorce or the death of one partner. In such cases, relatives in the extended family may step in to help take care of children.

- Read the text that introduces the next listening.

1. Prelistening Questions

- Have students look at the photo and talk about who the people are and their situation.
- Have the students read the questions and discuss them in pairs.
- Compare answers as a whole class.

2. Previewing Vocabulary

- Play the recording and have students listen for the underlined phrases.
- Have students complete the vocabulary preview individually.
- Compare their answers as a whole class and write the correct answers on the board.
- Ask students for additional synonyms (or examples) for each item, e.g., **1.** investigate **2.** go/set off/depart **3.** traditional **4.** getting shorter/not enough **5.** make sure
- Practice the pronunciation of new words or phrases.

ANSWER KEY

1. c **2.** e **3.** b **4.** d **5.** a

Listen

3. Comprehension Questions

- Explain that these questions will help students focus on the main ideas in the listening. They do not need to understand every word to answer the questions.
- You may want to write the questions on the board.
- Read the questions aloud.
- Play the recording.
- After listening, have students compare their answers in pairs.

ANSWER KEY

1. She wants him to babysit Joey; She has to go to the office;   2. She has a baby, but never got married;   3. She thought about having a baby before she got married;   4. It's very difficult for a single parent to raise a child; She's old-fashioned and could never bring up a baby by herself.

AUDIOSCRIPT

Jeff: Who's there?

Sharon: It's Sharon and Joey!

Jeff: Hi! Come on in. What's happening?

Sharon: Jeff, can you do me a big favor? I just got a call from the office. They want me to look into a computer problem right away. Would you mind watching Joey until I get back?

Jeff: Sure, no problem. Is he asleep?

Sharon: Yeah, he just fell asleep ten minutes ago. He usually sleeps for a couple of hours at this time of day. But if he wakes up, just give him a bottle.

Mari: Ooh, what a cute baby! He's so little!

Jeff: Mari, this is our neighbor, Sharon, and her son, Joey. Sharon, this is our new roommate, Mari.

Mari: Nice to meet you.

Sharon: You too. Listen, I've got to take off. Thanks so much, Jeff, for helping me out.

Jeff/Mari: Bye!

Mari: Hey, Jeff, I didn't know you liked babies.

Jeff: Well, Joey is special. I take care of him from time to time when Sharon's busy. And then she does favors for me in return. Like last week she lent me her car.

Mari: And her husband? Is he…

Jeff: She's not married. I don't think she ever was, actually.

Mari: Never?

Jeff: No, never. I think she's happy being a single mother.

Mari: Is that pretty common in America?

Jeff: Well, it's certainly becoming more and more common. Even Nancy talked about it. You know, before she got married.

Nancy: Hi, guys.

Mari/Jeff: Hi.

Nancy: Uh, what were you saying about me?

Jeff: That you used to talk about having a baby by yourself. Before you met Andrew.

Nancy: Oh yeah, I worried that time was running out. You know, like, what if I never got married?

Mari: Maybe I'm old-fashioned, but I could never bring up a baby by myself. I think it would be so difficult…

Nancy: Yeah, raising a child is tough. I'm really lucky I met Andrew.

Mari: And, if you have a baby, you'll have Jeff here to help you with babysitting.

Jeff: We'll see. Speaking of babysitting, I'd better check up on Joey.

PART 1

Student Book pages 103–105

Stress

FOCUS

Two- and Three-Word Verbs

- Have students read the instruction note.
- Have them read the three sentences aloud.
- Explain that these two- or three-part verbs (known as *phrasal verbs*) are very common in informal English. Sometimes the meaning is easy to guess from the individual parts of the verb (e.g., *take off* your coat), but sometimes the meaning is quite different (e.g., the plane *took off*). It is best to learn these verbs as separate vocabulary items.

8. I could never bring *up* a baby by myself.
9. I'd better check *up* on Joey.

5 Listening for Stressed Words (Part II)

- Play the recording, which is part of the conversation from Activity 3.
- Have students write the missing words.
- After listening, have students check their answers.
- Have students read the conversation with a partner, paying attention to stressed words in their pronunciation and intonation.

4 Listening for Stressed Words (Part I)

- Listen to the recording of selected sentences from the conversation.
- There will be a pause at the end of each sentence to allow time for students to repeat and write the missing words.
- After listening, have students check their answers with a partner.
- Have students read the sentences with their partner, paying attention to stressed words in their pronunciation and intonation.

ANSWER KEY

1. Come on *in*.
2. They want me to look *into* a computer problem right away.
3. If he wakes *up*, just give him a bottle.
4. Listen, I've got to take *off*.
5. Thanks so much, Jeff, for helping me *out*.
6. I take *care* of him from time to time when Sharon's busy.
7. I worried that time was running *out*.

AUDIOSCRIPT and ANSWER KEY

Mari: Hey, Jeff, I didn't know you liked *babies*.

Jeff: Well, Joey is *special*. I take care of him from time to time when Sharon's *busy*. And then *she* does favors for *me* in return. Like last week she lent me her *car*.

Mari: And her *husband*? Is he...

Jeff: She's not *married*. I don't think she *ever* was, actually.

Mari: Never?

Jeff: *No*, *never*. I think she's *happy* being a *single* mother.

Mari: Is that pretty *common* in America?

Jeff: Well, it's *certainly* becoming more and more common. Even *Nancy* talked about it. You know, before she got *married*.

Nancy: Hi, guys.

Mari/Jeff: Hi.

Nancy: Uh, *what* were you saying about me?

Jeff: That you *used* to talk about having a *baby* by yourself before you *met* Andrew.

Student Book pages 105–106

Nancy:	Oh yeah, I _worried_ that _time_ was running out. You know, like, what if I _never_ got married?
Mari:	Maybe I'm _old-fashioned_, but I could _never_ bring up a baby by _myself_. I think it would be so difficult...
Nancy:	Yeah, raising a _child_ is tough. I'm really _lucky_ I met Andrew.
Mari:	And, if you have a baby, you'll have _Jeff_ here to help you with _babysitting_.
Jeff:	We'll see. Speaking of babysitting, I'd _better_ check up on Joey.

FOCUS

Reductions

- Read aloud the instruction note about reductions.
- Read aloud each of the unreduced and reduced forms in sentences. Have students read them aloud.

6 Listening for Reductions

- Read the directions.
- Play the recording.
- There will be a pause after each sentence to allow students time to write their answers and repeat.
- After listening, have students check their answers with a partner.

ANSWER KEY

1. he, him   3. him   5. —
2. —   4. her   6. have, here

After You Listen

7 Using Vocabulary

- Have students work in pairs. Student A will look at page 249 in the Student Book. Student B will look at page 257.
- Have students read their section, and ask if there are any questions.
- Set a time limit of five minutes.
- Check the answers as a class.
- If there is time, have students choose one pair of sentences and continue the conversation.
- Have students discuss the three questions in pairs.

ANSWER KEY

A: It's 3 o'clock in the morning! Why aren't you sleeping?
B: I have to finish this paper by 10:00 A.M. Time is running out.
A: Are you leaving?
B: Yes, it's getting dark. I'd better take off.
A: Wake up, Sally. It's 10:00 A.M.
B: I'm tired! I don't want to go to school today!
A: Hello? Is anybody home?
B: Yeah, come on in.
A: Who takes care of your kids while you're working?
B: My mother.
A: What's wrong with this light? It's not working properly.
B: I know. I told the manager, and he's going to look into it.
A: How's the baby doing?
B: I just checked up on her. She's sleeping.
A: Why did George quit his job?
B: He decided to stay home for a couple of years and bring up his kids.

PART 1

Student Book pages 106–107

FOCUS

Asking for Help or a Favor

- Read the instruction note.
- Ask volunteers to model some of the expressions using a variety of "favors" (see examples below).
  - Lend me your cell phone.
  - Help me with my homework.
  - Show me how to use the computer.
  - Move your papers and books to another office.

8 Asking for a Favor

- Have students work in pairs. One student will look at page 249 in the Student Book. The other student will look at page 257.
- Set a time limit of five minutes for students to practice their conversations.
- Monitor the groups as they are doing the activity and make notes of errors.
- Invite volunteers to perform their conversation for the class.

Best Practice

Interacting with Others

Activity 9 is an example of collaborative learning to encourage fluency and confidence. In these role-plays, based around the topic of asking for and offering favors, communication is more important than grammar. Students can practice the role-plays in pairs and then improve their performance by switching roles or partners. By the time they perform the role-play for the class, they should feel more confident in the use of the new language.

9 Role-Play

- Have students work in pairs and read the seven situations.
- Check comprehension of any new vocabulary.

- Set a time limit of ten minutes for students to practice their conversations.
- Monitor the groups as they are doing the activity and make notes of errors. Tell the students the global errors at the end of the ten minutes. Do not focus on any student in particular, just note that the errors were heard and are things to be careful about.
- Invite volunteers to perform one of their conversations for the class.
- Next, have students work in groups to discuss the situations.
  - Which favors would they feel uncomfortable with and why?
  - What language would they use for each request?
- Rate the requests on a scale of 1 to 10, from *easy to ask* to *difficult or unlikely*.

REPRODUCIBLE — Expansion Activity

- The aim of this activity is to practice language for asking for and refusing favors.
- Please see Black Line Master "Can You Do Me a Favor?" on page BLM 14 of this Teacher's Manual. Photocopy and distribute one copy to each student.
- Model the example dialog with a student. Model writing the student's name and excuse on your chart. Encourage them to think of creative excuses.
- Have students walk around the room and ask each other favors so they can fill in the chart. Point out that they can use a classmate's name only once.
- When students have completed the worksheet, they can sit down and discuss part 2.

PART 2 Lecture: Changes in the American Family
Student Book pages 108–109

Before You Listen

Best Practice

Activating Prior Knowledge

The prelistening discussion is an example of personalization. This type of activity encourages students to relate the topic to their own experience. Asking students to predict what kind of differences they think there are between families in the 1950s and now will make it easier for them to assimilate the new information in the lecture.

1 Prelistening Discussion

- Have the students work in small groups and discuss each question. You can help students discuss each question by looking at the suggestions below.

  1. Brainstorm adjectives to describe each picture. How do you feel about the people in these pictures? Are they similar or different to your family?
  2. Make a chart outlining differences between American families in the 1950s and now.

Families in the 1950s	Families now
Father works	Mother and father both work
Mother does housework	Mother and father share housework

  3. Make a list of changes in families in the students' communities.

- Encourage students to explore various possible reasons for these changes.

2 Previewing Vocabulary

- Play the recording and have students listen for the words and phrases.
- Have students check the words they know and then compare answers with a partner. Explain that they will work out the meaning of the new words by listening to the lecture.

Listen

Strategy

Taking Notes on Examples

- Read the information in the Strategy box.
- Make some general statements and ask students to come up with examples. See below:
  - There are many changes in family life since the 50s. For example…
  - There are many difficulties in bringing up a child by yourself. To give one example…
  - Single parents might face problems at work. For instance…

3 Taking Notes on Examples

- Explain that students will listen to statements followed by examples and will take notes on the examples.
- Remind them to use key words, abbreviations, symbols, and indentation.
- Play the recording. Each sentence will be heard twice.
- Have students exchange notes with a partner, and using those notes, restate the items. Note that the important thing is not that they understand their partner's notes, but that they see some differences in note-taking. People develop their individual abbreviations and symbols for personal note-taking.

ANSWER KEY

1. ↑ 1/2 students in Am. med. school = women
2. childcare? shopping, cooking, cleaning? school volunteer jobs?
3. Canada–yes, U.S.–no

PART 2

Student Book pages 109–110

AUDIOSCRIPT

1. Women today are working in professions that were not as open to them 30 or 40 years ago. To give just one example, today more than half the students in American medical schools are women.

2. Most American homes don't have a full-time homemaker anymore. And that creates new problems for families; problems like who takes care of babies and old people; who shops, cooks, and cleans; who volunteers at the children's school; and so on.

3. In some countries, companies are required by law to give new parents a paid vacation when they have a new baby. Canada, for instance, has a law like that, but the United States does not.

4 Taking Notes (Part I)

- Read the questions or write them on the board.
- Have students close their books and take notes as they listen.
- Play the first part of the recording.

5 Outlining the Lecture

- Have students use their notes from Activities 3 and 4 to complete the outline.
- Play the recording again if needed.

ANSWER KEY

Topic: Changes in the American Family

I. "Typical" Am. fam
   A. 1950s: _father works, mother home, 2–3 children_

   B. Changes today:
   1. _families are smaller_

   2. _more single-parent families_

   3. _role of married mothers_
      Stats: _1950s 11% mothers worked, 2002 70%_
      Reasons:
      need money
      more opportunities available
      New problems:
      takes care of babies and grandparents?
      shops, cooks, and cleans?
      volunteers at school?

AUDIOSCRIPT

Have you ever seen the television show *Father Knows Best*? You probably haven't because it was a popular comedy show in the 1950s—way before you were born. It was about a family: a father, who went to work every day; a mother, who stayed home and took care of the house; and the children—two or three, I can't remember. Anyway, in those days that was considered to be a typical American family.

But today, the American family is very different. First, families are smaller today than before. I mean, people are having fewer children. Second, more and more children are growing up in single-parent families—families with only a mother or only a father. I'm not going to go into the reasons for that here because I want to focus on the third and biggest change in the American family: the role of married mothers and the effects of this new role. Consider these statistics: In the 1950s, only 11 percent of married mothers worked outside the home. In 2002, about 70 percent of mothers were employed.

Why is that? Well, there are two important reasons. The first one, very simply, is that they need the money. These days, the cost of living is so high that most families need two salaries in order to make ends meet.

Student Book pages 110–111

The other reason why married mothers are working in larger and larger numbers is that they have more opportunities than they did 30 or 40 years ago. There are laws in the United States that give women the same opportunity as men to go to college and get jobs. As a result, women today are working in professions that were not as open to them 30 or 40 years ago. To give just one example, today more than half of the students in American medical schools are women.

So, to summarize so far, we've seen that the American family has changed dramatically since the days of those old television shows. In the typical two-parent family today, both the father and the mother have jobs. This means that most American homes don't have a full-time homemaker anymore. And that creates new problems for families: problems like who takes care of babies and grandparents; who shops, cooks, and cleans; who volunteers at the children's school; and so on.

6 Taking Notes (Part II)

- Have students close their books and take notes as they listen.
- Play the second part of the recording.
- Have students use their notes to complete the outline.
- Play the recording again if needed.

ANSWER KEY

II. Company policies/programs:
 A. *paid maternity leave*
 B. If co. transfers worker, co. finds job for husb./wife
 C. *flextime = 9-5 or 7-3 or 10-6. work 8 hrs, choose start / finish time*
 D. *telecommuting / teleworking = working from home*
 15% of U.S. workers ↑ good for parents / childcare
 E. *daycare at office, children can go to work and go home w. parents*
 Concl: *very few cos can afford these progs, - gov shd help more*

AUDIOSCRIPT

To help families with working parents deal with these new problems, some American businesses have introduced new programs and policies to make it easier to work and raise children at the same time. Let me give you five examples of these policies and programs.

The first policy is paid maternity leave. What we're talking about is a woman taking time off from work when she has a baby. American law requires companies to give a woman up to 12 weeks of leave when she has a baby. But the problem is that the companies aren't required to pay for those 12 weeks. As a result, many women are forced to go back to work much sooner than they want to. Recently some companies, at least the big ones, have started to offer paid maternity leave. But it's still kind of rare. By the way, a small percentage of companies now also offer *paternity* leave—that means that fathers can take time off for a new baby. I would like to see a law that requires all companies to give paid leave to both mothers and fathers for a new baby. Canada, for instance, already has a law like that.

OK, moving along, here's another example of a policy that helps working families. As you know, big companies like IBM or General Motors often transfer their employees to other cities, right? Well, if a company transfers the husband, for instance, this might create a problem for the wife because now she has to find a new job, too. So now there are companies that will help the husband or wife of the transferred worker find a new job.

A third policy that many companies now offer is called *flextime*. Here's what that means. In the United States, a normal workday is from 9:00 A.M.

PART 2

Student Book page 111

until 5:00 P.M.—eight hours. With flextime, workers can choose the hour that they start work in the morning and can go home after eight hours. So, for instance, a worker who comes in at 7:00 can leave at 3:00. Or a worker can come in at 10:00 and leave at 6:00. You can imagine how useful this flexibility is for people who have children.

The fourth change I want to describe is *telecommuting*. Or sometimes we say *teleworking*. With telecommuting, people work at home and use the computer or phone to communicate with their workplace. It's estimated that about 15 percent of the U.S. workforce telecommutes now. But the percentage is growing all the time because it saves people time and money. And if parents are allowed to work at home, their children might not have to spend as much time in child care.

And speaking of child care, the fifth program offered by many of the best companies is daycare; that is, some companies have daycare centers at the office where trained people take care of the employees' children. This means workers come to work with their young children, leave them at the center, and can visit them during lunch or whatever. Then the parents and kids drive home together at the end of the day. With daycare at work, parents don't need to worry about their kids because they're right there.

OK, let me review what I've been talking about. I've given you five examples of company policies and programs that make life a little easier for working mothers and fathers. But it's important for me to tell you that only some large companies can afford these kinds of programs. For most people, trying to work and take care of a family at the same time is still very, very difficult. In my opinion, our government and our society need to do a lot more to help working parents and their children.

- Encourage students to use the new vocabulary in their discussion.
- Compare answers as a class.

ANSWER KEY

1. Why are more and more mothers in two-parent American families working these days?

   Families need money because the cost of living is high.

   There are more opportunities for work and education today than 30–40 year ago.

2. Challenges about who takes care of babies and grandparents; who shops, cooks, and cleans; who volunteers at the children's school

3. The five programs are:
   1. Paid maternity care (advantage to workers: can afford to take time off to care for young baby; advantage to companies: encourages working mothers to stay in their jobs; disadvantage to workers: usually only get half their salary; disadvantage to companies: expensive, workers may quit after maternity leave)
   2. Help the husband or wife of the transferred worker find a new job (advantage to workers: can transfer to higher paid jobs; advantage to companies: workers are more mobile; disadvantage to companies: expensive)
   3. Flextime (advantage to workers: can choose working hours; advantage to companies: no extra labor costs; disadvantage to companies: office hours may not coincide with busiest times)
   4. Telecommuting (advantage to workers: no commuting, can take care of children at home; disadvantage to workers: initial costs in setting up home office equipment; advantage to companies: lower costs; disadvantage to companies: possible communication problems)

After You Listen

7 Discussing the Lecture

- Have students work in groups of three or four to discuss questions 1–5.

Student Book pages 111–112

> 5. Daycare at the workplace (advantage to workers: can visit child at lunch break, can be close if there is an emergency; advantages to companies: encourages working parents to stay in their jobs, fewer parents forced to take sick leave when child is sick; disadvantage to companies: expensive)
> 4. Smaller companies cannot afford these programs.
> 5. Answers will vary.

8 Reviewing Vocabulary

- Refer students to Activity 2 on page 109 of the Student Book. Review any new items and have students check the meaning in a dictionary if necessary.
- Take a vote on the five most difficult words and have students give example sentences of how they are used.

On the Spot!

Best Practice

Cultivating Critical Thinking
This is an example of a collaborative team activity. This type of activity requires students to process the information from a reading and respond to it critically by generating different alternative solutions. This involves reinterpretation, synthesis, and application of concepts. The process of manipulating language and concepts in this way will create deeper processing of new material and allow students to develop and express their opinions on the topic of lifestyles.

9 What Would You Do?

- Have students read the first part of the article individually.
- Ask a student to summarize it for the class.

- Brainstorm possible predictions for the judge's response and write them on the board.
- Check the judge's response on page 261.
- Have students work in groups to discuss the second part of the article and part 2 of the activity.
- Set a time limit of five minutes.
- Ask representatives from each group to summarize their discussion for the class.
- Invite the whole class to discuss the third question together.

REPRODUCIBLE — Expansion Activity

- The aim of this activity is for students to use the Internet to develop skills using research to support their opinions and arguments.
- Please see Black Line Master "Starting a Workplace Daycare Center" on page BLM 15 of this Teacher's Manual. Photocopy and distribute one copy to each student.
- In this activity, students may access the same sites to get information, but they will have to adapt the information according to the point of view required by their role.
- Students can use a search engine, entering keywords like *workplace child care*.
- The research part of this activity can be done in a computer lab class or assigned for homework.
- Divide the students into small groups and have each person in the group choose one role.
- Students will research the topic on the web. Then re-form their groups to complete the worksheet. Encourage students to maintain their roles as they complete part 2.
- Finally, ask for volunteers to share the information from part 2 with the class.

PART 3 — Strategies for Better Listening and Speaking

Student Book pages 113–115

Focused Listening

FOCUS

Linking

- Read the instruction note.
- Practice the examples.

---

① Pronouncing Linked Phrases

- The recording has three sections. Each section practices a different rule for linking.
- Play the recording. There will be a pause after each section. Explain, or ask a student to explain, the rule.
- Have students listen and repeat each phrase.

② Pronouncing Sentences

- Before listening, have students read the sentences and mark which words they think are linked.
- Play the recording and have students listen carefully to the linked words.
- Play the recording again and ask students to repeat. They can also mark the linked words.
- Have students read the sentences in pairs.
- Move around the room and give feedback on pronunciation.

Getting Meaning from Context

Best Practice

Scaffolding Instruction

This is an example of an activity that raises metacognitive awareness of learning strategies. In real life, we use surrounding context clues to work out the meanings of unfamiliar words. This activity asks students to use the surrounding verbal clues in each conversation to work out the context. Asking students to write the clues will guide them through the steps of developing this important skill.

FOCUS ON TESTING — TOEFL iBT

Using Context Clues

- Read through the chart and check comprehension of any new items.
- Review the purpose of using clues to get meaning.
- This recording has five sections. Play each section of the recording. The recording will pause at the end of the conversation to allow time for students to circle their answers and write the clues.
- Then play the final part of each section, which gives the correct answer.

ANSWER KEY

	Answers	Clues
1.	B a retired person	pension, social security
2.	D her parents	come home, baby
3.	C is divorced	ex-wife, kids
4.	A with his parents	lost job, ran out of money, back home
5.	A a retirement home	privacy, friends my own age

AUDIOSCRIPT

Conversation 1

Senior Citizen Man: Well, I tell you, things get pretty tough by the end of the month. I don't have any pension—just Social Security—and that's only $800 a month. Sometimes the check is late, and the rent is due on the first of the month. Do you think the landlord cares?

Student Book pages 115–116

Question 1:	*The speaker is…*
Senior Citizen Man:	Sometimes I think no one cares about retired people in this country.
Conversation 2	
17-Year-Old Girl:	Sometimes I feel like I'm in a prison. "Come home by ten." "Don't go there." "Don't do that." "Turn down the music." They treat me like a baby. They have no respect for my privacy.
Question 2:	*The speaker is talking about…*
Girl:	My parents forget that I'm 17 years old. I'm not a child anymore.
Conversation 3	
Man:	My ex-wife and I agreed that the kids would live with me. At first it was hard with all the work and no help. But it's exciting to watch my kids grow up.
Question 3:	*This man…*
Man:	And fortunately, there are organizations to help divorced fathers like me.
Conversation 4	
Young Man:	I lived with my parents until I was 18, then I left home to go to college and lived with roommates in an apartment near the campus. When I graduated, I got a job with an engineering firm and got my own place. But last year, I lost my job and ran out of money. So what could I do? I came back home.
Question 4:	*This person probably lives…*
Young Man:	Boy, it's not easy living with your parents again after all these years.

Conversation 5	
Senior Citizen Woman:	After I broke my hip, it was too hard to go on living by myself. So I tried living with my son and his family for a while, but their house is small and noisy, and I want my privacy, too. So I came here. And it really isn't bad. I have my own doctor, good food, and plenty of friends my own age.
Question 5:	*This woman is living in…*
Senior Citizen Woman:	This retirement home is really the best place for me.

3 Discussing Lifestyles

- Read the descriptions of the five people on the recording.
- Have students answer the first question. You may want to ask students to choose which ones they find most interesting to talk about.
- Have students discuss Questions 2 and 3 in groups then report back on their discussion to the class.
- If there is time, you may want to have a debate on the third question, with each side of the class presenting arguments for and against.

PART 3

Expansion Activity

- The aim of this activity is to practice expressing opinions about lifestyle issues raised in this chapter.
- Please see Black Line Master "Questionnaire" on page BLM 16 of this Teacher's Manual. Photocopy and distribute one copy to each student.
- Explain that they will first read the statements silently and write their own opinions checking whether they agree or disagree.
- Divide students into groups. They will compare their opinions with their group and try to reach agreement. Have them make a note of the more difficult decisions or of the conditions that might have to exist in order for them to agree or disagree with the statement.
- Set a time limit of 15 minutes.
- At the end of the discussion, have representatives of each group report back on the most controversial issues.

PART 4 — Real-World Task: Using Numbers, Percentages, and Graphs Student Book pages 117–119

Before You Listen

FOCUS

Numbers and Percentages
- Read the instruction note about numbers and percentages, focusing on prepositions.

❶ Prelistening Discussion

- Read and discuss the questions with the whole class.
- If there is time, discuss information about several different communities.

Listen

Strategy

Graphic Organizer: Line Graph
- Read the information in the Strategy box.
- Point out the line graph on page 118 of the Student Book. They will complete this graph in the next activity.

Best Practice

Organizing Information

Activities such as this will teach students to organize information using a graphic organizer called a line graph. This allows students to understand and process information using statistics. In this case, students record statistics about the numbers of women who work, couples who divorce, and elderly people who live alone. Other types of graphic organizers are used throughout this book.

❷ Completing Line Graphs

- Discuss each graph individually, helping students understand what the numbers at the left and across the bottom of each graph mean.
- Read the captions and ask students to explain them in their own words to show that they understand what each graph is measuring.
- Play the recording and have students write their answers on the graphs.
- Point out that the third graph will have two kinds of marks, circles for women and Xs for men.

ANSWER KEY

Graph 1: 1960=37.8, 1980=51.1, 1990=57.5, 2003=61

Graph 2: 1960=2.2, 1970=3.5, 1980=5.2, 1990=4.7, 2003=3.8

Graph 3: 1970: women=35.9 men=10.8, 1980: women=31.9 men=8.1, 1990: women=51.8 men=21.5, 2000: women=40 men=17

AUDIOSCRIPT

Graph 1

Graph 1 gives statistics on American women in the U.S. labor force. In 1960, 37.8 percent of American women had jobs. By 1980, it had jumped to 51.1 percent. In 1990, it was 57.5 percent. And in 2003, 61 percent of American women were working.

Graph 2

Graph 2 shows the divorce rate in the United States. In 1960, the divorce rate was just 2.2 per 1,000 people. In 1970, it rose to 3.5, and in 1980, it jumped to 5.2. However, it declined in 1990 to 4.7, and in 2003 declined even more, to 3.8 per 1,000 people.

Graph 3

Graph 3 presents information on people over age 65 who lived alone from 1970 to 2000. You need to make two sets of points here. Use an O for men and an X for women.

In 1970, 35.9 percent of elderly women lived alone, compared to 10.8 percent of elderly men. In 1980, the percentage was 31.9 for women and 8.1 for men. In 1990, 51.8 percent of women lived alone, compared to 21.5 percent for men.

And finally, in 2000, 40 percent of women and 17 percent of men were living by themselves.

After You Listen

3 Talking About Statistics

- Have students read the directions and write their five true or false statements.
- Then ask them to work in pairs. Ask one pair of students to read the example aloud.
- Set a time limit of five minutes for students to read their statements to each other and respond.
- When they finish, they can go on to discuss the questions in part 2.
- Ask the class to come up with a variety of different explanations for the statistics in each graph.

Best Practice

Making Use of Academic Content

This is an example of collaborative problem-solving. Interpreting information from charts and graphs is an important academic skill. This type of activity requires students to work collaboratively to process information in order to complete the charts. They then have to synthesize and reach conclusions based on the data in order to answer the questions.

4 Comparing Lifestyles in Different Countries

- Read the instructions.
- Have students work in groups of three.
- Ask one graph of students to read the example.
- Explain that the three charts are the same except that some information is missing from each one.

- Each person will choose one chart and ask the others for the missing information.

ANSWER KEY

Charts A, B and C are combined below. The missing answers are boldfaced, and the chart letter that the answer is missing from is in parentheses in front of each answer.

Country	# Children per Woman	Life Expectancy	TV Sets per Person	Per Capita GDP
Korea	1.5	75.5	.4	**(B) $17,800**
United States	2.07	**(B) 77.43**	**(A) 1.00**	37,800
Argentina	2.24	75.7	.3	**(C) 11,200**
France	1.84	79.44	.6	27,600
Senegal	**(A) 4.84**	**(B) 56.56**	.08	1,600
Thailand	1.89	**(C) 71.41**	.5	7,400
Mexico	2.49	74.94	.3	9,000
Italy	1.27	79.54	.5	**(C) 26,700**
Saudi Arabia	4.11	75.23	.3	11,800
China (PRC)	**(B) 1.69**	71.96	.3	5,000
Egypt	**(C) 2.95**	70.71	.2	4,000
Iran	1.93	69.66	**(B) .1**	7,000
Russia	**(A) 1.26**	66.39	**(C) .5**	8,900
Japan	1.38	**(A) 81.04**	.8	28,200
Turkey	1.98	72.08	.4	**(A) 6,700**

5 Discussion

- When students have completed their charts, have them discuss the questions and write sentences as in the example.

ANSWER KEY
1. United States, Japan, France, Italy, Saudi Arabia
2. Senegal, Egypt, China, Iran, Thailand
3. Answers will vary.

Expansion Activity

- The aim of this activity is to practice the skills needed for making a line graph like the ones on pages 118-119 of this chapter and to practice research skills on the Internet or in the library. The research part of this activity can be given as homework.
- Brainstorm with your students possible topics for a line graph. The topics should relate to some development that takes place over a period of time. Here are some examples:

  The average retirement age over the last 50 years

  The number of university students over the last 20 years

  The number of women at university over the last 20 years

  The average age of getting married over the last 50 years

- Have students work in groups to design their line graph and plan their strategy for collecting this information. (It is important to draw out the graph at this stage so that students can plan the time scale of the graph and divide up the research.)
- Make sure all students know what data they need to research for the next class.
- In the next class, have students re-form their groups and transfer their information to the graph.
- Display the graphs on the wall of the classroom.
- Ask groups to tell the class what was most surprising or unusual and what possible theories might explain the patterns in the data.

Self-Assessment Log

- The purpose of the log is to help the students reflect on their learning.
- Read the directions aloud and have students check vocabulary that they learned in the chapter and are prepared to use.
- Have students check the strategies they understand.
- Put students in small groups. Ask students to find the information or an activity related to each strategy in the chapter.
- Tell students to find definitions in the chapter for any words they did not check, or they can look in their dictionaries.

CHAPTER 6
Global Connections

In this CHAPTER

Students will read about various topics related to international communication. In Part 1, they will talk about communication technology and learn to interrupt politely. In Part 2, they will listen to a lecture about cultural differences and body language. In Part 3, they will practice using context clues when listening to information about ways to travel. In Part 4, they will learn how to participate in and give a survey.

> "The question is no longer IF the Internet can transform learning in powerful ways."
>
> The Web-Based Education Commission

Chapter Opener

- Have students look at the photo and describe what is happening. Ask them the questions from the Connecting to the Topic section. Have students discuss as a class.
- Read and discuss the quote on page 124. Ask students to explain the quote in their own words. Ask how the Internet has transformed learning and in what ways it will continue to transform the way that people learn.

Chapter Overview

Listening Skills and Strategies
Listening for main ideas and details
Taking notes on similarities and differences
Identifying blended consonants
Listening to a phone survey

Speaking Skills and Strategies
Talking about taking courses online
Asking for help and permission, and information questions
Interrupting politely
Talking about body language customs in different cultures
Discussing pros and cons in different situations
Talking about different ways to travel
Conducting a phone survey

Critical-Thinking Skills
Interpreting body language in photos
Taking effective notes on a lecture to put into an outline

Getting meaning from context
Using a chart to conduct a phone survey with your classmates

Vocabulary Building
Expressions for interrupting
Expressions signaling similarity and difference
Expressions used in phone surveys

Pronunciation
Identifying and practicing stressed words
Identifying intonation patterns
Pronouncing names and sentences with blended consonants

Language Skills
Using context clues to guess about ways to travel

Vocabulary

Nouns	Verbs	Adjectives	Adverbs
authority	catch up on	affectionate	harmoniously
deadline	convey	convenient	unintentionally
feedback	get to know	horrified	
gestures	hug	invisible	**Expression**
overview	interrupt	offended	How come...?
potential	stay in touch	offensive	

PART 1 — Conversation: Taking Classes Online

Student Book pages 126–127

Can You Guess?

- Read the six statements below. Have students listen and write *True* or *False* for each statement. Go over the correct answers.
- What possible definitions of culture are suggested by these facts? What kinds of miscommunication can occur when people don't understand each other's cultures?

True or False?

1. Japan has the largest number of cell phone users in the world. (**A.** *False: It's China.*)
2. In the U.S., workers often call their bosses by their first names. (**A.** *True*)
3. In Egypt, it is polite to eat all the food on your plate. (**A.** *False*)
4. You should not give people from Iran yellow flowers. (**A.** *True: In many cultures, including Iran, Peru, and Mexico, the color yellow has a negative meaning.*)
5. In some countries, bribery is a normal part of doing business. (**A.** *True*)
6. The country with the largest number of newspapers is India. (**A.** *False: It's Japan.*)

Before You Listen

- Read aloud the text that introduces the conversation.

1 Prelistening Questions

- Discuss the prelistening questions as a class.
- Call students' attention to the photos on the page. Ask student to identify each type of technology (a tablet, a laptop, a cell phone).
- Have a student read aloud the two questions at the bottom of the page. Elicit answers from the class.

2 Previewing Vocabulary

- Play the recording and have students listen carefully for the underlined words and expressions. Point out to students that they should try to understand the meaning of the words from the context of the sentences.
- Have students complete the activity individually.
- Check answers as a whole class.

ANSWER KEY

1. c 2. g 3. e 4. f 5. b 6. d 7. h
8. a

Listen

3 Comprehension Questions

(The audioscript follows Activity 4.)

- Explain to students that these questions will help students focus on the main ideas in the listening. They do not need to understand every word to answer the questions.
- Read the questions with the class.
- Play the recording.
- After listening once (or twice if necessary), have students compare their answers in pairs.
- Check answers as a class.

ANSWER KEY

1. The regular classes were full.
2. It is convenient and he likes the people in his class.
3. They are people from all over the States and abroad.
4. He listens to their voice recordings and gives feedback.
5. He advises Mari to take an online class.

Student Book pages 127–129

Stress

4 Listening for Stressed Words

- Tell students that they will listen to the conversation from Activity 3 again and fill in the missing stressed words. Tell students to read the conversation first and notice the words that are missing.
- Play the recording again.
- Allow time for students to repeat and write the missing words.
- After listening, have students check their answers with the audioscript on page 283 in their books.
- Have students read the conversation with a partner, paying attention to stressed words in their pronunciation.

AUDIOSCRIPT and ANSWER KEY

Jeff: [saying some words in Chinese]

Mari: Oh, sorry, am I _interrupting_?

Jeff: No, that's okay. I'm just _catching up_ on my Chinese homework.

Mari: Oh, I didn't know you were taking _Chinese_.

Jeff: Yeah, I'm taking it _online_.

Mari: Online? Doesn't the college offer _Chinese_ classes?

Jeff: They do, but the regular _face_-to-_face_ classes were full. I like _this_ class better anyway.

Mari: Really? How _come_?

Jeff: Well, for one thing, it's so _convenient_. I mean, I don't need to _worry_ about fitting it into my schedule. I can just go online _whenever_ I want and do my work.

Mari: Whenever? Don't you have _deadlines_?

Jeff: Yeah, we have to _post_ the homework and _participate_ in group discussions by a certain date. But I don't feel _pressured_, you know, the way I do in a regular class.

Mari: I see what you _mean_. I'm not always _ready_ to participate in class.

Jeff: Uh-huh. And _another_ thing I like: the _people_ in the class. My classmates are from _all_ over the States and even from _abroad_. There's someone from Canada and people from _Germany_ and Brazil.

Mari: Wow. That's a lot of different _time_ zones! Seems like the _whole_ world wants to learn Chinese these days.

Jeff: Yup. And get this: the instructor is in _Beijing_.

Mari: That's so cool. But how does he correct your _pronunciation_? Don't you need the face-to-face _contact_?

Jeff: No, he listens to our _voice_ recordings and gives us _feedback_. And once a week we talk on Skype.

Mari: So you know what everyone _looks_ like?

Jeff: Sure. We've all become _friends_ and chat on Facebook all the time, too. And we've all agreed to stay in _touch_ after the course ends and meet next year in _China_!

Mari: Oh, so you'll get some face-to-face contact _after_ all!

Jeff: Of course. You _can't_ really get to know a culture without _traveling_ there.

Mari: True. That's _exactly_ why I came here. Not just to learn _English_ but also to get to know the _lifestyle_ and customs.

Jeff: Right. But anyway, you should _really_ try an online class some time. Almost all American _colleges_ and universities offer them, you know.

Mari: I probably will. You certainly got me _interested_.

Interactions 2 Listening/Speaking 99

PART 1

Student Book pages 129–131

Intonation

FOCUS

Intonation in Questions and Requests

- Read the instruction note.
- Model the intonation of the examples in the box. (You may want to emphasize the intonation by replacing the words with "dah.")

5 Practicing Intonation of Questions

- Play the recording and have students listen and read the questions.
- Play the recording again. This time, have students repeat the questions.

6 Identifying Intonation Patterns

- Explain that students will hear eight different questions. They must identify whether the intonation is rising or falling for each.
- Play the recording and have students circle the correct intonation pattern.
- After listening, check answers as a class.

AUDIOSCRIPT and ANSWER KEY

1. Don't you need face-to-face contact? (rising)
2. How much does the online class cost? (falling)
3. What countries are your classmates from? (falling)
4. May I interrupt? (rising)
5. Can you give me feedback? (rising)
6. Do you want to meet in Beijing next year? (rising)
7. Which hotel should we stay at? (falling)
8. Why do you want to study abroad? (falling)

Listen

7 Reviewing Vocabulary

- Have students work in pairs to discuss the questions. Monitor to make sure that they use the underlined words and expressions in their answers.
- Review answers as a class by asking student volunteers to give their answers.

Using Language Functions

FOCUS

Interrupting Politely

- Read the instruction note.
- Ask students to read the examples, using appropriate language to complete the sentences.

Content Note

In some cultures, it is considered extremely rude to interrupt anyone, particularly an older person in a position of responsibility, such as a teacher in the United States; however, it is common for students to politely interrupt a teacher if they don't understand something. Most teachers consider that an important part of the learning process is having students let them know when something is not clear.

Best Practice

Interacting with Others

Activity 8 is an example of collaborative learning to encourage fluency and confidence. In this type of activity, communication is more important than grammar. Students practice interrupting politely in groups of three. They can then improve their confidence by switching roles or partners and practicing the same situations again. By providing feedback to each other, they learn skills of self-evaluation.

Student Book pages 131–132

8 Role-Play

- Read the instructions to the class. Then read through the situations and check comprehension of any new vocabulary.
- Have students work in groups of three to practice the role-plays.
- Set a time limit of five minutes.
- Move around the room to monitor and provide feedback. Take notes on any errors. Point out and correct any common errors with the whole class at the end of the activity.
- Ask for volunteers to perform conversations for the class.

9 The Interrupting Game

- Prepare a list (or ask students for ideas) of popular conversational topics, e.g., baseball, TV, music, computers. Write the list on the board.
- Have students work in groups of four to five. Each person in the group should think of a story about one of the topics.
- Have three students role-play the example for the class.
- Set a time limit of ten minutes.
- Move around the room to monitor and provide feedback.

10 Survey: Find Someone Who...

- Remind students of the rules of this activity, or ask a student to explain the procedure to the class.
- Read aloud the instructions. Then read through the chart and check comprehension of any new vocabulary.
- Set a time limit of 15 minutes.
- Move around the room to monitor and provide feedback.
- Ask for volunteers to summarize what they discovered.

Expansion Activity (REPRODUCIBLE)

- The purpose of this activity is to practice strategies for interrupting politely and using new vocabulary on the topic of communication technology.
- See Black Line Master "Interrupting Politely" on page BLM 17 of this Teacher's Manual. Photocopy one page for each group of four students.
- Cut each copy into squares and distribute one set of squares to each group of students.
- Students will place the squares face down in the center of the group.
- Each student in turn will pick up a square and answer the question.
- The other students will try to prevent the first student from finishing the sentence by interrupting (politely!).
- Students gain one point for every successful and polite interruption and one point for answering the question.

PART 2 Lecture: Body Language Around the World

Student Book pages 132–135

Before You Listen

- Read the text that introduces the lecture. Ask students to explain body language. Mime examples as necessary.

1 Prelistening Discussion

- Have students describe the photos.
- Have students work in small groups to answer the questions, or give one question to each group of students.
- Review the responses as a class and compare some of their experiences.

2 Previewing Vocabulary

- Play the recording and ask students to listen to the words.
- Have students check any words that they don't know. Then have students compare answers with a partner and explain words to each other if they can.
- Ask for explanations or paraphrases of each word.

Listen

Strategy

Taking Notes on Similarities and Differences

- Read aloud the information in the Strategy box.
- Ask students for additional examples of similarities or differences.
- Write some of these examples on the board, using the expressions in the box.

3 Taking Notes on Similarities and Differences

- Have students read the directions.
- Play the recording and have students write the notes for each item.
- In pairs, have students try to recreate the original sentences from their notes.
- Ask for volunteers to write their notes on the board.
- Sample answers are below.

ANSWER KEY

1. <u>U.S.</u> rule: people stand arm's length (=70 cm) apart when talking.

   Latin Americans: <u>stand much closer when talking</u>

2. Arab culture: <u>men sit/stand very close to each other</u>

   E. Asia: <u>people stand farther apart than Americans</u>

3. U.S.: <u>look at a person's eyes when speaking to them</u>

   Africa, Carib: <u>children look down when speaking to parent or teacher</u>

4. <u>Japan</u>: no eye contact w/<u>employer; disrespectful</u>

5. Mexico/Italy: it's normal to <u>hug on happy occasions</u>

   France: everybody <u>kisses in greeting</u>

   Japan: <u>no touching in public, not even married people</u>

AUDIOSCRIPT

1. In the U.S. there is kind of a general rule, which is that people stand about one arm's length or about 70 centimeters apart when they are talking. In contrast, Latin Americans usually stand much closer to each other.

2. In Arab cultures, for instance, you will also notice that men sit and stand very close to each other. On the other hand, in East Asia, people usually stand farther apart than Americans do.

3. Next let's talk about eye contact, which is the way people look at each other, or don't look at each other, when they're talking. In the U.S. the rules are simple. You should look at a person's eyes when you speak with them. To Americans this is a sign of respect and attention. If I'm talking to you in class and you're looking away from me, I might think you're not listening to me. But the exact opposite is true in many cultures. In some parts of Africa and the Caribbean, for example, children are taught to look down when they're talking to a person with greater authority, such as a parent or a teacher.

4. Similarly, in Japan an employee would not make direct eye contact with an employer. It would be disrespectful.

5. The rules for touching are very different from one culture to another. Some cultures are more affectionate than others. So, in Latin cultures such as Mexico and Italy, it's normal for strangers to hug each other on happy occasions. And it's similar in France, where, maybe you know, everybody, even total strangers, kiss each other as a form of greeting. But in Japan and many other countries it is not proper for strangers to touch each other, and even married people may avoid touching in public.

4 Taking Notes (Part 1)

(The audioscript follows Activity 5.)

- Remind students of the keys to good note-taking. (See Student Book Chapter 1, pages 13 and 14.)
- Tell students they are going to take notes in any way they choose in their notebook or on a piece of paper.

Best Practice

Scaffolding Instruction

The lecture outline helps students to organize the lecture into main and secondary ideas. By providing students with part of the outline as a support, they can see how this note-taking technique helps the listener to structure the content of the talk. This guided activity prepares them for the skill of identifying main and secondary ideas without the help of an outline.

5 Outlining the Lecture

- Ask students to use their notes from Activity 4 to complete the outline.
- Play the recording again.
- Have students fill in any missing information.
- Check the answers as a class.

ANSWER KEY

Part 1

Topic: <u>Nonverbal Communication / Body Language</u>

Intro: <u>we convey info w/o words, by head, hands, eyes. differs from culture to culture; can cause misunderstandings</u>

A. Movement (gestures, <u>movement of head & feet</u>)

  1. U.S. "OK" gesture = <u>zero</u> in Russia, <u>offensive</u> in Brazil
  2. Pointing: OK in U.S., <u>rude in Indonesia</u>
  3. Show bottom of shoe: <u>disrespectful in Arab cultures</u>

PART 2

Student Book pages 135–136

> **B.** Distance
> 1. Every culture people have <u>personal space</u>
> 2. Standing:
>   a. U.S. + <u>N. Europe</u>: arm's length (=70 cm) when talking
>   b. Latin Cultures: <u>much closer</u>
>   c. Arab (men): <u>men sit/stand very close</u>
>   d. East Asia: <u>stand farther apart than Americans</u>

AUDIOSCRIPT

Professor: Good afternoon, class. As I announced last time, we're starting a new unit today, and the topic is nonverbal communication or body language as it's often called. As you know, we humans convey a lot of information without using any words, by using our heads, our hands, our eyes, and so on. The thing is, body language, like spoken language, differs from culture to culture; and there is a lot of potential for misunderstandings if people aren't aware of these differences. So today I'm going to give you an overview, an introduction, to four categories of nonverbal communication. Those categories are movement, distance, eye contact, and touching. I'll define each of the categories and give examples. And I'll be asking you for examples as well.

OK, the first category I mentioned is movement, and this includes gestures, um, movements of the hands and arms, and also movement of the head and even the feet. There's a famous photo of Bill Clinton, who was president from 1993 to 2001, making the American gesture for OK: you make a circle with your first two fingers, and you hold up the other three fingers, like this. And this photo caused some confusion in other countries, like Russia, where this gesture means "zero." And in Brazil, where it's a really offensive gesture. This is just one example of how the same gesture can mean different things in different places. Can someone give me another example? Yes, Adi?

Adi: When I first came here I saw American people pointing with the second finger, and I was really shocked because in my country, Indonesia, this is very rude. If you want to point at someone you use your thumb or your open hand.

Professor: Thank you, that's interesting. Does anyone have another example? Maybe something that involves another part of the body? OK, Moussa?

Moussa: In Arab cultures you never, never, show the bottom of your shoe or even point to someone's feet. It's really terrible. I was so surprised the first time I saw a teacher sitting with one foot on his knee, and I could see the bottom of his shoe. I thought he was so disrespectful.

Professor: Another great example. Thank you, Moussa. All right, I think we need to move on to the second category I mentioned, and that's distance. I mean how close or far people are comfortable sitting or standing from each other. In every culture people have what we call their personal space, which is like an invisible bubble around them. And if a stranger steps inside their personal space, they feel uncomfortable. In the U.S. there is kind of a general rule, which is that people stand about one arm's length or about 70 centimeters apart when they are talking. This is also true for Northern European countries like Sweden. In contrast, in Latin cultures, people usually stand much closer to each other.

So imagine a party where, let's say, a person from Sweden is talking to a person from Italy. The Italian stands close to the Swede because that's normal in his culture, but the Swede keeps moving backwards because to him the Italian is standing too close for comfort. The conversation may have started in the middle of the room but soon the Italian has unintentionally pushed the Swede against a wall. The poor Swede looks really uncomfortable and the poor Italian is confused because he doesn't understand what he's doing wrong!

Other cultures also differ from Americans in their use of personal space. In Arab cultures, for instance, you will also notice that men sit and stand very close to each other. On the other hand, in East Asia, people usually stand farther apart than Americans do.

Student Book page 136

6 Taking Notes (Part 2)

- Play the second part of the recording. Have students take notes in their own way, on paper or in their notebooks.
- Have students use their notes to complete the outline.
- Play the recording again if necessary.
- Check answers as a class.

ANSWER KEY

C. Eye contact
1. U.S.: always look at person you're speaking to
2. Africa, Carib: children look down when talking to parent/teacher
3. Japan: no eye contact with employer

D. Touching
1. Latin: normal for strangers to hug/kiss on happy occasions
   a. E.g. France: everybody kisses in greeting
2. Japan: no touching in public, not even married people

Conclusion: important to know about nonvbl comm. in other cultures to avoid misunderstandings

AUDIOSCRIPT

Professor: Next let's talk about eye contact, which is the way people look at each other, or don't look at each other, when they're talking. In the U.S. the rules are simple. You should look at a person's eyes when you speak with them. To Americans this is a sign of respect and attention. If I'm talking to you in class and you're looking away from me, I might think you're not listening to me. But the exact opposite is true in many cultures. In some parts of Africa and the Caribbean, for example, children are taught to look down when they're talking to a person with greater authority, such as a parent or a teacher. Similarly, in Japan an employee would not make direct eye contact with an employer. It would be disrespectful. Yes, Angie? You want to say something?

Angie: I read about a case where a woman didn't get a job because the employer said she didn't look at him during the interview, so he felt like she was hiding something, like she was dishonest.

Professor: Exactly. That is how most Americans would react, I think. All right, finally I want to introduce the topic of touching. First let me tell you a little story. A young woman from Mexico, let's call her Inez, is invited to the wedding of her Japanese classmate, Yuki. After the wedding ceremony everyone stands in line to greet the bride and groom and their families. When Inez is introduced to Yuki's mother, she leans in and tries to hug her. Yuki's mother looks horrified and immediately steps away from Inez. Inez looks hurt. Can someone explain what happened here?

Female: I think Inez was trying to offer congratulations to Yuki's mother, but maybe the mother wasn't comfortable touching someone she didn't know.

Professor: That's correct. The rules for touching are very different from one culture to another. Some cultures are more affectionate than others. So in Latin cultures, like Mexico and Italy, it's normal for strangers to hug each other on happy occasions. And it's similar in France, where, maybe you know, everybody, even total strangers, kiss each other as a form of greeting. But in Japan and many other countries it is not proper for strangers to touch each other, and even married people may avoid touching in public. You can see why Yuki's mother was uncomfortable and Inez was offended in the example I gave you. All right, let's review what we've discussed so far. I've introduced four categories of nonverbal communication—uh, movement, distance, eye contact, and touching. Next time we'll look at each of these categories in greater detail. For now, what I hope you've gotten is the general message that body language differs from culture to culture in the same way that spoken language does, and because of these differences there is always the potential of people misunderstanding one another.

PART 2

Student Book pages 136–137

In today's globalized world, where we are interacting with one another in business, in the classroom, and in the workplace, it's important to know something about nonverbal communication in other cultures so that we can work together harmoniously and avoid misunderstandings.

Expansion Activity

REPRODUCIBLE

- The purpose of this activity is to practice using the Internet for research and to gain an understanding of naming practices in different countries.
- Students can use a search engine, typing in keywords such as *naming practices* and the name of their chosen country.
- The research part of this activity can be done in a computer lab class or assigned for homework.
- See Black Line Master "Naming Practices" on page BLM 18 of this Teacher's Manual. Photocopy and distribute one copy to each student.
- Divide students into groups of four and have each person in the group choose one country. (They can choose alternative countries if they wish.)
- Students will research their chosen topic on the web. Then they will re-form their groups to report what they found and complete the worksheet.
- Ask a representative from each group to summarize the differences and similarities in naming practices.

After You Listen

Best Practice

Activating Prior Knowledge

This is an example of an activity that encourages students to make text-to-self connections. The discussion questions ask students to relate the content of the lecture on cultural differences and similarities to their own lives. This aids understanding and retention of new material.

7 Discussing the Lecture

- Have students discuss the questions in groups.
- Encourage students to use the new vocabulary in their discussion.
- Ask for representatives from each group to report to the class about their group's discussion.

8 Reviewing Vocabulary

- Have students test each other on the new vocabulary, working in small groups.
- Ask for volunteers to give example sentences using the new vocabulary in Activity 2 on page 134 of the Student Book.

PART 3 Strategies for Better Listening and Speaking   Student Book pages 137–140

Focused Listening

FOCUS

Blending Consonants

- Review the meaning of vowel and consonant.
- Read the instruction note and practice the examples.

① Pronouncing Names with Blended Consonants

- Have students read the directions. Then have them read silently the 12 names.
- Play the recording and have students repeat each example.

② Listening for Blended Consonants

- Read the sentences and have students try to identify the blended consonants before listening.
- Play the recording and have students circle the blended sounds.
- Play the recording again and ask students to repeat the sentences.
- Review the answers as a class.

ANSWER KEY

1. Jamil lives in a small town.
2. Yesterday Linda had a really bad day.
3. Michelle texted her mother eight times.
4. Susanna's birthday is August tenth.
5. Let's see the movie at the Friss Cinema.
6. Would you like some hot tea and cookies?
7. Kevin needs a tall ladder to reach that high window.
8. Malik Khan hosts a popular radio show.

③ Pronouncing Sentences

- Review the meaning of blended consonants, linked sounds, stressed and reduced sounds, and intonation.
- Read the sentences and have students try to identify the blended consonants before listening.
- Play the recording and have students mark their answers, circling the blended consonants and linking the linked sounds.
- Play the recording again and ask students to repeat the examples.
- Review the answers as a class.

ANSWER KEY

1. Whose black car are you driving?
2. Pat told me to have a good day.
3. The yard was full of fall leaves.
4. Chris said, "We're ready to take a walk."
5. This story is so sad.
6. I forgot to write down Ned's phone number.
7. I received a letter with three stamps on it.
8. Did you forget to make our dinner reservations?

Getting Meaning from Context

FOCUS ON TESTING TOEFL® iBT

Using Context Clues

- There are five conversations on this recording. There is a question at the end of each conversation.
- Play each conversation. Stop the recording after the question, and give students time to fill in the circle next to their answer choice and write the clues that helped them.
- Check answers as a class.

AUDIOSCRIPT

Conversation 1
A: I want to go overseas next summer but I can't afford it.
B: You can—if you stay at a hostel.
A: How is that different from a hotel?
B: A hostel, especially a youth hostel, is more like a dormitory. You share a room with a bunch of other travelers, often from all over the world.
A: Wow, it sounds like a great way to meet new people.
B: Yeah. And it's a lot cheaper than a hotel.

Question 1: *A hostel is probably...*

Conversation 2
A: How was your vacation?
B: Fantastic! We stayed at a great apartment in the center of Paris, totally free.
A: A free apartment in Paris? Wow. How did you do that?
B: We exchanged apartments with a French family.
A: Oh, so your friends stayed at your place in New York while your family stayed at theirs?
B: Well, yeah, but they're not our friends. Actually, we met them online through a company called homeexchange.com.
A: That sounds great. Can I find an apartment in Bangkok that way? I'm planning to visit Thailand next summer.
B: Definitely. Just sign up online and pay a small fee.

Question 2: *What is probably true about home exchanges?*

Conversation 3
A: After I graduate, I want to see and learn about other parts of the world.
B: Me too. But I don't want to be just a tourist. Have you heard about something called volunteer travel?
A: I think so. You go abroad and do volunteer work, like at a hospital, a school, an orphanage, places like that. Right?
B: Yeah. There are all sorts of organizations you can join, depending on where you want to go and what kind of work you want to do.
A: Are they all free?
B: I don't think so. When my cousin volunteered at a hospital in Mexico, he had to pay for his travel expenses. But the housing and food were free.
A: How long was he there?
B: A year, I think. But you can volunteer for short periods, too. Let's look into it.

Question 3: *Volunteer travel is probably a good experience for...*

Conversation 4
A: Wow. Look at this advertisement: "Discover nature, protect the environment and help improve the lives of local people."
B: Sounds like a travel ad.
A: Yes, it's an ad for a trip to Brazil. Not to famous cities like Rio, though, but to natural areas. Like the rainforest.
B: Hmm. Isn't the rainforest disappearing very quickly? How does it help the environment to have more and more tourists visiting there?
A: Well, the purpose of this trip is to teach visitors about nature, how to protect it and not to damage it. And some of the money from the tourists will go directly to the local people.
B: Oh, I get it. I think this kind of travel is called "ecotourism."

Question 4: *What are "eco-tourists" interested in?*

Conversation 5
A: Where are you going to stay when you go to Tokyo?
B: I'm going to try couch surfing.
A: Couch what?
B: Couch surfing. It's a kind of international club. Members volunteer to host you in their homes, give you a tour of their city, or just give you advice. And you host people in your home, too.
A: It sounds wonderful. But aren't these people total strangers?

Student Book pages 139–142

B: Yup. But it's really safe. I've stayed with people in Europe and Asia. And I've hosted people from Sweden, Russia and Japan.

A: Hm. I'll check out their website and see if this is for me.

Question 5: *Couch surfing is an organization for...*

ANSWER KEY

Answers	Clues
1. B	youth hostel; young people; dormitory; share a room
2. D	free apartment; homeexchange.com; sign up; pay fee
3. A	volunteer work; hospital; school; orphanage
4. C	nature; environment; rainforest; teach; protect
5. A	host you in their homes; stayed with people; hosted people

Using Language Functions

FOCUS

Expressing Pros and Cons

- Read the instruction note.
- As a class, continue the discussion about youth hostels. Draw a T-chart on the board and elicit additional pros and cons of youth hostels from the students.
- Have students use the expressions from the chart in their answers.

Talk It Over

4 Comparing Different Ways to Travel

- Read the instructions. Call students' attention to the chart on page 142 that they will fill in. Also, have students turn back in their books to page 134 to remind them of the expressions of similarity and difference.
- Have students look at the photos on the page. Call on volunteers to describe each photo and the type of travel they represent.
- Have students work in small groups to discuss the pros and cons of the five types of travel and complete the chart.
- Discuss answers and compare charts as a class.

5 Discussion

- Have students work in small groups to discuss the questions.
- Move around the room to give feedback and help.
- Ask a volunteer from each group to report back to the class on their group's discussion.

Expansion Activity

- The aim of this activity is to practice the language of expressing similarities and differences.
- Elicit topics from the students and write them on the board, e.g., studying abroad. Allow each group to choose a different topic from the list.
- Have groups discuss and list the pros and cons of their topic in a T-chart like the one in the Student Book on page 142.
- At the end of the activity, ask a representative from each group to present their list to the class.

PART 4 Real-World Task: Participating in a Survey

Student Book pages 143–144

- Read the introductory note about participating in a survey on the top of page 143.
- Have two volunteers read aloud the example conversation.
- Read aloud the nouns and verbs in the box and elicit paraphrases or examples to display their meaning. Confirm that students understand all of the vocabulary.
- Elicit sentences using the vocabulary words that describe the photos on the page.

Before You Listen

1 Prelistening Questions

- Read and discuss the questions as a class. Or, divide the class into three groups. Assign each group one of the questions. Assign a group leader for each group to lead the discussion. Have the groups discuss their question. Have a representative from each group report back to the class about their discussion.

Listen

2 Listening to a Phone Survey

- Read the instructions to the class.
- Give students time to read over the survey. Tell them that reading the survey first will help them focus on listening for the correct answers.
- Play the recording. Have students fill in their answers. Play the recording again if necessary for students to confirm their answers.
- Students will compare answers with a partner in Activity 3.

ANSWER KEY

Respondent's Name: Julie Salsedo

Respondent's Age: 40–50 yrs

Yearly Income: [no answer given]

1. Donated money: NO **2.** Volunteered: YES **3.** Helped a stranger: YES **4.** Country with most generous people: Switzerland **5.** Life satisfaction: 8

AUDIOSCRIPT

A: Hello?

B: Yes, I'd like to speak to Ms. Julie Salsedo.

A: Speaking.

B: Oh. Ms. Salsedo, my name is Ken. I'm calling from the International Gallop Poll organization. I wonder if you have a few minutes to participate in a survey.

A: Um, a survey? What kind of survey?

B: A survey about charity and volunteering. It's very short, just five questions.

A: OK, I guess I can do that. Go ahead.

B: Terrific. OK, my first question is: In the past month, have you donated money to an organization?

A: What kind of organization? Like a charity, or…?

B: It can be any organization—a charity, or a school, or even a political organization.

A: No, I haven't. Not since the economy has gone down, you know, it's been hard…

B: I see. That's OK. You can just give yes/no answers. So, here is my second question. During the past month, have you volunteered time to an organization?

A: Yes, I have. I volunteered at my daughter's school.

B: OK. Next, in the past month, have you helped a stranger? Or someone you didn't know who needed help?

A: Hmm. Let's see. I think so.

B: So your answer is "Yes"?

A: Yes. Some tourists asked me for directions, and I helped them out. I actually took them to the place they were looking for.

B: Great. OK, next: Which country do you think has the most generous people?

A: Oh, that's a tough one. I think you can find generous people and selfish people everywhere.

B: Right. But which country do you think has the most generous people?

A: Hmm. I suppose the richest countries because they have the most money and time to give. So I'm going to pick, um, Switzerland.

B: OK, thank you. Next, can you tell me how you feel about your life? How satisfied are you with your life on a scale of 1 to 10? One means very unhappy, and 10 means very happy, very satisfied.

Student Book pages 144–147

A: Hmm. I guess I'm pretty happy. I'd say 8.

B: OK, Ms. Salsedo. That's all the questions I have. I just need some personal information. What is your age range? Are you between 20 and 30? Between 30 and 40? Between 40 and 50?

A: The last one. Between 40 and 50.

B: And your income level? Is your yearly income between 20,000 and 40,000…

A: I'm sorry, I'm really not comfortable answering that.

B: Oh, that's OK. No problem. Thank you very much for your time, Ms. Salsedo.

A: You're welcome.

B: Bye-bye.

After You Listen

3 Discussing the Survey Questions

- Have students work in pairs. Ask them to compare answers to the survey questions and take the survey themselves. Have students switch roles asking the questions and answering.
- If pairs have questions about the answers to the survey, refer them to the audioscript on page 287 of the Student Book.
- Call attention to the chart on page 145 and demonstrate how to read it, e.g., *In Australia, 38 percent of the people volunteered when this survey was taken.* Elicit other statements about the chart from the class as additional examples.
- Have students continue to work in pairs to answer questions 2–5.
- Review answers as a class.

ANSWER KEY

3. Which country has…

   the highest percentage of people who volunteered = United States

   the highest percentage of people who gave money to charity = Thailand

   the highest percentage of people who helped a stranger = United States

Talk It Over

4 Conducting a Survey

- Read the instructions with the class.
- Have students work in groups to prepare 5–10 questions for their survey.
- Tell each student to prepare a chart or blank survey form to complete. Tell them to use the example given. Give students a number of people to survey, (e.g., at least five), so that they know how many columns to add to their chart.
- Have students walk around the room, asking their survey questions to classmates for practice. Tell them to use the introductory sentences given in Step 4.
- Have students survey people outside of the classroom and bring their results back to class.
- Have students summarize the results of their survey for the class. Discuss the results and make generalizations about your community's generosity.

Self-Assessment Log

- The purpose of the Self-Assessment Log is to help students reflect on their learning.
- Read the directions aloud and have students check the vocabulary they learned in the chapter and are prepared to use.
- Have students check the strategies they practiced in the chapter and the degree to which they learned them. Have students work individually to complete the sentences at the bottom of the page.
- Put students in small groups. Ask students to find the information or an activity related to each strategy in the chapter.
- Tell students to find definitions in the chapter for any words they did not check, or they can look in their dictionaries.

CHAPTER 7
Language and Communication

In this CHAPTER

Students will read about various topics related to language and communication. In Part 1, they will talk about cultural stereotypes and learn to contradict politely. In Part 2, they will listen to a lecture about differences between American and British English. In Part 3, they will practice listening to conversations and learn to understand the meaning of interjections. In Part 4, they will practice spelling.

> "To have another language is to possess a second soul."
>
> Charlemagne
> King of the Franks,
> Emperor of the West (742?–814)

Chapter Opener

- Have students look at the photo of a couple in their kitchen having a discussion, or possibly an argument. Ask students the questions in the Connecting to the Topic section. Discuss the answers as a class.
- Read and discuss the quote. What knowledge do you gain by learning another language? Do people think differently in different languages?

Chapter Overview

Listening Skills and Strategies
Listening for main ideas and details
Making inferences
Understanding statements with rising intonation
Identifying correct spellings in a spelling bee

Speaking Skills and Strategies
Discussing the meaning of friendship
Comparing American and British English
Contradicting politely
Talking about stereotypes
Using interjections
Using expressions for guessing

Critical-Thinking Skills
Getting meaning from context
Taking notes on classifications

Vocabulary Building
Terms used to talk about friendship vs. friendliness
Terms used for talking about languages and dialects
Examples of vocabulary differences between American and British English
Interjections
Expressions for guessing
Slang expressions

Pronunciation
Identifying and practicing stressed words

Language Skills
Using context clues to guess about language and communication

Vocabulary

Nouns
- category
- dialect
- friendliness
- friendship
- majority
- sample
- standard

Verbs
- catch on
- make friends

Adjectives
- identical
- in the dark
- noticeable

- two-faced
- unique

Adverbs
- whereas
- while

Expressions
- Have a seat.
- It's hard to say.

PART 1 — Conversation: What Do People Really Mean?

Student Book pages 150–152

Can You Guess?

- Ask students to discuss the questions below in groups and compare their answers with the correct answers.
- Discuss the issues raised by these questions: Why do we have so many languages in the world? What would happen if we all spoke the same language?

1. How many languages are spoken in the world? **A.** *Roughly 6,500.*
2. Can you name one language that is not related to any other language in the world? **A.** *The best known language "isolate" is Basque, spoken in north-western Spain and south-western France. Others are Ainu, spoken in Japan, Burushaski (northern Pakistan), and Korean.*
3. What are the world's top five languages, based on number of native speakers?
   A. 1. Mandarin Chinese 6. Bengali
   2. Spanish 7. Portuguese
   3. English 8. Russian
   4. Hindi 9. Japanese
   5. Arabic 10. German

Before You Listen

- Read the text aloud that introduces the next conversation.

1 Prelistening Questions

- Have the students read the questions and discuss them in pairs.
- Compare answers as a whole class.
- As a whole class, make a list of different ways of showing friendliness in different cultures.

2 Previewing Vocabulary

- Play the recording and have students listen for the underlined words and expressions.

- Have students complete the activity individually.
- Compare their answers as a class and write the correct answers on the board.

ANSWER KEY
1. b 2. h 3. f 4. a 5. g 6. d 7. c 8. e

Listen

3 Comprehension Questions

- Read the questions aloud.
- Play the recording and have students write their answers.
- After listening, have students compare their answers in pairs.
- Check the answers as a class.

ANSWER KEY
1. They are acquaintances but not friends.
2. Mari is confused because Katrina seems friendly but never has time to meet. 3. People are friendly, but that doesn't mean they want to be friends. 4. No. 5. *How are you?* means "Hello."

AUDIOSCRIPT

Mari:	Yolanda! Hi!
Yolanda:	Hi, Mari, how are you?
Mari:	Fine, thanks. Um, is anyone sitting here?
Yolanda:	No, have a seat.
Mari:	Thanks. So how have you been?
Yolanda:	Oh, you know, busy. I've got school, and work, and I'm getting ready for my brother's wedding next month.
Mari:	Oh, yeah.
Yolanda:	Anyway, it's going to be a huge wedding and…

114 CHAPTER 7

Student Book pages 152–153

Mari:	Oh, excuse me, uh... Nancy! Over here!
Nancy:	Hi!
Mari:	Nancy, this is Yolanda. She works in the library. Yolanda, this is my housemate, Nancy. She teaches English here.
Nancy:	Nice to meet you, Yolanda.
Yolanda:	You too. Well, listen, actually, I've got to go. I have to be at work in ten minutes. I'll see you soon, Mari. We'll go to a movie or something.
Mari:	Sure. How about Thursday night?
Yolanda:	Uh, I have to check my calendar. I'll call you, OK?
Mari:	OK, see you.
Mari:	I don't understand Americans.
Nancy:	Huh?
Mari:	Did you hear what she said? "We'll go to a movie. I'll call you." But every time I try to pick a specific day or time, she says she's busy, she has to check her calendar. And then she doesn't call.
Nancy:	Mm hmm...
Mari:	Why do Americans say things they don't mean? They act so nice, like they always say, "How are you," but then they keep on walking and don't even wait for your answer. They're so... how do you say it... two-faced?
Nancy:	I know it seems that way sometimes, Mari. But it's not true. It's just that for Americans, friendliness and friendship aren't always the same thing.
Mari:	What do you mean?
Nancy:	Well, you know how Americans can be very open and friendly. Like, they invite you to sit down, they ask you questions, they tell all about their families. So naturally you think they're trying to make friends with you. But actually, friendship, real friendship, doesn't happen so quickly.
Mari:	So, when people say "How are you," they're just being polite? They don't really care?
Nancy:	Not exactly. The thing you have to understand is that "how are you" isn't a real question. It's more like a way of saying hello.
Mari:	Aha, I get it! And "Have a nice day" is just a friendly way to say good-bye?
Nancy:	Exactly. Now you're catching on.
Mari:	But I'm still in the dark about Yolanda. Does she want to be my friend or not?
Nancy:	It's hard to say. Maybe she's just too busy these days. I guess you'll just have to be patient.
Mari:	Hmm. That's good advice, I guess. Thanks.

Stress

4 Listening for Stressed Words

- Play the recording again.
- Have students write the missing words.
- After listening, have students check their answers with the audioscript in their books.
- Have students read the conversation with a partner, paying attention to stressed words in their pronunciation.

AUDIOSCRIPT and ANSWER KEY

Mari:	I don't understand Americans.
Nancy:	Huh?
Mari:	Did you _hear_ what she said? "We'll go to a _movie_. I'll call you." But every time I try to pick a _specific_ day or time, she says she's _busy_, she has to check her _calendar_. And then she _doesn't_ call.

PART 1

Student Book pages 152–154

Nancy:	Mm hmm…
Mari:	Why do Americans say things they don't *mean*? They *act* so nice, like they *always* say "How are you," but then they keep on *walking* and don't even wait for your *answer*. They're so… how do you say it… *two*-faced?
Nancy:	I know it *seems* that way sometimes, Mari. But it's *not true*. It's just that for Americans, friendliness and friendship *aren't* always the same thing.
Mari:	What do you *mean*?
Nancy:	Well, you know how Americans can be very *open* and friendly. Like, they *invite* you to sit down, they *ask* you questions, they *tell* you all about their families. So naturally you think they're trying to make *friends* with you. But actually, friendship, *real* friendship, doesn't happen so *quickly*.
Mari:	So, when people say, "How are you," they're just being *polite*? They don't really *care*?
Nancy:	Not exactly. The thing you have to *understand* is that "how are you" isn't a *real* question. It's more like a *way* of saying hello.
Mari:	Aha, I *get* it! And "Have a nice day" is just a *friendly* way to say good-bye?
Nancy:	Exactly. *Now* you're catching on.
Mari:	But I'm *still* in the dark about Katrina. Does she *want* to be my friend or *not*?
Nancy:	It's *hard* to say. Maybe she's just too *busy* these days. I guess you'll just have to be *patient*.
Mari:	Hmm. That's good *advice*, I guess. Thanks.

Intonation

FOCUS

Statements with Rising Intonation

- Read the instruction note.
- Model the intonation of the examples. You may want to emphasize the intonation by replacing the words with *dah*.

5 Understanding Statements with Rising Intonation

- Read the directions for the activity.
- Play the recording while students listen and write questions.

ANSWER KEY

1. Are you going?
2. Do you remember my friend Yolanda?
3. Hasn't he done his homework yet?
4. Is it at the intersection of First and Main?
5. Is Jack Rose's brother?

AUDIOSCRIPT

1. You're going?
2. You remember my friend Yolanda?
3. He hasn't done his homework yet?
4. It's at the intersection of First and Main?
5. Jack is Rose's brother?

Student Book pages 154–155

After You Listen

6 Using Vocabulary

- Have students work in pairs. Student A should look at page 250 in the Student Book. Student B should look at page 258.
- Set a time limit of five minutes.
- Review the answers as a class.

ANSWER KEY

1. **A:** Do you understand tonight's homework assignment? I don't.
   B: No, I'm in the dark, too.
2. **A:** When do you think you'll be able to speak English fluently?
   B: That's hard to say. In just a few years, I hope.
3. **A:** I'm here to see Dr. Brown at 3 P.M.
   B: Please have a seat. The doctor is with another patient right now.
4. **A:** Jerry is a two-faced liar. He told my girlfriend I was seeing another woman!
   B: He did? I thought he was your best friend.
5. **A:** Claudette's friendliness is the reason everyone likes her.
   B: I agree. She always smiles when I see her.
6. **A:** I've known my best friend since we were three years old.
   B: Really? You're lucky to have such a close friendship.
7. **A:** I've told John six times that I don't want to go out with him, but he keeps asking me.
   B: I guess he's a little slow to catch on.
8. **A:** Why is it so hard to make friends with Americans?
   B: You have to be patient. Friendships don't happen so quickly.

Using Language Functions

FOCUS

Contradicting Politely

- Read the instruction note.
- Ask students to read the examples.
- Give some additional statements (see examples below) and ask students to contradict you using the expressions from the box.

Examples:

Video games are too violent.
Fast food is bad for you.
It's easier to learn a language when you are young.
People with college degrees earn more money.

Best Practice

Interacting with Others

This type of activity is an example of collaborative learning to encourage fluency and confidence. In this activity, communication is more important than grammar. Students can improve their confidence to contradict politely by switching roles or partners and practicing the same situations again. By providing feedback to each other, they learn skills of self-evaluation.

7 Contradicting Stereotypes

- Read the directions and have students read the Language Tip. Clarify any questions.
- Have students work in pairs to discuss the questions.
- Compare answers as a class.

PART 1

Student Book page 156

Talk It Over

Best Practice

Cultivating Critical Thinking
This is an example of an activity that encourages students to examine their own cultural assumptions. By trying to define their personal and social concepts of friendship, and comparing them with others, they can develop a more critical awareness of the cultural relativity of these kinds of concepts.

8 What Is Friendship?

- Read the list of situations and check comprehension of any new vocabulary.
- Have students work in groups to discuss the questions.
- You can set a time limit of 10 to 15 minutes.
- Invite volunteers to summarize their discussion.

Expansion Activity

- The purpose of this activity is to practice strategies for contradicting politely and expressing opinions on the topic of language and communication.
- Please see Black Line Master "Do You Agree?" on page BLM 19 of this Teacher's Manual. Photocopy and distribute one copy to each student.
- Have students complete the sentences individually. Have them choose either the positive or negative phrase in sentences 1, 5, 6, 7, and 8, depending on their opinions.
- Have students work in groups to read their sentences using contradicting strategies to disagree with each other.
- Set a time limit of 10 to 15 minutes.
- Move around the room to monitor and provide feedback.
- Invite volunteers to read out the most controversial statements.

PART 2 — Lecture: Differences Between British and American English Student Book pages 157–158

Before You Listen

- Have students describe the pictures. What sort of misunderstanding is being illustrated? Can they think of any other similar examples?

1 Prelistening Discussion

- Have students work in groups to answer the questions.
- Review the responses as a class and compare some of their experiences.
- Ask for some examples of British, Australian, or Canadian English (vocabulary, grammar, or pronunciation).

2 Previewing Vocabulary

- Play the recording and have students listen to the words.
- Have students check the words they know.
- Ask students to compare answers with a partner. They will find out the meanings of these words by listening to the lecture.

Listen

Best Practice

Organizing Information

Activity 3 is an example of a graphic organizer. In this exercise it is used to classify lecture organization. This type of study tool helps students to organize new information so that it is easier to recall. It will also help them when they want to review their notes. There are many types of graphic organizers used in this book.

Strategy

Classifying and Taking Notes on Classification

- Read the information in the Strategy box.
- Introduce the graphic organizer.

3 Classifying Lecture Organization

- Ask for some suggestions for subtopics for each of the main topics.
- Play the recording and have students write key words.
- Compare answers as a class and write the answers on the board.

Best Practice

Scaffolding Instruction

This is an example of an activity that raises awareness of learning strategies. In real life, we use a combination of different strategies to identify and interpret information. In this exercise, students focus on one strategy for identifying and classifying lecture organization. These short guided tasks will help students to use this strategy independently in the context of a lecture.

ANSWER KEY

1. Computers: at home, in business, in education
2. U.S. population: growth and characteristics
3. Differences between BE and AE: pronunciation, vocabulary, grammar

PART 2

Student Book Student Book pages 158–159

AUDIOSCRIPT

Lecture 1
Personal computers have revolutionized the way people work and communicate. I could talk for hours about the wide use of personal computers, but today we only have time to introduce three major uses of computers: at home, in business, and in education.

Lecture 2
In today's lecture, I will provide the most recent information concerning the growth and characteristics of the U.S. population.

Lecture 3
You may have guessed by now that my topic for today's lecture is differences between American and British English. In particular, I want to examine three categories of difference. First, and most obvious, is pronunciation; second, vocabulary; and third, grammar.

FOCUS

Some Vocabulary Differences Between American and British English
- Compare the words in each of the lists.
- Have students circle the words they've heard.

4 Taking Notes (Part I)

(The audioscript follows Activity 5.)

- Remind students of the keys to good note-taking. (See Student Book Chapter 1 pages 12 and 13.)
- Tell students they are going to hear part of a lecture about differences between British and American English.
- Play the recording.
- Go over the word lists in the box.

5 Outlining the Lecture

- Ask students to use their notes to complete the outline.
- Play the recording again.
- Have students fill in any missing information.
- Check the answers as a class.

ANSWER KEY

Differences between American and British English

I. Pronunciation

Sound	Am.E.	B.E.
1. 'a' e.g. can't	/kænt/	/kant/
2. 'r' e.g. car	/kar/	/ka/
3. 'd' e.g. little	liddle twenny-one	little twenny-one

AUDIOSCRIPT

Part 1

Lecturer: Good afternoon. To introduce my topic today, I'd like you to listen to two speech samples and tell me where the speakers are from. Ready? OK, here's the first one.

Speaker 1: "Today's weather forecast calls for partly cloudy skies in the morning, clearing by mid-afternoon with winds up to 15 miles an hour out of the west. The high temperature will be 80 degrees Fahrenheit, and the low will be 64."

Lecturer: OK. Now, where do you think that speaker was from?

Audience: America... the United States... Canada.

Lecturer: Yes, most of you got it. That was what we call a standard American accent, which means the accent that is spoken by the majority of people who live in the United States and Canada.

Now, listen to a different speaker reading the same text.

Speaker 2: "Today's weather forecast calls for partly cloudy skies in the morning, clearing by mid-afternoon with winds up to 15 miles an hour out of the west. The high temperature will be 80 degrees Fahrenheit, and the low will be 64."

Lecturer: And where is that speaker from?

Audience: England... the United Kingdom... Great Britain.

Lecturer: Yes, of course. That was British English. So you may have guessed by now that my topic for today's lecture is differences between standard American and British English. In particular, I want to examine three categories of difference. First, and most obvious, is pronunciation; second, vocabulary; and third, grammar.

So to begin, let's go back to the subject of accent, or pronunciation. You had no trouble identifying the North American and British accents because each of them has a unique sound. What is it? Well, one obvious difference is in the pronunciation of the letter *a*. For example, most Americans say /kænt/, but the British say /kant/. Or Americans say /bæth/ and the British say /bath/. The /æ/ sound is very common in American English, but not very common in British English.

Another noticeable difference between American and British pronunciation is the /r/ sound. In British English, the /r/ sound is very often dropped; it disappears. To give some examples, Americans say /kar/ but the British say /ka/. Americans say /fɣrst/ but British say /fʌst/. A big American city is New /yɔrk/ for Americans, but New /yok/ to the British. In the two speech samples you heard at the beginning of this lecture, the American speaker said /forkæst/, but the British said /fohkast/. In that single word, you can hear the difference both in the a vowel and in the pronunciation of /r/. Listen again: /forkaest/, /fohkast/.

A third difference is the pronunciation of the /t/ sound in the middle of words. In British English, it is normally pronounced, but in American English, it changes to a /d/ or disappears. For example: a British person will say "little," but an American says "liddle." You can hear this difference particularly with numbers: Brits say "twenty one, twenty two," and so on, but Americans drop the /t/ and say "twenny one, twenny two," and so on.

So there you have just three of the differences that give American and British pronunciation their unique sounds. There are many more. But now let's go on to talk about vocabulary.

6 Taking Notes (Part II)

- Play the second part of the recording. Have students take notes in their own way on paper or in their notebooks.
- Have students use their notes to complete the outline.
- Play the recording again if necessary.
- Check the answers as a class.

PART 2

Student Book page 160

ANSWER KEY

II. Vocabulary

- Eng. has over <u>1 m.</u> words
- # of vocab diffs between Am.E. and B.E.: <u>small</u>
- Examples:

Am.E.	B.E.
truck	lorry
elevator	lift
wash up = wash hands and face	wash up = wash dishes
sausages and mashed potatoes	bangers and mash

III. Grammar

- Am.E. almost = B.E.
- few diffs.:

Grammar	Am.E.	B.E.
1. Verbs	gotten	got
2. have	do you have?	have you?
3. prepositions	different from	different than

IV. Br. E and Am. E. are 2 varieties of 1 language

AUDIOSCRIPT

Part 2

Some people believe that American-English vocabulary and British-English vocabulary are very different, but actually they are not. The English language has more than one million words. Yet there are only a few hundred words and expressions that are different in American and British English. You can see a few of them in the chart right here. So for instance, Americans say *truck*, but the Brits say *lorry*. Another well-known example is *elevator*, which is used in the United States and *lift*, which is the British term. Now, although the number of vocabulary differences is small, funny misunderstandings can sometimes occur. For instance, if an American says, *I'm going to wash up*, he would go into the bathroom and wash his hands and face. But a British person may be quite surprised to see him go to the bathroom because in England, to *wash up* means to wash the dishes.

Vocabulary differences can also create some confusing situations in restaurants. If an Englishman traveling in the United States enters a restaurant and orders "bangers and mash," the American waiter would be totally confused. He wouldn't know that the man wanted sausage and mashed potatoes.

Finally, let's talk a bit about grammar. I've left this category for last because in the area of grammar, standard American and British English are nearly identical. One common difference, however, involves the past participle of the verb *get*. For example, an American might ask, "Have you gotten your grade yet?" whereas a Brit would ask, "Have you got your grade yet?" Another difference is in the use of the verb *have*, especially in questions. Americans say, "Do you have any ideas?" but the British might say, "Have you any ideas?" or "Have you got any ideas?" There are also differences in prepositions. So for instance in the United States, it's correct to say that John is different *from* Mary, but the British will say that John is different *than* Mary. But these differences are very small and few in number.

And this brings me to my conclusion, which is this: Standard British and standard American English are so similar that most speakers of these two types will have no trouble understanding one another. American and British English are not two different languages. Rather, they are two dialects, two varieties, of the same language, English.

Student Book pages 161–162

After You Listen

> **Best Practice**
>
> **Activating Prior Knowledge**
> Activity 7 is an example of an activity that encourages students to make text-to-self connections. The discussion questions ask students to explore their existing knowledge on the topic of differences between different varieties of English. They can then add the new information to their existing knowledge framework. This aids understanding and retention of new material.

7 Discussing the Lecture

- Have students discuss the questions in groups.
- Encourage students to use the new vocabulary in their discussion.
- Ask for representatives from each group to report to the class on the discussion.

8 Summarizing Your Discussion

- You may want to have students write individual summaries or a group summary.
- Call on volunteers to present their summaries. Discuss them as a class.

9 Reviewing Vocabulary

- Ask students to look back at the vocabulary in Activity 2 on page 157 of the Student Book and to test each other in pairs.
- Invite volunteers to give examples of sentences using the new vocabulary.

Talk It Over

10 Comparing American and British English

- Ask students to complete the activity individually.
- Have students compare their answers.

- If the sentence is in British English, how would they change it to American English (and vice versa)?

> **ANSWER KEY**
> 1. British
> 2. American
> 3. British
> 4. American
> 5. British
> 6. British
> 7. British
> 8. American

 **Expansion Activity**

- The purpose of this activity is to practice using the Internet for research and to gain an understanding of different varieties of English spoken around the world.
- Students can use a search engine to find the vocabulary items or use keywords, for example, *Australian English*.
- You can also have them use this website: www.wordwebonline.com, but check it first to make sure you want to introduce it to them.
- The research part of this activity can be done in a computer lab class or assigned for homework.
- Please see Black Line Master "Varieties of English" on page BLM 20 of this Teacher's Manual. Photocopy and distribute one to each student.
- Have students work in groups to complete as much as they can. Assign the rest of the worksheet for homework.

PART 3 Strategies for Better Listening and Speaking

Student Book pages 163–164

Getting Meaning from Context

FOCUS ON TESTING — TOEFL® iBT

Using Context Clues

- Explain that students will hear three different conversations.
- Play the recording and have students write their answers.
- Check the answers as a class. Note that the answers for the clues will vary.

ANSWER KEY

Answers	Clues
Conversation 1	
1. B a language	language, Where is it spoken? Who speaks this language now? 15 million people speak Esperanto.
2. D from a magazine article	the article, it says here
3. B It has no native speakers.	artificial, comes from lots of different languages
Conversation 2	
4. B to kill the bees	beehive under the roof, exterminator, kill
5. D taste	where, how far away, how much
6. B the study of insects	learn about bugs
Conversation 3	
7. B to save time	dictation, slow typist
8. A try Rita's software	Can I try it? I should get one
9. C It's useful for students and writers.	don't have to type, I have three term papers

AUDIOSCRIPT

Conversation 1

A: Have you ever heard of Esperanto?
B: Huh?
A: Esperanto. It's a language.
B: Really? I've never heard of it. Where is it spoken?
A: Lots of places. According to this article, it's actually an artificial language; it was invented in 1887 by a man from Poland.
B: That's interesting. So who speaks this language now?
A: Well, it says here that there may be as many as 15 million people who speak Esperanto as a second language.
B: What does *Esperanto* mean, anyway? It doesn't sound like Polish.
A: It's not. The vocabulary of Esperanto comes from lots of different languages. *Esperanto* means "hope" in Latin.
B: Well, I hope I never have to learn it. It's hard enough trying to learn English.

Question 1: What is Esperanto?
Question 2: Where did the woman get her information about Esperanto?
Question 3: Which of the following is probably true about Esperanto?

Conversation 2

A: Look, there's a beehive under the roof.
B: I guess we'd better call an exterminator.
A: Yeah, you're right... But I really don't want to kill them. Did you know bees can communicate with one another?
B: Really? How?
A: They use body language to show where food is, how far away it is, and how much food is available.
B: No kidding...

A:	Yeah, see that one there? See how she's going around and around in circles, like she's dancing? That means the food is nearby. If the food is farther away, the bee points to it with her body. And the faster she dances, the more food is available.
B:	How do you know so much about bees?
A:	I took an entomology class in college. I was a biology major, and I thought it would be interesting to learn something about bugs.
Question 4:	Why does the man want to call an exterminator?
Question 5:	Which information about food is *not* conveyed by the bee's body language?
Question 6:	What is entomology?

Conversation 3

Man:	Why are you talking to your computer?
Woman:	I'm not talking to it. I'm giving a dictation.
Man:	What do you mean?
Woman:	It's this great software program. It understands what I'm saying and writes down the words.
Man:	Wow. So you don't have to type at all?
Man:	No, that's the point. I'm a slow typist, so this program is a lifesaver.
Man:	Can I try it?
Woman:	Well, first you have to train the computer to recognize your voice.
Man:	Oh. Why?
Woman:	Because everybody's pronunciation is different. If it doesn't know your voice, it makes mistakes.
Man:	I see. I should get one of these for my computer. I have three term papers due this month.
Question 7:	Why does the woman use this software program?
Question 8:	What will the man probably do next?
Question 9:	What is probably true about this computer program?

Focused Listening

FOCUS

Interjections

- Read the instruction note about interjections.
- Ask if students can think of any other examples or different meanings for the ones given.

❶ Understanding Interjections

- Explain that they will listen to six different conversations and write the meanings of the interjections they hear.
- Play the recording while students write their answers.
- Review the answers as a class.

ANSWER KEY

1. Yes. 2. That hurts. 3. I dropped something. 4. What? (or What does that mean?) 5. No. 6. I forgot.

AUDIOSCRIPT

Conversation 1
Student:	Can we use a dictionary on the test?
Teacher:	Uh-huh.

Conversation 2
Mother:	Here, let me brush your hair.
Child:	Ouch! Not so hard!

PART 3

Student Book pages 165–166

Conversation 3
Father: Could you please carry this bag of groceries into the house? Be careful; it's heavy.
Son: Sure… oops! Sorry.

Conversation 4
A: The computer is down because of a virus that crashed the hard drive.
B: Huh?

Conversation 5
A: I'm expecting an important letter. Has the mail arrived yet?
B: Uh-uh.

Conversation 6
A: Did you remember to buy stamps when you went to the post office?
B: Uh-oh.

❸ Guessing Meanings of Slang Expressions

- Review the meaning of the word *slang*. When is slang appropriate or inappropriate?
- Have students work in pairs to guess the meanings of these slang expressions.
- When they have finished, they can check their answers on page 261.

Using Language Functions

FOCUS

Guessing

- Read the instruction note about *Guessing*.
- Read the example aloud. Substitute the expressions in B. For example, "Hmm. I'd say it's something Scandinavian. It could be Swedish, but it might be Danish."

❷ Using Interjections

- Have students work in pairs.
- Student A should look at page 250 in the Student Book. Student B should look at page 258.
- Set a time limit of five minutes.
- Move around the room to monitor and provide feedback.
- Review the answers as a class.

PART 4 Real-World Task: Spelling Bee

Student Book pages 167–168

Before You Listen

- Read the text in the box about spelling bees. This is what the next conversation is about.

1 Prelistening Questions

- Discuss the idea of a spelling bee and find out if students have ever participated in a spelling competition.
- Discuss some of the reasons why English spelling can cause problems (vowels have different sounds, some vowels are silent, some consonants are silent e.g., *r* in *hour*, *l* in *half*).
- Discuss the questions in groups or as a class.

Listen

2 Identifying Spellings

- Explain that students will hear a recording of a spelling bee.
- As they listen, they will try to identify the answers given by the participants.
- Play the recording.
- Compare answers as a class.

ANSWER KEY

1. C right 2. A wrong 3. A right 4. C right
5. B wrong 6. B right 7. B wrong 8. A right
9. A wrong 10. C right

AUDIOSCRIPT

Teacher:	Our contestants in today's spelling bee are Jack, Marisa, Yolanda, Evan, and Tony. As you know, I will say the word and then say it in a sentence. Are you ready to begin?
All:	Ready. Yes.
Teacher:	All right. The first word is for Tony. The word is *tries*. "He always tries to do a good job."
Tony:	Tries. OK, T-R-I-E-S.
Teacher:	Correct. All right. The next word is for Jack. Your word is *choose*. "Which flavor ice cream will you choose?"
Jack:	Choose. C-H-O-S-E.
Teacher:	I'm sorry, but that is wrong. The correct spelling of *choose* is C-H-O-O-S-E. Good try, Jack. OK, the next word goes to Marisa. Your word is *effect*. "Jogging has a good effect on our health."
Marisa:	Effect. E-F-F-E-C-T.
Teacher:	Right! Marisa, you stay in the game. The next word is for Evan. Your word is *quizzes*. "We had two grammar *quizzes* last week."
Evan:	OK, quizzes. Uh, Q-U-I-Z-Z-E-S.
Teacher:	Yes, that's right. Now, for Yolanda, your word is *succeed*. "You must study hard if you want to succeed."
Yolanda:	Hmm. Succeed. S-U-C-C-E-D-[pause]-E.
Teacher:	I'm sorry, Yolanda, that's wrong. It's S-U-C-C-E-E-D. Good try. OK, let's see who's still in the game: Marisa, Evan, and Tony. Are you ready for the second round?
All:	Yes, yeah, let's go.
Teacher:	OK, Tony. Your word is *ninety*. "The shoes cost ninety dollars."
Tony:	N-I-N-E-T-Y. Ninety.
Teacher:	You're right! Well done. The next word is for Marisa. *Analyze*. "After a test, you should analyze your mistakes."
Marisa:	Wow, that's hard. OK: A-N-A-L-I-Z-E. Analyze.
Teacher:	Sorry, Marisa. It's A-N-A-L-Y-Z-E. Please sit down. Evan, you're next. Your word is *possibility*. "There is a possibility of snow tonight."

PART 4

Student Book pages 168–170

Evan:	Possibility. OK. P-O-S-S-I-B-I-L-I-T-Y.
Teacher:	Great! OK, it's down to Tony and Evan. First Tony. Your word is *mysterious*. "During the night we heard mysterious noises."
Tony:	Um, M-I-S-T-E-R-I-O-U-S. I think.
Teacher:	Oh no, that's not correct. It's M-Y-S-T-E-R-I-O-U-S. You almost got it. Well, that leaves Evan. If you spell this word correctly, you'll be the winner today. The last word is *lightning*. "We were scared by the thunder and lightning."
Evan:	L-I-G-H-T-N-I-N-G. Lightning.
Teacher:	Right! Congratulations, Evan! You're our winner today.

After You Listen

Content Note

The National Spelling Bee in the U.S. is a competition sponsored by newspapers and educational foundations. The participants are school children and they go through many local and regional rounds before reaching the final round, which is shown on national television. The winner gets a cash prize. The basic rules are that once the contestant has started to spell a word, he or she may start over, but the letter or sequence of letters already spoken may not be changed. If a contestant fails to spell a word correctly, he or she is disqualified. The competition is conducted in rounds until only one contestant remains.

3 Class Spelling Bee

- Organize the class into teams.
- Set a time limit of five minutes for each team to prepare a list of words (you may want to assign certain chapters of the book to each team to avoid overlap).
- Have team leaders read out the words and keep score.

Talk It Over

Best Practice

Making Use of Academic Content
This type of activity is an example of using real-world global content to help students identify English language errors and understand why they might have been made. In academic contexts, students must always analyze their own writing. This activity can help them understand subtleties of language and why certain errors are made, helping them to avoid these errors in their own work.

4 Creating Dialogues

- Have the students read the directions and look at the photos on pages 169 and 170 of the Student Book. Clarify any questions.
- Have students create a dialogue for each photo. Encourage them to use as many of the expressions as possible from the box in each dialogue.
- You can decide if you want students to read their dialogues or perform them (or one of them) with a partner.

Student Book page 171

Expansion Activity

- The aim of this activity is to practice the spelling of some commonly misspelled words.
- Please see Black Line Master "Spelling Bee" on page BLM 21 of this Teacher's Manual. Photocopy one for each pair. Cut each copy in half.
- One student will be A and the other will be B. Students will take turns reading out a word and asking the other student to spell it. You may ask students to write their partner's spelling next to each word, as a kind of dictation.
- Compare notes as a class. Which words were most commonly misspelled?
- For more commonly misspelled words, you might want to check this website:

www.yourdictionary.com/library/misspelled.html

Self-Assessment Log

- The purpose of the log is to help the students reflect on their learning.
- Read the directions aloud, and have students check vocabulary that they learned in the chapter and are prepared to use.
- Have students check the strategies they understand.
- Put students in small groups. Ask students to find the information or an activity related to each strategy in the chapter.
- Tell students to find definitions in the chapter for any words they did not check, or they can look in their dictionaries

CHAPTER 8
Tastes and Preferences

In this CHAPTER

Students will read about various topics related to tastes and preferences. In Part 1, they will talk about likes and dislikes and practice making an impromptu speech. In Part 2, they will listen to a lecture about changing fads and fashions and learn to recognize paraphrasing. In Part 3, they will practice listening to conversations and learn to express approval and disapproval. In Part 4, they will practice writing an online profile.

"Markets change, tastes change, so the companies and the individuals who choose to compete in those markets must change."

Dr. An Wang
Chinese-American inventor,
co-founder of Wang Laboratories,
1920–1990

Chapter Opener

- Have students look at the photo of the two young men listening to music. Ask the students the three questions in the Connecting to the Topic section. Discuss with the class.
- Discuss the quote. What shapes our tastes and preferences? Do our tastes influence fashions, or do fashions influence us?

Chapter Overview

Listening Skills and Strategies

Listening for main ideas and details

Making inferences

Understanding reduced questions

Distinguishing between present and past yes/no questions

Understanding comparisons of people

Recognizing paraphrases

Speaking Skills and Strategies

Talking about likes and dislikes

Giving an impromptu speech

Comparing the characteristics of generations

Talking about fads

Expressing approval and disapproval

Describing your ideal partner

Critical-Thinking Skills

Getting meaning from context

Speculating about hypothetical situations

Evaluating people's positive and negative qualities

Interpreting the language of personal ads

Taking notes in columns

Predicting note organization

Vocabulary Building

Expressions for likes and dislikes

Expressions of approval and disapproval

Terms signaling paraphrases

Ways to say that something is popular

Pronunciation

Identifying and practicing stressed words

Language Skills

Using context clues to identify people's tastes and preferences

Using intonation to identify feelings

Vocabulary

Nouns
- brand
- conflict
- consumer
- developed country
- dish
- income
- phenomenon
- standard of living

Verb
- identify with

Adjectives
- Caucasian
- confident
- diverse
- hip (informal)
- loyal
- optimistic
- significant
- tolerant

Expressions
- can't stand
- don't/doesn't care for
- have a good time
- I'm crazy about it!
- see eye to eye

PART 1 — Conversation: What Do You Like to Do for Fun?

Student Book pages 174–175

Can You Guess?

- Ask students to discuss the questions below in groups and compare their answers with the correct answers.
1. What is the most popular children's educational television program in the world? **A.** *Sesame Street. It is broadcast to 180 countries.*
2. What is the most popular sport in the world? **A.** *Soccer.*
3. What is the most-recorded pop song in history? **A.** *"Yesterday" by John Lennon and Paul McCartney.*

Before You Listen

Best Practice

Activating Prior Knowledge
The prelistening questions activate students' prior knowledge. This activity will help students relate their own likes and dislikes to the new language in this chapter. When students activate their prior knowledge before learning new material, they are better able to map new language onto existing concepts, which aids understanding and retention.

1 Prelistening Questions

- Have the students read the questions and discuss them in pairs.
- Compare answers as a whole class.
- Make a list of ways to ask about people's likes and dislikes. Ask students to classify these according to whether they are slang, informal, or formal.

2 Previewing Vocabulary

- Play the recording and have students listen for the underlined words and phrases.

- Have students complete the exercise individually.
- Compare their answers as a whole class and write the correct answers on the board.

ANSWER KEY
1. c **2.** e **3.** f **4.** b **5.** d **6.** a

Listen

3 Comprehension Questions

- Explain that these questions will help students focus on the main ideas in the listening. They do not need to understand every word to answer the questions.
- Read the questions aloud.
- Play the recording.
- After listening, have students compare their answers in pairs.
- Check the answers as a class.

ANSWER KEY
1. Mari and Dan disagree on most things.
2. They agree to go to a science fiction movie.
3. (Answers in chart below.)

	Dan likes	Mari likes
Music	rock	jazz
Food	Mexican, American	Japanese, Indian
Art	modern art	19th-century art
Sports	American football	basketball
Movies	science fiction	science fiction

132 CHAPTER 8

Student Book pages 175–177

AUDIOSCRIPT

Jeff:	Come in!
Dan:	Hi.
Jeff:	Hey, Dan, how ya doin'?
Dan:	Great, thanks. Hey, I burned you some new CDs.
Jeff:	Cool.
Dan:	Hi. You were at our show last night, right?
Mari:	Yeah, I was.
Jeff:	Sorry, Mari, this is Dan. Dan, this is Mari.
Mari:	It's nice to meet you.
Dan:	Nice to meet you too.
Jeff:	Oh, let me get that. I'll be right back.
Dan:	OK. So Mari, did you have a good time at the club last night?
Mari:	Yeah, it was pretty wild.
Dan:	What did you think of our band?
Mari:	Well, your music is great for dancing, but to tell you the truth, it was kind of loud. I guess I really prefer jazz.
Dan:	Do you go to concerts much?
Mari:	No, not very often. I can't afford them. They're so expensive!
Dan:	Yeah, I know what you mean. Well, what do you like to do for fun?
Mari:	I love to eat! I love going to different ethnic restaurants and trying new dishes.
Dan:	What's your favorite kind of food?
Mari:	Well, Japanese, of course. What about you?
Dan:	Well, I'm not crazy about sushi or sashimi. But I really like Mexican food.
Mari:	Ooh, I can't stand beans, and I don't like cheese. Uh… What about Indian food?
Dan:	I don't care for it. Too spicy. Um… you like American food? You know, hamburgers, hot dogs, French fries…
Mari:	Yuck! All that fat and salt and sugar… We don't see eye to eye on anything, do we?
Dan:	Well, let's see. What's your opinion of modern art? There's a wonderful show at the county museum right now.
Mari:	To be honest, I don't get the modern stuff. I prefer 19th-century art, you know, Monet, van Gogh, Renoir.
Dan:	Hmm. How do you feel about sports? Are you interested in football?
Mari:	American football? I hate it!
Dan:	Basketball?
Mari:	It's OK.
Dan:	How about tall musicians with curly hair?
Mari:	It depends.
Dan:	OK, I got it. How about tall musicians with curly hair who invite you to a movie?
Mari:	Science fiction?
Dan:	Sounds great!
Mari:	Finally, we agree on something!

Stress

4 Listening for Stressed Words

- Play the recording again.
- Have students repeat the phrase or sentence and write the missing words.
- After listening, have students check their answers with the audioscript in their books.
- Have students read the conversation with a partner, paying attention to stressed words in their pronunciation.
- Explain that students will hear five short conversations. They will rewrite the sentences as questions.
- Play the recording, allowing time for students to write.
- Ask volunteers to write their answers on the board and compare answers as a class.

PART 1

Student Book pages 176–177

AUDIOSCRIPT and ANSWER KEY

Dan: What did you think of our _band_?

Mari: Well, your music is _great_ for _dancing_, but to tell you the truth, it was kind of _loud_. I guess I really prefer _jazz_.

Dan: Do you go to _concerts_ much?

Mari: No, not very often. I _can't afford_ them. They're _so_ expensive!

Dan: Yeah, I know what you _mean_. Well, what do you like to do for _fun_?

Mari: I _love_ to _eat_! I love going to different _ethnic_ restaurants and trying new _dishes_.

Dan: What's your _favorite_ kind of food?

Mari: Well, _Japanese_, of course. What about you?

Dan: Well…. I'm _not crazy_ about sushi or sashimi. But I really like _Mexican_ food.

Mari: Ooh, I _can't stand_ beans, and I don't like _cheese_. Uh… What about _Indian_ food?

Dan: I don't _care_ for it. Too _spicy_. Um… Do you like _American_ food? You know, hamburgers, hot dogs, French fries…

Mari: _Yuck_! All that fat and salt and sugar… We don't see eye to eye on _anything_, do we?

Dan: Well, let's see. What's your opinion of _modern_ art? There's a _wonderful_ show at the county _museum_ right now.

Mari: To be _honest_, I don't _get_ the modern stuff. I prefer _19th_-century art, you know, Monet, van Gogh, Renoir.

Dan: Hmm. How do you feel about _sports_? Are you interested in _football_?

Mari: _American_ football? I _hate_ it!

Dan: Basketball?

Mari: It's OK.

Dan: How about tall musicians with _brown_ hair?

Mari: It _depends_.

Dan: OK, I got it. How about _tall_ musicians with _brown_ hair who invite you to a _movie_?

Mari: Science fiction?

Dan: Sounds _great_!

Mari: _Finally_, we agree on _something_!

FOCUS

Reductions

- Read the instruction note.
- Ask students if they can think of any other examples.

5 Listening for Reductions

- Have students read the directions.
- Play the recording and have students write the full questions for the reduced ones in each of the five dialogues.

ANSWER KEY

1. Do you like Japanese food?
2. Are you tired?
3. Is anybody home?
4. Are you leaving already?
5. Does he have kids?

AUDIOSCRIPT

1. **A:** Do you like Chinese food?
   B: Not really.
   A: Japanese?

2. **A:** Whew! What a day!
   B: Tired?

3. **A:** Anybody home?
   B: I'm here. I'm in the kitchen.

4. **A:** I guess it's time to go.
   B: Leaving already?

5. **A:** Does he have a wife?
   B: Yes.
   A: Kids?

Student Book pages 177–179

After You Listen

6 Reviewing Vocabulary

- Have students work in pairs. Student A will look at page 251 in the Student Book. Student B will look at page 259.
- Set a time limit of five minutes.
- Review the answers as a class.

ANSWER KEY

1. **A:** What is this delicious dish?
   B: It's humus. It's from the Middle East. I love it, too.
2. **A:** Sally has a new boyfriend. To be honest, I'm not crazy about him.
   B: Really? What's his name?
3. **A:** What do you think of action movies?
   B: I can't stand them. I prefer comedies.
4. **A:** Did you have a good time in San Diego last weekend?
   B: No. It rained all day Saturday and Sunday, so we came home early.
5. **A:** Why did you break up with your girlfriend?
   B: Because we didn't see eye to eye on anything.
6. **A:** I don't care for this new chair you bought. It's not very comfortable.
   B: OK, I'll take it back to the store.

Using Language Functions

FOCUS

Talking About Likes and Dislikes

- Read the instruction note.
- Ask students to read the examples.
- Practice pronunciation and intonation by giving topics to which students can respond with one of these expressions, e.g. *Mexican food? Jazz music? Ice hockey?*

7 Asking About Likes and Dislikes

- Read the directions for the activity.
- Have students complete the questions individually.
- Practice the questions and answers in pairs.
- Remind students to use the expressions from the language box, along with the appropriate intonation, to answer the questions.

ANSWER KEY

1. *What did you think of* our band?
2. *What's your favorite* kind of food?
3. *Do you like* American food?
4. *What's your opinion of* modern art?
5. *How do you feel about* sports?
6. *Are you interested in* football?
7. *How about* tall musicians with brown hair?

Best Practice

Interacting with Others

Activity 8 is an example of collaborative learning to encourage fluency and confidence. In this activity, communication is more important than grammar. Students can improve their confidence in talking about likes and dislikes by switching roles or partners and practicing the same situations again.

8 Talking About Likes and Dislikes

- Have students work in pairs to complete the chart and discuss each topic.
- Set a time limit of five minutes.
- Move around the room to provide feedback and encouragement.
- Ask volunteers to retell their conversation to the class.

PART 1

Student Book page 179

Talk It Over

Best Practice

Making Use of Academic Content
This is an example of an activity that encourages students to practice impromptu speaking skills. When participating in debates or discussions in class, they may sometimes be asked to defend their opinions without having a lot of preparation time. This activity provides an opportunity to practice this skill.

9 Giving an Impromptu Speech

- Read the instructions and ask one or two students to explain the activity to the rest of the class.

- Have students choose a topic from the box and write one question about that topic. Read the example questions to point out the difference between the general and specific questions.

- Collect the questions and put them in a box or a bag.

- One at a time, have students pick a question from the box and talk about it for one minute.

- You may do this activity in groups or as a whole class.

Expansion Activity

- The purpose of this activity is to practice asking and answering questions about likes and dislikes.

- Please see Black Line Master "What Kind of Person Are You?" on page BLM 22.1 and BLM 22.2 of this Teacher's Manual. Photocopy one set for each pair of students.

- Have students ask their partner questions to fill out the questionnaires.

- Move around the room to monitor and provide feedback.

- When students have finished asking the questions, have them add up the points for their partner and read the result to their partner.

PART 2 Radio Interview: Generation Y

Student Book pages 180–183

Before You Listen

1 Prelistening Discussion

- Have students describe the pictures and talk about the information.
- Have students work in pairs to answer the questions.
- Review the responses as a class and compare some of their experiences.

2 Previewing Vocabulary

- Play the recording and have students listen for the words.
- Have students check the words they know.
- Ask students to compare answers with a partner and define or explain the words they know.

Listen

Strategy

Recognizing Paraphrases
- Read the information in the Strategy box.
- Review the meaning of paraphrasing and give some examples, using the phrases in the box.

3 Practicing Paraphrase Signals

- Read the directions for the activity and have students match each sentence with a paraphrase and then write the sentence.

ANSWER KEY
1. b 2. c 3. d 4. e 5. a

4 Predicting Note Organization

- Explain that students will be listening to an interview rather than a lecture as in previous chapters.
- Ask for some suggestions about how they will organize their note-taking.

Best Practice

Scaffolding Instruction
This outline helps students to organize their notes into main and secondary ideas. By providing students with the outline as a support, they can see how key words and numbering can be used to structure the content of the interview. This guided activity prepares them for the skill of identifying main and secondary ideas without the help of an outline.

5 Taking Notes (Part I)

(See the audioscript following Activity 6.)

- Ask students to take notes in their own as they listen.
- Play the recording.

6 Rewriting Your Notes

- Ask students to complete the outline using their notes.
- Play the recording again if necessary.

ANSWER KEY

Questions/Topics	Generation Y Answers
Meaning of Gen Y?	1. Young Am. born late 1970s– early 1990s, i.e. 1977–1994 2. Number = _70 mil._
B. Number— significant?	Yes. Reason: _now 2nd lgst. by 2020 lgst._ → _future mkt_ → _imp. for marketing_

Interactions 2 Listening/Speaking

PART 2

Student Book pages 182–184

C. Characteristics	1. *1/4 from single-parent homes*
	2. *3/4 have mothers who work*
	3. *1/3 not Caucasian*
D. Tolerant?	*yes*
	Also *optimistic, confident, independent, rich*
E. rich	Stats:
	1. Total income/yr: *$211 bil.*
	2. Spend *av. $30 on a trip to the mall*

AUDIOSCRIPT

Host: Dr. Harris, thank you for joining us today.

Dr. Harris: My pleasure.

Host: To begin, could you tell us the meaning of the term *Generation Y*?

Dr. Harris: Sure. Generation Y refers to young Americans who were born between the late 1970s and the early 1990s, uh, that is between 1977 or 1978 and 1993 or 1994. In other words, the youngest ones are still teenagers, and the oldest ones are young adults. And there are more than 70 million of them.

Host: Is that number significant?

Dr. Harris: It is extremely significant. Generation Y is the second-largest generation in U.S. history, and by the year 2020 it will be the largest. So this generation is the future market for almost all consumer brands. Marketers know they have to stay in touch with this generation if they want their products to succeed.

Host: What are some of the most important characteristics of this generation?

Dr. Harris: Well, first let me give you some statistics, OK? One-fourth, that is one in four people in this generation, grew up in single-parent homes. Three-fourths, I mean 75 percent, have mothers who work. And one-third are not Caucasian. To put it another way, this is the most diverse generation in U.S. history.

Host: Would you say they are tolerant?

Dr. Harris: Very tolerant. Also optimistic, confident, independent, and… rich!

Host: Rich? Explain that.

Dr. Harris: OK. Here are some more statistics: According to a study by the Harris company, members of Generation Y have total incomes of $211 billion a year. These kids spend an average of $30 on every trip to the mall. And if you have teenagers, you know that this generation practically lives at the mall.

7 Taking Notes (Part II)

- Play the second part of the recording.
- Have students take notes in their own way as before.
- Then have students use their notes to complete the outline.
- Play the recording again if necessary.

ANSWER KEY

F. *spend money on?*	Fashion, fast food, *movies, CDs, electronics, concert tickets.*
G. *Preferred brands?*	*Change brands fast, whatever is in fashion*

138 CHAPTER 8

Student Book page 184

H. <u>Internet gen.</u>	1. grow up w/ media → smart shoppers
	2. Don't like trad. advert.
	3. <u>not loyal to brands</u>
	4. <u>love fads</u>
I. <u>only U.S.?</u>	No. Internat'l, but diff. in other countries, e.g.:
	1. <u>E. Europe 1st gen. w/o communism</u>
	2. <u>Korea/Greece hi stand. of living</u>

AUDIOSCRIPT

Host: Two hundred and eleven billion. That's an incredible amount of money. What do they spend it on?

Dr. Harris: Fashion, fast food, movies, CDs, electronics, concert tickets. Generation Y-ers like to have fun.

Host: Are there special brands that this generation prefers?

Dr. Harris: No, not in the way that their parents preferred Levis jeans or SUVs. Generation Y-ers like anything that's hip or hot at the moment, but that can change very fast.

Host: So what do marketers need to know if they want to sell to this group?

Dr. Harris: I think the main thing to remember is that this is the Internet generation, the generation of instant messaging. They have grown up with the media, so they are very smart shoppers. They don't like traditional advertising techniques. And as I said, they are not loyal to specific brands. And they love fads, like right now graphic T-shirts and flip-flops are totally in.

Host: Is Generation Y found only in the U.S., or is it in other countries as well?

Dr. Harris: Generation Y is actually an international phenomenon, although it has different characteristics in different countries. In Eastern Europe, for example, it's the first generation to grow up without communism. And in other countries like, oh, Korea and Greece, this is the first generation to grow up with a high standard of living. These young people want to be modern. I mean they are not interested in the traditional way of life. Also, they identify more closely with the West, and that can cause conflict between them and the generations that came before them.

Host: Dr. Harris, before we conclude, may I ask you a personal question?

Dr. Harris: Go ahead.

Host: What generation are you?

Dr. Harris: I'm a baby boomer, born in 1960. But my daughter, who was born in 1984, is Generation Y. And believe it or not, she loves listening to my old Beatles records.

Host: No kidding. Dr. Harris, this has been very interesting. Thank you for being with us today.

Dr. Harris: You're welcome.

After You Listen

8 Discussing the Lecture

- Have students discuss the questions in groups.
- Encourage students to use the new vocabulary in their discussion.
- Ask for representatives from each group to report to the class on the discussion.

PART 2

Student Book pages 184–186

9 Reviewing Vocabulary

- Ask students to look back at the vocabulary in Activity 2 and to test each other in pairs.
- Invite volunteers to give examples sentences using the new vocabulary.

Talk It Over

Best Practice

Organizing Information

Activities such as this will teach students to organize information by completing a chart. This specific activity allows students to understand and process information by categorizing. Here, students identify and list specific items within broader categories. Seeing information in a chart like this helps students organize the information and see the relationship of the items to each other.

10 Talking About Fads

- Brainstorm ideas for different types of fads.
- Have students read the directions and the questions.
- Have them read the FYI note and the Language Tip. Clarify any questions.
- Have students work in groups of three or four people.
- Have students fill in the charts and answer the questions.
- Ask for volunteers to give examples to the class.
- Other related questions might be: Who starts fads? Are they started by young people or by companies trying to sell new products? What makes a fad popular?

Expansion Activity (REPRODUCIBLE)

- The purpose of this activity is to practice paraphrasing.
- Please see Black Line Master "What Do You Mean?" on page BLM 23 of this Teacher's Manual. Photocopy and distribute one to each student.
- Have students work in groups or pairs to complete the sentences.
- Set a time limit of ten minutes.
- Compare answers as a class. The focus should be on accuracy of meaning, rather than grammar.
- Take a vote on the best sentence completions and write them on the board.

ANSWER KEY

Answers will vary. Possible answers:

1. don't require computer skills
2. about 66 percent of U.S. teens have cell phones
3. go online and download the latest music
4. go to the cinema to see movies
5. buying big cars because gas is expensive
6. more people are taking sport vacations far away
7. more people are thinking about how much salt and sugar they eat
8. you can save time by shopping online
9. watch movies on TV or listen to music on a stereo
10. wait to read the news in a newspaper

CHAPTER 8

PART 3 — Strategies For Better Listening and Speaking

Student Book pages 187–189

Focused Listening

FOCUS

Yes/No Questions with *Do*, *Does*, or *Did*

- Read the instruction note.
- Read aloud the examples.

1. Yes/No Questions with *Do*, *Does*, or *Did*

- Read the directions for the activity.
- Play the recording and have students repeat the questions.

2. Distinguishing Among *Do*, *Does*, and *Did*

- Read the instructions.
- Play the recording and have students circle their answers.

ANSWER KEY

1. A   5. B
2. A   6. B
3. B   7. B
4. A   8. A

AUDIOSCRIPT

1. Do you have time to eat lunch?
2. Does he play the piano?
3. Did they need help?
4. Do I look like my sister?
5. Did she understand the instructions?
6. Do we sound good?
7. Did they own a house?
8. Do we need to rewrite the composition?

3. *Do*, *Does*, and *Did* in Questions

- Play the recording.
- Allow time for students to write the missing words.
- Compare answers as a class.

ANSWER KEY

1. <u>Did he</u> decide to take the job?
2. When <u>do we</u> eat?
3. <u>Do I</u> have to rewrite this composition?
4. Where <u>did we</u> park the car?
5. <u>Do they</u> know what to do?
6. <u>Did she</u> miss the bus again?
7. <u>Do you</u> usually walk to school?
8. <u>Did you</u> remember to turn off the light?

FOCUS ON TESTING — TOEFL® iBT

Using Context Clues

- Review strategies for getting meaning from context.
- Explain that students will hear five different conversations.
- Play the recording and have students write their answers.
- Check the answers as a class.

PART 3

ANSWER KEY

Answers	Clues
1. B a painting	look at that; colors and shapes; it's modern
2. B a tie	don't wear the brown one; suit
3. D snowboarding	cold and windy; flying down a mountain; one thin piece of wood
4. B She does not like it.	different
5. A She likes it.	(There are no specific words, but the speaker's intonation and tone show excitement and approval.)

AUDIOSCRIPT

Conversation 1

Woman: Look at that! Isn't it interesting? I love the colors and shapes.

Man: What's it supposed to be?

Woman: It's not supposed to *be* anything. It's modern. Don't try to analyze it.

Man: Well how much does it cost?

Woman: Let's see. Five thousand dollars. What do you think?

Question 1: *What are the speakers talking about?*

Man: Five thousand dollars? For *that* painting? I don't think so.

Conversation 2

Woman: Don't wear the brown one.

Man: Why not? What's wrong with it?

Woman: Well, it doesn't go with your suit. Brown and black don't look good together.

Man: Well, what if I wear it with my other suit?

Question 2: *What are the man and woman talking about?*

Woman: No, you should just wear a different tie. I don't really like brown anyway.

Conversation 3

A: Do you want to try it? It's really fun!

B: No thanks. It's too cold and windy. And honestly, I'm not crazy about the idea of flying down a mountain on one thin piece of wood.

A: But that's the fun part!

Question 3: *What sport are the people talking about?*

B: I'm sorry, snowboarding isn't for me. I'd rather stay inside by the fire.

Conversation 4

Teen Girl: You colored your hair.

Teen Boy: Yeah, I finally did it. Do you like it?

Girl: Uh, you look so… different.

Boy: What do you mean, "different"?

Question 4: *How does the girl feel about the boy's hair?*

Girl: Uh, I'm not crazy about it. Sorry.

Conversation 5

Teen Girl: You colored your hair!

Teen Boy: Yeah, I finally did it. Do you like it?

Girl: You look so different!

Boy: What do you mean, "different"?

Question 5: *How does the girl feel about the boy's hair?*

Girl: I love it! It's so cool!

Student Book pages 190–191

Using Language Functions

FOCUS

Expressing Approval and Disapproval
- Read the instruction note.
- Review the difference in meaning between *approve/disapprove* and *like/dislike*.

4 Practicing Expressions of Approval and Disapproval

- Read the directions for the activity and have students work individually to complete the sentences.
- Have students discuss their answers with a partner.
- Compare answers as a class.

On the Spot!

5 What Would You Do?

- Give students time to read the instructions.
- Ask one student to explain the instructions in their own words.
- Have students complete the chart individually.
- Help students to form groups and have them discuss their charts by answering the three questions.
- Encourage them to use expressions from page 190 of the Student Book.
- Set a time limit of 20 minutes.
- Move around the room to provide encouragement and feedback.
- At the end, invite a representative from each group to report on the most controversial topic in their discussion.

Expansion Activity

- The aim of this activity is to practice the language of expressing approval and disapproval on the topic of fads and fashions.
- Please see Black Line Master "Fads and Fashions" on page BLM 24 of this Teacher's Manual. Photocopy and distribute one to each student.
- Have students work in groups to discuss one of the topics in the box. Point out that the topics are written like short advertisements.
- As a group, they should try to think of reasons why each group of people in the chart might approve or disapprove of this topic.
- Have students fill out the chart with their ideas.
- Each group member should then choose one of the roles.
- The group will then role-play a discussion using the information they have gathered.
- Set a time limit of 15 minutes.
- Ask a representative from each group summarize the main points of the discussion.

PART 4 — Real-World Task: Choosing Someone to Date

Student Book pages 192–193

Before You Listen

1. Describing Your Ideal Partner

- Set a time limit of three minutes for students to write their lists.
- Have students compare lists with their partner.
- Discuss the questions in groups or as a class.

Listen

2. Comparing People's Qualities

- Look at the photos and brainstorm a list of adjectives about each person.
- Play the recording and have students complete the chart.
- Play the recording again if necessary.
- Ask a volunteer to write the answers on the board.

ANSWER KEY

	Katherine	Jean
Positive qualities	parents like her	smart
	intelligent	loves sports
	interesting to talk with	good sense of humor, tells funny jokes
	loves kids	good at managing money, shares cost of dates
Negative qualities	sensitive, gets offended	quiet
	not good at managing money	not easy to talk with
	has a bad temper, gets angry	not sure about having kids

AUDIOSCRIPT

I don't know what to do. Katherine and Jean are both wonderful women. So how am I supposed to choose between them? Take Katherine. We went to the same high school and college, and my parents are crazy about her. Also, Katherine is very intelligent, and she's interesting to talk with; we spend hours discussing art and politics and books.

Now Jean is also very smart, but she's much quieter than Katherine. It's not as easy to talk to her. But even though she's quiet, she's crazy about sports, just like me, and she has a great sense of humor; I mean, she tells the funniest jokes, and I love the way she laughs. On the other hand, Katherine is sometimes too sensitive; what I mean is, she doesn't understand that I'm just joking, so she gets offended.

And another thing I don't like about Katherine is that she's not good at managing money. She has a very good job and a good salary, but somehow she never seems to have any money! That's not very responsible, is it? But Jean is great with money. She even insists on sharing the cost of our dates.

On the other hand, I want to have children, but Jean says she's not sure. That could be a problem later on. Katherine loves kids, but sometimes she has a bad temper; she gets angry whenever I'm five minutes late!

I'm really confused. Katherine and Jean—they're so different and I really like them both. But you know, I don't know if either one is serious about me anyway. What do you think I should do?

After You Listen

3. Discussion

- Have students work in pairs to discuss the answers.
- Compare answers as a class.

Student Book pages 193–195

Talk It Over

Best Practice

Cultivating Critical Thinking

This is an example of a collaborative team activity resulting in a final product. This type of activity requires students to process the information they have learned and apply it to a new situation. The process of manipulating language and concepts in this way will create deeper processing of new material which will allow students to evaluate whether they have understood the new material and help them remember it better.

4 Reading Personal Ads

- Explain the context of personal ads (see the Content Note below).
- Read the ads and check comprehension. Have them choose the most interesting ad and explain their choice to a group.

Content Note

Although meeting people through personal ads in the newspapers or online is fairly common in the U.S. and other Western countries, there are still risks associated with it, and many people in the U.S. would disapprove of or be suspicious of meeting people in this way. It is unusual and may be considered unacceptable in other cultures.

5 Writing an Online Profile

- Read the information in the boxes. Explain that each student will write an online profile for him or herself. Set a time limit of ten minutes.
- Move around the room to provide feedback.
- Collect the profiles and pin them to the wall. You may want to give each profile a number.
- Have students read all the profiles and guess who wrote them.

Expansion Activity

- The aim of this activity is to practice vocabulary for describing personal characteristics.
- Write the following list of words on the board. Students may use their dictionaries.

adventurous	bad-tempered	confident
considerate	have a sense	independent
optimistic	of humor	sensitive
responsible		

- Each pair of students can choose three words. They will prepare a question for each word to find out if their classmates have this characteristic. They must not use the word in their questions.

Example: generous

Question: How much do you usually spend on a birthday present for your best friend?

- Set a time limit of five minutes. Move around the room to monitor progress and provide feedback.
- At the end of the time limit, ask students to choose someone in the class and read out their questions. The chosen student will try to answer truthfully. The other students will try to guess which characteristic is being described.

Self-Assessment Log

- Have students check vocabulary that they learned in the chapter and are prepared to use.
- Have them check strategies they understand.
- Put students in small groups. Ask students to find the information or an activity related to each strategy in the chapter.
- Tell students to find definitions in the chapter for any words they did not check, or they can look in their dictionaries.

CHAPTER 9
New Frontiers

In this CHAPTER

Students will read about various topics related to advances in science. In Part 1, they will talk about living in a "smart" house and learn to introduce surprising information. They will also practice pronouncing the *th* sounds. In Part 2, they will listen to a lecture about facial recognition software. They will also practice giving a speech to persuade. In Part 3, they will discuss inventions and discoveries and learn to express interest or surprise. They will also practice the pronunciation of *-ed* endings. In Part 4, they will listen and track a journey on a map.

Chapter Opener

- Have students look at the photo and describe what is happening. (This is a photo of a "smart" house and a person is using a cell phone to turn the lights on or off inside.) Discuss the questions in the Connecting to the Topic section.

- Read and discuss the quote by Andre Gide (1869–1951) on page 196. Ask students to explain the quote in their own words. Ask students to think of examples that support this statement.

> "Man cannot discover new oceans unless he has the courage to lose sight of the shore."
>
> Andre Gide
> French writer, humorist, and moralist

Chapter Overview

Listening Skills and Strategies
Listening for main ideas and details
Recognizing persuasive language
Distinguishing between -ed endings
Following a journey on a map

Speaking Skills and Strategies
Talking about "smart" houses
Introducing surprising information
Giving a persuasive speech
Talking about new inventions and technological trends
Expressing interest or surprise
Talking about personal discoveries

Critical-Thinking Skills
Getting meaning from context
Taking notes and outlining based on a lecture
Recognizing signposts in a speech or lecture

Vocabulary Building
Terms for talking about home efficiency
Terms for technological advancements
Expressions for persuasive language
Terms for talking about voyages and discoveries
Expressions that signal surprise

Pronunciation
Identifying and practicing stressed words
Pronouncing the *th* sound
Pronouncing *-ed* endings

Language Skills
Recognizing signal words to guess the correct answer

Vocabulary

Nouns
- antidepressant
- appliances
- aspect
- billboard
- display
- impact
- potential
- privacy
- riot
- utility bill
- width

Verbs
- display
- install
- leave on
- match
- scan
- turn into

Adjectives
- convenient
- efficient
- essential
- facial

Adverb
- remotely

Expression
- for ages
- in the meantime

PART 1   Conversation: Living in a "Smart" House   Student Book pages 198–199

Can You Guess?

- Write the following questions on the board. Ask students to discuss them in groups. After a few minutes, write the answers on the board and have students compare their answers with the correct answers.

1. Who was the first woman in space and what country did she come from? **A.** *Valentina Tereshkova, Russia*
2. What do the following inventions have in common: the yo-yo, Post-it notes, dynamite, and Velcro? **A.** *They were all accidental inventions.*
3. Where were the following things invented: piano, chocolate, toothbrush? **A.** *piano—Italy; chocolate—Central America/Mexico; toothbrush —China*

Content Note

- The piano (originally known as pianoforte) was developed from an older instrument, the harpsichord, in or around 1720 by Bartolomeo Cristofor of Padua, Italy.
- The Olmec Indians of Central America are believed to have grown cocoa beans as early as 1500 B.C. In 600 A.D., Mayans and Aztecs took beans from the cacao tree and made a drink they called *xocoatl* (chocolate).
- Toothbrushes were first invented by the ancient Chinese who made them from pig's hair.

Source: http://inventors.about.com/od/famousinventions

Before You Listen

- Read aloud the text that introduces the conversation.
- As a class, look at the photos. Have volunteers read aloud the question next to each. Discuss the answers.

Content Note

The following are a few ideas for conserving energy in the home:

- Use a thermostat to control the heat and air conditioning.
- Let your dishes air dry instead of using the dishwasher's drying cycle.
- Turn things off when you're not using them. This includes lights, TVs, entertainment systems, and computers.
- Plug electronics into power strips and turn the power strips off when you're not using them. TVs, DVD players, computers, and printers still use power when they are in standby mode.
- Take quick showers, not baths.
- Wash only full loads of dishes and clothes.
- Hang your clothes to dry instead of using the dryer.
- Make sure your windows and doors are closed when the heat or air conditioner is on.
- Plant trees around your home. They provide shade to keep your home cooler in the summer and block the wind to keep your home warmer in the winter.

Source: http://www.energysavers.gov/tips/save_energy.cfm

Best Practice

Activating Prior Knowledge

The prelistening questions in Activity 1 activate students' prior knowledge. This activity will help students relate their own knowledge about saving energy to the new language in this chapter. When students activate their prior knowledge before learning new material, they are better able to map new language onto existing concepts, which aids understanding and retention.

1 Prelistening Questions

- Read the directions.
- Have students read the questions and discuss them in small groups.

Student Book pages 199–201

- Ask volunteers to share their group's answers with the whole class.

2 Previewing Vocabulary

- Play the recording and have students listen carefully to the underlined words and expressions. Point out to students that they should try to understand the meaning of the word from the context of the sentence.
- Have students complete the activity individually.
- Check answers as a whole class.

ANSWER KEY
1. d 2. j 3. b 4. a 5. e 6. g 7. h 8. i
9. f 10. c

Listen

3 Comprehension Questions

(The audioscript follows Activity 4.)

- Read the directions and the questions with the class.
- Explain to students that these questions will help them focus on the main ideas in the listening. They do not need to understand every word to answer the questions.
- Play the recording.
- After listening once (or twice if necessary) have students compare their answers in pairs.
- Check answers as a class.

ANSWER KEY
1. It is too high, or expensive.
2. It is automatically controlled.
3. It is too expensive.
4. In Japan, they are careful about conserving energy.
5. Everyone should be smart about saving energy.

Stress

4 Listening for Stressed Words

- Tell students that they will listen to the conversation from Activity 3 again and fill in the missing stressed words. Tell students to read the conversation first and notice the words that are missing.
- Play the recording again.
- Allow time for students to repeat and write the missing words.
- After listening, have students check their answers with the audioscript on pages 296–297 in their Student Books.
- Have students read the conversation with a partner, paying attention to stressed words in their pronunciation.

AUDIOSCRIPT and ANSWER KEY

Andrew: Nancy!

Nancy: Yeah?

Andrew: Look at this _utility_ bill. We're spending _way_ too much on _electricity_.

Nancy: Ugh, I know. It's because _some_ people in this house never remember to turn off _lights_.

Mari: Um, _I_ turn off lights all the _time_. In Japan, we're very _careful_ about saving energy.

Andrew: Well, if we had a _smart_ house, we wouldn't have to _worry_ about this so much.

Mari: A smart house?

Nancy: Yeah, we've been talking about that for _ages_. Go ahead, Andrew, explain what it _is_.

Andrew: Well, a _smart_ house is a house that has _automatic_ systems for controlling the lights, _temperature_, windows and doors…

Mari: You mean the lights turn off by _themselves_?

Andrew: Yes, they can turn on or off at a _specific_ time that you decide.

Interactions 2 Listening/Speaking 149

PART 1

Student Book pages 200–203

Nancy:	Or the *system* can tell if someone is in the *room* or not. If the room is empty, the lights go *off*.
Andrew:	And the heating and *air conditioning* work the same way.
Mari:	That's very cool.
Andrew:	And you can program other *appliances* to do stuff, too.
Mari:	Like which *ones*? How?
Andrew:	Like your security system *recognizes* you and opens your door, your *music* turns on when you enter a *room*, your refrigerator tells you when you *run* out of food…
Mari:	So it's all *computerized*, right?
Nancy:	Right. And get this, you control *everything* remotely from your phone or *tablet*.
Andrew:	So let's say you're on *vacation* or at work, but don't remember if you turned off your *stove*, it's all very convenient.
Nancy:	And *efficient*!
Mari:	You just need an *app* on your phone and that's it?
Andrew:	Well, yes, an *app*, but you also have to *install* a control system, you know, the hardware, then some *software*…
Nancy:	Yeah, it can get a little *complicated*. And expensive!
Andrew:	But we will *definitely* turn this house into a *smart* one eventually…
Nancy:	OK, but in the *meantime*, let's all be smart about *saving* energy. Um, who left the TV on in the *bedroom*?
Andrew:	Oops.

After You Listen

5 Using Vocabulary

- Read the directions and the vocabulary words in the box.

- Point out that these are the same vocabulary words that were practiced in Activity 2: Previewing Vocabulary. Students will now practice using them in new contexts.

- Have a volunteer read aloud the examples.

- Have students work in groups to practice telling stories about the pictures using the vocabulary words. Tell students to listen as their classmates tell their story and check off the vocabulary words they have used.

- At the end of the activity, find out which student used the most vocabulary words in his or her story. Invite the student to retell their story for the class.

Pronunciation

FOCUS

Pronouncing TH

- Read the instruction note.
- Model the pronunciation of the voiced and voiceless *th* sounds
- Practice the pronunciation of *th*. Call on individual students to pronounce the sounds. Give feedback and encouragement as necessary.

6 Pronouncing Voiced and Voiceless *th*

- Play the recording. Allow time for students to repeat all together.
- Select students to pronounce the words individually. Provide feedback on their pronunciation.

7 Distinguishing Between Voiced and Voiceless *th*

- Have students read the sentences silently and try to predict which *th* sounds are voiced or voiceless.
- Play the recording and have students mark the sentences.
- Check answers as a class.
- Practice saying the sentences.

ANSWER KEY

1. <u>Th</u>at's going to happen on October <u>th</u>ird.
2. Brea<u>th</u>e out when you pronounce the /th/ sound.
3. Next <u>Th</u>ursday is my bir<u>th</u>day.
4. The wea<u>th</u>er is getting warmer on Ear<u>th</u>.
5. Elizabe<u>th</u> takes a ba<u>th</u> every night.
6. There's some<u>th</u>ing to <u>th</u>ink about.
7. Tom's bro<u>th</u>er gave him a new too<u>th</u>brush.

Using Language Functions

FOCUS

Introducing Surprising Information

- Read the instruction note. Model the expressions with appropriate intonation to introduce surprising information.
- Brainstorm some ways of completing the sentences.
- Ask students to read the example, using appropriate questions to complete the sentences.

Best Practice

Making Use of Academic Content

Activity 8 is an example of an activity that encourages students to practice impromptu speaking skills. When participating in debates or discussions in class, they may sometimes have to come up with ideas without having a lot of preparation time. This activity provides an opportunity to practice this skill.

8 Fact or Fiction Game

- Prepare ahead of time one card or slip of paper for each student in the class. Each card should say either "Fact" or "Fiction."
- Read the instructions to the class and ask one or two students to explain the activity to the rest of the class.
- Model the activity with two or three students first.
- Set a time limit of ten minutes.

Expansion Activity

- The purpose of this activity is to practice telling and asking questions about surprising stories from the newspaper.
- Ask students to find one funny, interesting, or strange story from the newspaper (or online source) and bring it to the next class.
- Have students work in pairs to tell each other their stories, using the expressions from the Focus list on page 204.
- The listener should ask questions about the details of the story to make sure they understand.
- Then have students change partners and retell their *partner's* story to their new partner.
- Student A tells story to Student B. Student B tells Student A's story to Student C. Student C pairs up with A and tells A's story back to A.
- To check comprehension, the new partner should now pair up with the person who told the original story.
- Set a time limit of 15 minutes.
- Move around the room to monitor and provide feedback.
- When students have finished, ask for volunteers to tell the most surprising or most unusual story.

PART 2   Lecture: Facial Recognition Software

Student Book pages 205–207

Before You Listen

- Read the text that introduces the next lecture.
- Have students look at the photos. Ask a volunteer to read aloud the information next to each photo.
- Ask the class what they think about this use of Facial Recognition Software. Elicit ideas.

1 Prelistening Discussion

- Have students work in small groups to answer the questions, or give one question to each group of students.
- Review the responses as a class and compare some of their experiences.
- Ask a volunteer to write on the board all the facts they know about identity theft and how people can avoid it.

2 Previewing Vocabulary

- Play the recording and ask students to listen to the words.
- Have students check any words that they don't know. Then have students compare answers with a partner and explain words to each other if they can.
- Students will find out the meanings of these words by listening to the lecture.

Listen

Strategy

Recognizing Persuasive Language

- Read aloud the information in the Strategy box.
- Using identify theft as the example issue, model correct intonation of the expressions for convincing people that a problem exists.
- Continuing to use identify theft as the example issue, ask students to complete the expressions for persuading people to take action.

3 Listening for Persuasive Language

- Read aloud the directions.
- Play the recording and have students write *P* for *problem* or *A* for *action* for each context.
- Check answers as a class.

ANSWER KEY

1. P   2. A   3. A   4. A   5. P

AUDIOSCRIPT

1. According to a study published in the *New York Times* newspaper, the average American teenager now spends more than 11 hours each day using some kind of electronic device to get information, communicate with friends, listen to music, or watch videos. You might think that sounds totally normal. But in reality, this amount of media use, day in and day out, can have very serious consequences.

2. Unless the people in town start conserving water right away, we are going to face serious water shortages as early as next summer. We all need to take action to avoid running out of water. Here are three things you need to do starting today. First...

3. **A:** That's a pretty bad sunburn.
   B: Yeah. I went to the beach yesterday.
   A: You really need to start using sunscreen.
   B: I don't like the way it feels.
   A: You'll get used to it. Believe me, with your light skin and blue eyes, it's crucial to use sunscreen every day, unless you want to get skin cancer.

4. If you're concerned about protecting your privacy on the Internet, it's essential to write your government representatives and say you want them to pass laws that protect people's privacy. Do it today!

5. The police have estimated that approximately 72 miles of city property such as walls, fences, freeway overpasses, park benches, and so on, are covered in graffiti. Now I know some people say that graffiti is a kind of street art, that people have a right to freedom of expression. But it's a fact that graffiti attracts crime and lowers property values.

Best Practice

Organizing Information

The next two activities, Activities 4 and 5, use a graphic organizer to categorize information. Using an outline encourages students to process and organize information while they are listening and also provides a record for them to refer to when reviewing their notes. This type of graphic organizer emphasizes listing and categorizing skills. Other types of graphic organizers are used throughout this book.

Best Practice

Scaffolding Instruction

The next two activities, Activities 4 and 5, support scaffolding. This outline helps students to organize their notes into main and secondary ideas. By providing students with the outline as a support, they can see how key words and numbering can be used to structure the content of the lecture. This guided activity prepares them for the skill of identifying main and secondary ideas without the help of an outline.

4 Taking Notes and Outlining (Part I)

- Ask students to take notes as they listen.
- Remind them to use abbreviations and symbols.
- Play the recording.
- Ask students to complete the outline using their notes.
- Play the recording again, if necessary.
- Check the answers as a class.

ANSWER KEY

Part I

I. Intro

   A. Situation: You're walking <u>in mall</u>, see digital <u>ad display</u> w/ ads for <u>deodorant, energy drink</u>.

   B. Billboard "knows" <u>you're 20- yr-old guy likes sports</u>. Uses computer software to <u>scan your face</u>, match ads to <u>age, sex, body</u>.

   C. Lecture topic: facial recognition software (FRS)

     1. <u>What is it?</u>

     2. positive uses

     3. <u>negative aspects</u>

     4. argument: <u>we & govt. need to control it carefully</u>

PART 2

Student Book pages 207–208

> II. Two kinds of facial recognition software
>   A. Recognizes <u>human faces, but can't identify person</u>
>   1. used in <u>advertising</u>
>   2. used in bars to <u>tell how many male and female customers</u>
>   B. <u>Identifies people</u>
>   1. measures <u>distance between eyes, shape of nose, width of mouth</u>
>   2. useful for <u>catching criminals & potential terrorists</u>
>   a. e.g. <u>in London, 2011, identified people in riots</u>

AUDIOSCRIPT

Part 1

I want you to imagine this situation. Let's say you're in a shopping mall, and you walk by one of those digital advertising displays, and you decide to stop and look. Suddenly an ad appears for running shoes, followed by an ad for men's deodorant. And then one for an energy drink. It's like the sign "knows" that you're a 20-year-old guy who loves sports. Well, guess what: It *does* know! That's because, um, when you looked at the sign, a computer scanned your face and selected ads that matched your age, sex, and body. The technology that does this is called facial recognition software.

In my speech today I'm gonna explain what facial recognition technology is and some of the positive ways that we can use it. But then, in the second part of my speech, I'm gonna tell you about some negative aspects of this technology. Especially the negative impact on privacy. And I'm gonna argue that this technology is something that we and the government need to control very carefully.

OK. To begin, what is facial recognition software? Well, actually, there are two kinds of facial recognition technology. One kind recognizes human faces, but it can't identify who the person is. This is the kind of software that I told you about in my introduction. It's already being used in advertising, for example, in subway stations in Tokyo. Another interesting use of this software is in bars in the city of Chicago. It's used to identify the number of men and women in a bar at one time. So then the bars send out this information, for example on Twitter, and then customers can decide if they want to go there or not. Cool, huh?

OK. Now the second kind of software *does* have the ability to recognize who you are. It works by measuring the distance between your eyes, the shape of your nose, the width of your mouth, etc., and it's really useful for catching criminals and potential terrorists. In London, for example, in England, you know, there are cameras in most public places. In the fall of 2011, police used facial recognition software to analyze photos of people who were involved in riots.

Now, I can imagine what you are thinking. Facial recognition software is great! It can help businesses sell products, and it can help police fight crime! What's wrong with that? Well, I agree that those are excellent uses of facial recognition software.

5 Taking Notes and Outlining (Part II)

- Play the second part of the lecture.
- Have students take notes in their own way, as before.
- Then have students use their notes to complete the outline.
- Play the recording again, if necessary.
- Check the answers as a class.

ANSWER KEY

III. Problem with FRS: <u>potential to take away privacy</u>

IV. Explanation
   A. Your name & photo on <u>Facebook</u>
   B. Public camera takes a photo of you > someone can match that photo w/ your Internet photo > <u>get your name, age, city, likes, dislikes, etc.</u>

V. Dangerous
   A. Strangers can know <u>name, age, political beliefs, employment history, etc.</u>
   B. Can steal <u>identity</u>
   C. "Smart" billboards can display <u>ads for medication/medical issue</u> > embarrassing

VI. What to do
   A. <u>limit photos online connected to name</u>
   B. <u>support laws that protect privacy</u>

AUDIOSCRIPT

Part 2

The problem is that facial recognition software also has the potential to take away your privacy.

I mean, everybody here has a Facebook account, right? I read that each month, 2.5 *billion* photos get posted to Facebook. So probably there is a photo of you, either on Facebook or somewhere else on the Internet, and that photo probably has your name and other information attached to it. So, let's say you're walking down the street and a camera takes a picture of you. Someone could use face recognition software to match that photo to your photo on the Internet. And in that way they can get your name, your age, your city, your likes and dislikes, and all kinds of other private information.

Maybe you think that this is not a big deal, but to me, well, I think it's dangerous. Imagine a world where a picture of your face will allow anybody to know your name, your age, your political beliefs, your employment history, your shoe size… And remember those digital billboards in malls that I talked about at the beginning? Imagine if those billboards could match your face with your medical history and display an ad for an antidepressant or heart medication right there for anybody to see. I think that would be incredibly embarrassing, don't you?

All right, so if you are concerned about protecting your privacy, what can you do about it? Well, there are two things you need to do right away. First, try to limit the number of photos online that are connected with your name. Like, don't let people tag your photos on Facebook.

In the second place, it's essential to support laws that protect people's privacy. In Germany, private companies have to get your permission before they're allowed to store your photo or information about you in their databases. But we don't have a law like that in the U.S., and I think we should.

In conclusion, facial recognition software already exists, and there is no way to go back in time and make it disappear. But if you care about your privacy and want to keep your freedom to walk down the street without people knowing all your secrets, then you and the government should take steps to control it before it's too late.

After You Listen

Best Practice

Activating Prior Knowledge
Activity 6 is an example of an activity that encourages students to make text-to-self connections. The discussion questions ask students to relate the content of the lecture on facial recognition software to their own lives. This aids understanding and retention of new material.

PART 2

Student Book pages 208–209

6 Discussing the Lecture

- Have students discuss the questions in groups.
- Encourage students to use new vocabulary from the chapter in their discussion.
- Ask for representatives from each group to report to the class about their group's discussion.

7 Reviewing Vocabulary

- Ask students to look back at the vocabulary in Activity 2 on page 206 of the Student Book and test each other in small groups.
- Ask for volunteers to give example sentences using the new vocabulary.

- Once students have all of their information, tell them to prepare a full outline to organize their speech. Tell them to follow the model given in the Student Book on page 209.
- Tell students to include language and expressions for stating the problem and encouraging action from page 206 of the Student Book. Also tell them to use signposting.
- Have students work with a partner to practice their speech.
- Allow time for all students to present their speech to the class.

Talk It Over

Strategy

Signposting
- Read aloud the information in the Strategy box.
- Ask students to discuss how helpful they find signposting when they are listening to lectures or give other examples.
- Tell students that they will practice signposting when they give a speech in Activity 8.

8 Giving a Speech to Persuade

- Read through the directions and the steps with the class.
- Brainstorm a few additional possible topics for their speeches. Write them on the board.
- Give students time in class or outside of class to research their topic and gather information. Elicit ways to gather information, e.g., Internet research, surveying people in community or school.

PART 3 Strategies for Better Listening and Speaking

Student Book pages 210–211

Getting Meaning from Context

FOCUS ON TESTING — TOEFL® iBT

Signal Words for Guessing the Correct Answer

- Read the information in the box and check comprehension of *infer*, *imply*, and *conclude*.

Using Context Clues

- Explain that students will hear five different talks about recent inventions, discoveries, or trends.
- Play the recording. Pause the recording after each talk and allow time for students to fill in the circle next to the answer and write down the clues they used to find the answer.
- Check the answers as a class.

ANSWER KEY

Answers	Clues
1. A	accidents caused by human error; could prevent thousands of deaths
2. C	uses 90% less water; nearly waterless machine
3. B	reduce global warming; reduce need for air conditioning and save energy
4. C	Don't expect it to taste like McDonalds!
5. B	30 miles per gallon; park it in the garage

AUDIOSCRIPT

Passage 1

Someday soon, your car may be able to drive itself. In 2010, Google introduced a fully automated, driverless car that went 140,000 miles without an accident. According to the World Health Organization, more than 1.2 million people die every year in traffic accidents. Nearly all these accidents are caused by human error; therefore, driverless cars, which are controlled by computers, could prevent thousands of deaths each year. Driverless cars could also give greater freedom to disabled people and reduce the need for parking spaces, since the cars could drive themselves home after dropping off passengers.

Question 1: *What can we conclude from this information?*

Passage 2

Each year Americans use more than 330 billion gallons of water to wash their clothes. Now a British company called Xeros has developed a machine that uses 90 percent less water than normal washing machines. It cleans clothes with reusable nylon beads that remove stains and dirt. This is good news both for the environment and for your monthly water bill. The nearly waterless machine became available in 2011.

Question 2: *The passage implies that the new washing machine...*

Passage 3

"Geo-engineering" is the process of changing things in our environment in order to reduce global warming. A simple example of geoengineering is the practice of painting buildings, roofs, and streets white. In hot countries like Greece, people have been doing this for generations. Professor Steven Chu, who won the Nobel Prize for Physics in 1997, explains that white surfaces are cooler because they reflect sunlight back into space.

PART 3

Student Book pages 210–214

Painting both houses and cars white would reduce the need for air conditioning and save a lot of energy. In the U.S. it would be like taking all cars off the roads for a period of 11 years.

Question 3: *What can we infer from the passage?*

Passage 4
Would you eat a hamburger that was grown in a laboratory? Maybe not today. However, by the year 2050, the world will have 9 billion people, and finding ways to feed them will be a major challenge. One answer may be artificial food. In fact, scientists in Holland and Britain have already succeeded in developing artificial meat in laboratories, and the first artificial hamburger could be developed soon. But don't expect it to taste like McDonald's!

Question 4: *What can we conclude from the passage?*

Passage 5
Imagine a car that flies. Or is it an airplane that you can drive? Both, according to the builders of the Transition—the world's first vehicle that can travel both in the air and on land. The Transition gets 30 miles per gallon, almost 13 km per liter on land, and it can fly two passengers about 500 miles, 805 km, at a speed of 105 miles, about 170 km per hour. It can fly in and out of any airport. Once it lands, the wings fold up and the pilot can drive it home and park it in the garage. The vehicle, which has both airbags and a parachute, costs $200,000.

Question 5: *We can infer that the greatest advantage of the Transition is…*

❶ Talking About New Frontiers

- Read the directions.
- Have students form small groups to discuss each of the discoveries and inventions listed. Ask which they think will play the largest role in their lives.
- Which might be the most useful and why? What is good and bad about each?
- Discuss which are inventions and which are trends.

Focused Listening

FOCUS

Pronunciation of *-ed* Endings

- Read the information about the pronunciation of *-ed* endings.
- Model correct pronunciation of the endings with emphasis.
- Play the recording. Have students repeat the examples aloud.

❷ Practicing *-ed* Endings

- Read the directions for the activity and then play the recording.
- Have students repeat all together after the recording.
- Select individual students to practice selected words.

❸ Distinguishing Among *-ed* Endings

- Read the directions and call students' attention to the chart.
- Play the recording.
- Allow time for students to check the column of the pronunciation they hear.
- Select individual students to practice selected words.
- Review the answers as a class.

AUDIOSCRIPT and ANSWER KEY

1. smoked	/t/	9. added	/id/
2. rubbed	/d/	10. surfaced	/t/
3. lifted	/id/	11. solved	/d/
4. mopped	/t/	12. selected	/id/
5. changed	/d/	13. erased	/t/
6. directed	/id/	14. telephoned	/d/
7. wished	/d/	15. numbered	/d/
8. removed	/d/		

Student Book pages 214–215

4. Pronouncing -ed Endings

- Have students work in pairs to pronounce each word and decide on their answers.
- Play the recording. Have students listen and check their answers.
- Play the recording again and ask students to repeat the words.
- Compare answers as a class and write the answers on the board.
- If there is time, have students make up sentences and practice the pronunciation of -ed forms in a sentence.

ANSWER KEY

1. emptied	/d/
2. used	/d/ [This may vary depending on how the word *used* is pronounced. With a voiceless s, the ending is /t/. If the s is pronounced as a z, then the ending is /d/.
3. stayed	/d/
4. worked	/t/
5. passed	/t/
6. waited	/id/
7. benefited	/id/
8. judged	/d/
9. identified	/d/
10. drummed	/d/

Using Language Functions

FOCUS

Expressing Interest or Surprise
- Read the instruction note.
- Practice the expressions using the appropriate intonation.

Best Practice

Making Use of Academic Content
Activity 5 is an example of an activity that requires students to draw on their own experience to give examples of abstract ideas and concepts. In this activity, they are asked to talk about examples of discoveries they have made in their own lives. This provides each student with an opportunity for authentic individualization, which makes their interaction more meaningful.

5. Talking About Discoveries

- Give students time to read the instructions and the information in the chart.
- Ask students to think quietly for one minute and make a list of discoveries they have made.
- Help students to form groups.
- Set a time limit of ten minutes.
- Move around the room to provide encouragement and feedback.
- At the end, have volunteers to talk about their discoveries.

PART 3

Student Book page 215

Expansion Activity

- The aim of this activity is to practice the language of expressing interest and surprise by using real information.

- See Black Line Master "That's Amazing!" on page BLM 25 of this Teacher's Manual. Photocopy and distribute one copy to each group.

- Have students read the directions. Then form groups of three.

- Have groups discuss their skills and abilities. If necessary, brainstorm a few examples on the board; for example: baking cakes, telling funny stories, playing the piano.

- Students will fill in the diagram together as a group.

- You can tell students to label A, B, and C in the diagram with each student's name in the group.

- Set a time limit of ten minutes.

- Ask students to share their amazing facts with other groups

- Encourage students to think of imaginative ideas for their enterprises.

PART 4 — Real-World Task: Tracking a Journey on a Map

Student Book pages 216–217

Before You Listen

1 Prelistening Questions

- Read aloud the questions and ask students to look at the photo and think about the answers.
- Have students form small groups to discuss their answers.
- Tell students that they will hear the words in question 3 in the listening. Tell them to listen for the words and the context in which they are used.

Listen

2 Reading Background Information

- Read aloud or ask a student volunteer to read aloud the paragraph in the box.
- Check comprehension of the paragraph by asking a few simple comprehension questions, e.g., *What did Zac do in 2009?*

3 Following a Journey on a Map

- Read the instructions to the class.
- Make sure that all students are starting on the correct point on the map: Marina del Rey, California.
- Play the recording and allow time for students to circle the points on the map.
- Play the recording again if necessary. Then have students connect the circles to mark Zac's route.

AUDIOSCRIPT and ANSWER KEY

One. Zac started his voyage across the Pacific Ocean from a place called Marina del Rey, in California. He crossed the Pacific Ocean to his first stop, _Hawaii_.

Two. Next, he sailed to the _Marshall Islands_, where he met the president of that country.

Three. Next, he traveled to _Papua New Guinea_, a country in Australia.

Four. After leaving Australia, he ran into some pirates in the Indian Ocean. Luckily, he escaped without any problems and continued to his next destination, the island nation of _Mauritius_. At this point, he was halfway through his journey.

Five. Near the eastern coast of Africa, strong storms damaged Zac's boat. However, he was able to repair the damage and sail on to _Durban, South Africa_.

Six. In South Africa, he also stopped at _Cape Town_, where he met the oldest person to sail around the world: Minoru Saito, age 75, from Japan.

Seven. After leaving South Africa, Zac sailed across the Atlantic Ocean and landed in _Panama_.

Eight. He crossed the Panama Canal to the Pacific Ocean, and after a couple of stops in _Mexico_, he sailed up the coast back to _California_, completing his journey in 13 months and two days.

PART 4

Student Book page 218

After You Listen

4 Discussion

- Have students work in small groups. Ask them to compare maps and the route they have marked.
- If groups have questions about the route and stops Zac made, refer them to the audioscript on page 300 of the Student Book.
- Check answers as a class by calling out the number of the stop, e.g., *1*. The students will respond with the place that Zac stopped, e.g., *Hawaii*.
- Have students discuss the questions with their group.
- At the end of the activity, call on volunteers to report back about their group's discussion for the whole class.

Best Practice

Making Use of Academic Content

Activity 5 is an example of an activity that exposes students to situations that they will face in an academic setting. Students at a university will often have to research information and give presentation on what they learned. This activity will give the students the authentic practice that they will need to develop this skill.

5 Presentation

- Read the instructions with the class. Read the topics and tell students to each choose one to research.
- Have students do their Internet research during computer lab time or outside of class. Tell students to take notes on the information they find and to organize their notes into outline form. Tell them that using an outline will organize their information and make giving the presentation easier.
- Ask students to present their findings to the class. Encourage the class to ask questions of the presenter and discuss the new information they learn from each other.

Expansion Activity

REPRODUCIBLE

- The purpose of this activity is to practice talking about inventions and discoveries.
- See Black Line Master "Inventions and Discoveries" on page BLM 26 of this Teacher's Manual. Photocopy one for each group of about four people.
- Cut each page into squares. Give one set of squares to each group.
- Put the squares face down in the center of the table.
- Each student in turn will pick up one square. They will make statements about the discovery or invention (without saying its name) and the others
- will try to guess the discovery or invention that is being described.
- Score one point for each correct guess.
- After using all the squares, students may continue using their own ideas.
- You may assign one student in each group to be a fact checker; his or her job will be to query any facts that might be incorrect. These can be checked later for homework.

Student Book pages 219

Self-Assessment Log

- The purpose of the Self-Assessment Log is to help students reflect on their learning.
- Read the directions aloud and have students check the vocabulary they learned in the chapter and are prepared to use.
- Have students check the strategies they practiced in the chapter and the degree to which they learned them. Have students work individually to complete the sentences at the bottom of the page.
- Put students in small groups. Ask students to find the information or an activity related to each strategy in the chapter.
- Tell students to find definitions in the chapter for any words they did not check, or they can look in their dictionaries.
- Set a time limit of ten minutes.

CHAPTER 10 Ceremonies

In this CHAPTER

Students will read about various topics related to ceremonies in different cultures. In Part 1, they will talk about a baby shower and learn how to make, accept, and decline offers. They will also practice stress in compound nouns. In Part 2, they will listen to a lecture about the use of water in traditional ceremonies in different parts of the world. They will learn to recognize digressions from the main topic. In Part 3, they will listen to conversations about ceremonies and practice affirmative tag questions. They will also practice offering congratulations and sympathy. In Part 4, they will talk about weddings.

"There is nothing like a ritual for making its participants think beyond their own appetites, and for making them feel that they belong to something greater, older and more important than themselves."

Tom Utley
British journalist (1921–1988)

Chapter Opener

- Have students look at the photo of Olympic athletes receiving their medals at the award ceremony. Then ask students the questions from the Connecting to the Topic section. Have students discuss as a class.
- Read and discuss the quote. How can the word *culture* be defined? How do cultures influence each other? Ask students for some examples from the past or the present.
- Brainstorm a list of adjectives to describe the picture.

Chapter Overview

Listening Skills and Strategies
Listening for main ideas and details

Making inferences

Recognizing the meaning of affirmative tag questions

Taking notes on wedding preferences

Speaking Skills and Strategies
Using expressions to offer, accept, or decline help

Talking about water in ceremonies around the world

Asking and answering affirmative tag questions

Offering congratulations and sympathy

Critical-Thinking Skills
Getting meaning from context

Recognizing digressions in a lecture

Comparing celebrations across cultures

Vocabulary Building
Expressions to offer, accept, or decline help

Terms to express congratulations and sympathy

Expressions signaling digressions in a lecture

Terms related to ceremonies

Pronunciation
Identifying and practicing stressed words

Using correct stress in compound phrases

Language Skills
Using context clues to identify ceremonies

Vocabulary

Nouns
- mother-to-be
- prayer
- priest
- ritual
- sin
- symbol
- symbolism

Verbs
- cleanse
- focus on
- host
- involve
- narrow (something) down
- play a part in

- pour
- pray
- purify
- register
- shower
- sprinkle
- symbolize

Adjectives
- allowed
- due
- fascinating
- pregnant
- pure
- silly

Expression
- go "ooh and ah"

PART 1   Conversation: A Baby Shower   Student Book pages 222–223

Can You Guess?

- Ask students to discuss the questions below in groups and compare their answers with the correct answers.
- Discuss the issues raised by these questions: Why are ceremonies important? What kinds of ceremonies are more important in the U.S. and in other cultures?
    1. In which culture are women wedding guests not allowed to wear white or black? **A.** *China*
    2. What are the three most popular honeymoon places for Americans? **A.** *The Caribbean, Hawaii, and Mexico*
    3. What culture celebrates a death with a three-day party of singing and drinking? **A.** *Irish*

Before You Listen

1 Prelistening Questions

- Ask students to describe the photo. Who are these people? What are they doing? What are they talking about? thinking? feeling? What kind of ceremony is it and why is it important?
- Discuss similar ceremonies in other cultures.

2 Previewing Vocabulary

- Play the recording and have students listen for the underlined words and expressions.
- Have students complete the exercise individually.
- Compare their answers as a whole class and write the correct answers on the board.

ANSWER KEY
1. d   2. a   3. f   4. g   5. c   6. b   7. h
8. i   9. e

Listen

3 Comprehension Questions

- Explain that these questions will help students focus on the main ideas in the listening.
- You may want to write the questions on the board.
- Read the questions aloud.
- Play the recording.
- After listening, have students compare their answers in pairs.
- Check the answers as a class.

ANSWER KEY
1. an invitation to a baby shower;   2. Sharon and Carolyn;   3. Jeff isn't invited because baby showers are usually only for women;   4. at the end of May;   5. give gifts, play silly games, eat cake;   6. In Japan, people don't usually open their gifts in front of the person who gave the gift;   7. online

AUDIOSCRIPT

Mari: Hi Jeff. Hi Sharon. Look what I got in the mail.

Jeff: Hey.

Sharon: Hi, Mari.

Jeff: "Join us for a baby shower honoring Nancy Anderson, April 5th, 11:00 A.M.... hosted by Sharon Smith and Carolyn Freeman..."

Sharon: Oh good, you got the invitation. So can you make it?

Mari: I think so, but, well, what is a baby shower exactly?

Jeff: You know, it's a party for a woman who's going to have a baby. Um, it's like a welcoming ceremony for the new baby.

166   CHAPTER 10   Copyright © McGraw-Hill

Mari:	It's a party? Then why do you call it a *shower*?
Jeff:	Because the custom is to *shower* the woman with gifts for the baby. Get it?
Mari:	I see. Are you invited too, Jeff?
Jeff:	No way! No men allowed!
Mari:	Really?
Sharon:	Well, not exactly. Lots of baby showers include men these days, but traditionally showers are hosted by a woman's girlfriends or female relatives, and they're only for women.
Mari:	Hmm. But isn't Nancy and Andrew's baby due at the end of May? And this invitation says April 5th.
Sharon:	Well, yes. The custom is to have a shower *before* the baby is born, when the woman is seven or eight months pregnant.
Mari:	Very interesting. And everybody brings a gift?
Sharon:	Right. Something for the baby: you know, toys, or clothes, or something for the baby's room.
Mari:	OK. The invitation says it's for lunch, so…
Sharon:	Yeah, we'll have lunch, and afterwards, we'll play games.
Mari:	Games? What kind of games?
Jeff:	Girl games…
Sharon:	Yeah, silly games, like bingo, or guessing games, or baby trivia games. And the winners get small prizes.
Mari:	It sounds like fun.
Sharon:	It is. And then, at the end of the party, there's usually a cake with baby decorations, and then the mother-to-be opens her presents.
Mari:	While the guests are still there?
Sharon:	Sure. That's my favorite part! Everybody gets to see the gifts.
Jeff:	And go oooh, aaah…
Sharon:	And see how happy the woman is.
Mari:	Wow. That's so different from our custom. In Japan, we usually don't open a gift in front of guests.
Sharon:	Really? That *is* different.
Mari:	Well what kind of gift do you think I should get for her?
Sharon:	She's registered online, so you can see what she's already gotten and what she still needs. Would you like me to write down the Internet address for you?
Mari:	Sure, that would be great.
Mari:	Uh, is there anything I can do to help with the party? Maybe do the flower arrangements or something?
Sharon:	Oh, thanks, but it's not necessary. Everything is all taken care of. Just come and have fun.

Stress

4 Listening for Stressed Words

- Review the meaning of stressed words from the previous unit.
- Play the recording again.
- Have students write the missing words.
- After listening, have students check their answers with the audioscript in their books.
- Have students read the conversation with a partner, paying attention to stressed words in their pronunciation.

AUDIOSCRIPT and ANSWER KEY

Mari:	Hmm. But isn't Nancy and Andrew's baby due at the end of *May*? And this invitation says April *5th*.
Sharon:	Well, yes. The custom is to have a shower *before* the baby is born, when

PART 1

Student Book pages 224–226

	the woman is seven or eight months pregnant.
Mari:	Very interesting. And everybody brings a *gift*?
Sharon:	Right. Something for the baby: you know, *toys*, or clothes, or something for the baby's *room*.
Mari:	OK. The *invitation* says it's for lunch, so...
Sharon:	Yeah, we'll have lunch, and *afterwards*, we'll play *games*.
Mari:	Games? What *kind* of games?
Jeff:	*Girl* games...
Sharon:	Yeah, *silly* games, like bingo, or guessing games, or baby trivia games. And the *winners* get small prizes.
Mari:	It *sounds* like fun.
Sharon:	It is. And then, at the *end* of the party, there's usually a cake with *baby* decorations, and then the mother-to-be opens her *presents*.
Mari:	While the *guests* are still there?
Sharon:	Sure. That's my *favorite* part! Everybody gets to see the gifts....
Jeff:	And go oooh, aaah...
Sharon:	... and see how *happy* the woman is.
Mari:	Wow. That's so *different* from our custom. In Japan, we usually *don't open* a gift in front of guests.
Sharon:	Really? That *is* different.
Mari:	Well, what kind of gift do you think I should *get* for her?
Sharon:	She's registered *online*, so you can see what she's already *gotten* and what she still needs. Would you like me to write down the *Internet* address for you?
Mari:	Sure, *that* would be great.

After You Listen

5 Using Vocabulary

- Have students work in pairs to ask and answer these questions.
- You may want to set a time limit of ten minutes.
- Compare answers as a class.

Pronunciation
FOCUS

Stress in Compound Phrases

- Read the instruction note about noun + noun combinations, and adjective + noun combinations.
- Review the difference between syllable stress and word stress.

---

6 Pronouncing Noun + Noun Combinations

- Play the recording and have students repeat each phrase.

7 Pronouncing Adjective + Noun Combinations

- Read the directions.
- If necessary, read the information in the box about adjective + noun combinations.
- Play the recording and have students repeat each phrase.

8 Predicting Stress

- Read the examples in the list.
- Have students mark the stress in each phrase before listening.
- Play the recording and have students check their answers.
- Check the answers as a class.

Student Book pages 226–228

ANSWER KEY

1. yo’ung mo’ther   stepmo’ther
2. co’ffeepot   large po’t
3. ni’ce pla’ce   fi’replace
4. fla’shlight   green li’ght
5. we’dding cake   delicious ca’ke
6. ha’ir dryer   dry ha’ir
7. bu’sboy   tall bo’y
8. fa’st rea’der   mind rea’der

Using Language Functions

FOCUS

Offering to Do Something

- Read the instruction note.
- Practice pronunciation and intonation of the phrases.
- Write the following list on the board and nominate students to offer, accept, and decline. Examples:
  bring you a cup of coffee
  help you with your homework
  give you a lift home
  help you fix your computer
  visit you at home this weekend

Best Practice

Interacting with Others

Activity 9 is an example of collaborative learning to encourage fluency and confidence. In this activity, communication is more important than grammar. Students can improve their confidence in offering, accepting, and declining offers by switching roles or partners and practicing the same situations again. By providing feedback to each other, they learn skills of self-evaluation.

9 Role-Play

- Have students work in pairs to discuss the photos and create a conversation about each one.
- Make sure they look at and use some of the expressions from page 227.
- Set a time limit of five minutes.
- Invite volunteers to role-play their conversations for the class.

REPRODUCIBLE — Expansion Activity

- The purpose of this activity is to practice strategies for making, accepting, and declining offers.
- Please see Black Line Master "May I Help You?" on page BLM 27 of this Teacher's Manual. Photocopy enough so you have one strip for each student. (There are 10 strips on the page.)
- Cut the copies into strips so that you have one strip for each student.
- Have students walk around the room and say their sentence to each person they meet. The other students must respond with an offer. The first student will accept or decline the offer.
- Remind students to keep notes of what kinds of offers were made in response to their sentences. (They may summarize them later as a class in order of highest frequency.)
- Set a time limit of 10 to 15 minutes.
- Move around the room to monitor and provide feedback.
- Invite volunteers to summarize the offers that were made in response to their statements.

Copyright © McGraw-Hill   Interactions 2 Listening/Speaking   **169**

PART 2 Lecture: Water in Traditional Ceremonies

Student Book pages 229–231

Before You Listen

- Read the text that introduces the next listening.
- Ask the students what they see in the photos.

1. Prelistening Discussion

- Have students work in small groups to discuss the list of meanings and add their own ideas.
- Review the responses as a class.

> **Best Practice**
>
> **Making Use of Academic Content**
> This type of activity encourages students to connect personal and abstract knowledge. In academic lectures, content is often unrelated to students' daily lives. Students have to learn to connect the content to their own experiences in order to make it more meaningful and memorable. This exercise helps students to use their real-world knowledge and relate it to abstract concepts.

2. Previewing Vocabulary

- Play the recording and have students listen to the words and phrases.
- Have students check the words they know.
- Ask students to compare answers with a partner.

Listen

> **Best Practice**
>
> **Scaffolding Instruction**
> This is an example of an activity that raises awareness of learning strategies. In real life, we use a combination of different strategies to identify and interpret information. In this exercise, students focus on recognizing digressions. Focusing on one strategy in this short section of the audio will help students to use this strategy independently in the context of the lecture.

> **Strategy**
>
> **Digressing from (Going off) and Returning to the Topic**
> - Read the information in the box.
> - Read the expressions aloud and ask students to say them aloud.
> - Have them circle the expressions they've heard of. Remind them that they will hear all of them in the next activity.

3. Recognizing Digressions

- Explain that students will hear part of a lecture where the speaker digresses from the main topic. Their task is to identify the digressions by crossing them out.
- Play the recording.
- Have students cross out the appropriate topics.
- Play the recording again if necessary.
- Compare answers as a class.

> **ANSWER KEY**
>
> **A.** Thailand
>
> Speaker's experience
> — April: hottest time of year
> — ~~Thail. doesn't have four seasons.~~
> — ~~dry season: Nov.–Feb.~~
> — ~~hot season: March–June~~
> — ~~rainy season: July–Oct.~~
> — spkr was walking down street & teens threw water on him
> — reason: April 13th = Songkran
> Songkran = water festival
> — people throw water on each other
> — wash hands of elders w/ scented water
> — belief = water will wash away bad luck

Student Book page 231

AUDIOSCRIPT

So I thought I'd focus on that today: the role of water in celebrations around the world.

Let's take Thailand as an example. I'll never forget my first time there. It was April, the hottest part of the year. And by the way, Thailand doesn't have four seasons like we do here. Um, depending on which part of the country you're in, there are three seasons, the dry season from November to February, the hot season from March to June, and the rainy season from about July to October. Um, so anyway, back to our topic, I was walking down the street in the small village where I lived and suddenly, two teenagers walked past me and as they did, they threw water on me! I was kind of shocked but didn't really mind because it was so hot. Then I realized that it was the 13th, which is Songkran, the Water Festival in Thailand. On that day, people throw water on each other, and also wash the hands of their elders with scented water. It's a custom based on the belief that water will wash away bad luck.

4 Taking Notes

- Remind students of the keys to good note-taking. (See Chapter 1 pages 12 and 13.)
- Tell students they are going to hear a lecture about the use of water in ceremonies around the world.
- Play the recording.
- Students can take notes in their own way.

Culture Note

Go over the Culture Note about the Peace Corps. This will help give context for the next lecture.

AUDIOSCRIPT

Host: And now I'd like to introduce our speaker, Josh Harrison. Josh has just returned from his latest overseas assignment as a Peace Corps volunteer. He's served in at least three different countries and has traveled to many more than that; that's why I thought he'd be the perfect speaker for today's topic: ceremonies and celebrations around the world. Welcome, Josh.

Speaker: Thank you, Diane. And thanks for inviting me. Well, I've thought about the topic and I thought, gosh, how am I going to narrow this down? I mean, I have seen and participated in so many fascinating celebrations in many fascinating celebrations in many different cultures. Then I remembered something I noticed just recently: Even though the cultures I experienced were completely different, many of their ceremonies had something interesting in common: the use of water. Yeah, water. Some ceremonies involve drinking the water, some involve pouring it, and some involve dunking or going under water. To me, that was a very interesting discovery.

So I thought I'd focus on that today: the role of water in celebrations around the world.

Let's take Thailand as an example. I'll never forget my first time there. It was April, the hottest part of the year. And by the way, Thailand doesn't have four seasons like we do here. Um, depending on which part of the country you're in, there are three seasons, the dry season from November to February, the hot season from March to June, and the rainy season from about July to October. Um, so anyway, back to our topic, I was walking down the street in the small village where I lived and suddenly, two teenagers walked past me and as they did, they threw water on me! I was kind of shocked but

PART 2

Student Book pages 231–232

didn't really mind because it was so hot. Then I realized that it was the 13th, which is Songkran, the Water Festival in Thailand. On that day, people throw water on each other, and also wash the hands of their elders with scented water. It's a custom based on the belief that water will wash away bad luck.

Now, this idea of washing away bad things, of cleansing or purifying, is also found in Islamic cultures. For example, when I lived in Saudi Arabia, I learned that traditional Muslims pray five times a day, and before they do, they always wash their faces, hands, and feet with water. And the water has to be very clean and pure. This ritual washing symbolizes the removal of sin and disease, in other words, the cleansing of both body and soul, before speaking to God.

All right, now, another religion where water plays an important role is Christianity. And one particular ritual that comes to mind is baptism. Baptism is a ceremony that welcomes a new baby into the Christian religion and the community. Now, since there are many branches of Christianity, there are also many different ways that baptism can be performed. When I lived in Latin America, I attended several Catholic baptisms. And what they do is they bring the baby to the church, where a priest pours or sprinkles some water on the baby's head. This water symbolizes the washing away of sin—somewhat similar to the meaning in Islam. And then, while pouring the water, the priest says a prayer and tells the parents to raise the baby as a good Christian.

So as you can see, water has different symbolic meanings in different cultures. In some cultures, it's believed to keep away bad luck, as in Thailand. In Islamic and Christian cultures, it's used to purify and wash away sin. Water has rich symbolism in nearly all cultures. So now I'd like to know what you think and see if you can share some of your own traditions. How does water play a part in celebrations in *your* culture?

5 Outlining the Lecture

- Ask students to use their notes to complete the outline.
- Play the recording again.
- Have students fill in any missing information.
- Check the answers as a class.

ANSWER KEY

I. Intro

   Speaker: *Josh Harrison, Peace Corps volunteer*

   General Topic: *ceremonies and celebrations around the world*

II. Specific Topic: *the role of water in celebrations around the world*

   A. *Thailand*
   April 13th, Songkran, the Water Festival in Thailand
   people throw water on each other
   wash hands of elders with scented water
   believe that water will wash away bad luck

   B. *Islamic cultures, e.g., Saudi Arabia*
   Muslims pray 5 x a day
   before they pray, wash faces, hands, & feet with water
   water v. clean and pure
   symbolizes the removal of sin & disease, cleansing of body and soul before speaking to God

Student Book pages 232–233

    C. Christian ceremony: baptism
       <u>welcomes new baby into Christian religion and community</u>

       <u>e.g., Latin America</u>
       <u>bring baby to church</u>
       <u>priest pours water on baby's head</u>
       <u>symbolizes washing away sin — similar to Islam</u>
       <u>while pouring water, priest says a prayer and tells parents to raise baby as a good Christian</u>

III. Conclusion
    <u>water has different symbolic meanings in diff. cultures:</u>
    <u>in Thailand: keep away bad luck</u>
    <u>in Islamic and Christian cultures: purify and wash away sin</u>

After You Listen

Best Practice

Activating Prior Knowledge

This is an example of an activity that encourages students to make text-to-self connections. The discussion questions ask students to explore their existing knowledge on the use of water in ceremonies. They can then add the new information to their existing knowledge framework. This aids understanding and retention of new material.

6 Discussing the Lecture

- Have students discuss the questions as a whole class or in groups.
- Encourage students to use the new vocabulary in their discussion.
- Ask for representatives from each group to report to the class on the discussion.

7 Reviewing Vocabulary

- Ask students to look back at the vocabulary in Activity 2 on page 230 in the Student Book and to test each other in pairs.
- Invite volunteers to give examples sentences using the new vocabulary.

Talk It Over

Best Practice

Organizing Information

This is an example of a graphic organizer called a multi-column chart. This type of study tool helps students to organize new information so that it is easier to recall. It will also help them when they want to review their notes. There are many types of graphic organizers used in this book.

8 Interview

- Go over the information in the Strategy box.
- Read the directions in the activity.
- Read the information in the multi-column chart.
- Ask for suggestions for completing the final box in the first row.
- Have students work in pairs to interview each other. If there is time, they can interview two or three students. You may want to assign this as homework.
- Invite students to present their findings to the class.

Expansion Activity

- The purpose of this activity is to practice using the Internet for research and to gain an understanding of ceremonies in different cultures.
- Students can use a search engine to find the vocabulary items or use keywords, for example, *birthday traditions*.
- The research part of this activity can be done in a computer lab class or assigned for homework.
- Please see Black Line Master "Ceremonies Around the World" on page BLM 28 of this Teacher's Manual. Photocopy and distribute one to each student.
- Have students work in groups to choose a ceremony (encourage groups to choose ceremonies that are different from each other) and complete as much of the chart as they can.
- Have students use the Internet to research the rest of the information.
- Have students re-form their groups and share their information to complete the chart.
- Invite volunteers to summarize their findings to the class.

PART 3 — Strategies for Better Listening and Speaking

Student Book page 234

Getting Meaning from Context

FOCUS ON TESTING — TOEFL iBT

Using Context Clues

- Review strategies for getting meaning from context.
- Explain that students will hear five different conversations about ceremonies.
- Read the list of ceremonies and check comprehension of each one.
- Play the recording, pausing after each one to allow time for students to write their answers.
- Check the answers as a class.
- Ask students to identify context clues in each conversation that helped them identify the topic.

ANSWER KEY

1. f   2. c   3. d   4. a   5. g

AUDIOSCRIPT

Conversation 1

Man 1: And now, on behalf of our entire staff, I'd like to present this gold watch to Mr. Harry Kim and express our appreciation for 35 years of dedicated service to our company. Congratulations, Mr. Kim!

Mr. Kim: Thank you, Mr. President. All I can say is, it's been a pleasure working with you all these years. This company has been like a second family to me.

Man 1: What are you going to do with your time from now on?

Mr. Kim: I'm going to play a lot of golf, work in my garden, and visit my grandchildren.

Conversation 2

Woman: Well, that was a very moving service. And I never saw so many flowers. She sure had a lot of friends.

Man: Yep. And the minister spoke beautifully, didn't he? I'm sure it was a comfort to the family.

Woman: I am really going to miss Myra. She was a good neighbor and a good friend.

Man: I can't imagine what Ralph is going to do without her. They were married, what, 40 years?

Woman: Something like that, yes. Poor Ralph.

Conversation 3

Girl: Here they come! Look Mommy, there's Shawna!

Mother: Where?

Girl: She's walking in behind that really tall guy, see?

Mother: Oh yes, yes, I see her. Doesn't she look elegant in her cap and gown, honey? So grown up…

Girl: What's going to happen now?

Father: After everyone sits down there'll be speeches, and then they'll give out the diplomas.

Mother: I can't believe that three months from now our little girl is going to be starting college.

Father: I know. Where did the time go?

Conversation 4

Daughter: And now I'd like to propose a toast. To my parents, Lena and Richard: May your next thirty years together be as happy and prosperous as the first thirty have been. Thanks for being an inspiration to us all. Cheers!

All: Cheers! Congratulations!

Father: Thank you, Betsy, and thank you all for coming out to celebrate with us on this happy occasion. You're the best

PART 3

Student Book pages 234–235

group of friends anyone ever had and we're very grateful. And now *I'd* like to propose a toast: To my wife Lena, who's as beautiful today as she was on our first date more than 30 years ago. To you, darling!

All: Cheers!

Conversation 5

Mother: How are the plans coming?

Daughter: I met with the caterer yesterday and tomorrow we'll order the flowers. We have the rings, and oh, my dress will be ready next Wednesday.

Mother: What about the band for the reception?

Daughter: We hired them months ago. And we ordered the cake too.

Mother: Speaking of cake... You and Robert aren't going to shove cake in each other's faces, are you?

Daughter: No, Mom, don't worry.

1 Talking About Ceremonies

- Have students work in groups to discuss their experiences of these ceremonies.
- Make a list of other ceremonies that are important in their cultures.
- As a class, discuss why ceremonies are important in society. What is their function and purpose? Are they becoming more or less important?

Focused Listening

Strategy

Affirmative Tag Questions
Read the instruction note and practice the intonation of the examples.

2 Recognizing the Meaning of Affirmative Tag Questions

- Explain that students will hear eight different questions. They will listen and choose the correct interpretation of each question.
- Play the recording while students write their answers.
- Review the answers as a class.

ANSWER KEY

1. B   2. A   3. B   4. A   5. B   6. B
7. A   8. B

AUDIOSCRIPT

1. Alia didn't forget to buy flowers again, did she? (rising)
2. That wasn't a very long ceremony, was it? (falling)
3. We don't need to bring a present, do we? (rising)
4. You're not going to wear that shirt to the party, are you? (rising)
5. There aren't many people here, are there? (falling)
6. You're not bringing your dog, are you? (rising)
7. The wedding hasn't started yet, has it? (rising)
8. You didn't like the party, did you? (falling)

Student Book pages 236–237

Using Language Functions

> **FOCUS**
>
> **Offering Congratulations and Sympathy**
> - Read the information about offering congratulations and sympathy.
> - Practice the expressions using appropriate intonation.

> **FOCUS**
>
> **Answering Affirmative Tag Questions**
> - Read the information in the box.
> - Read the questions and answers. Then have students practice asking and answering them in pairs.

3 Asking and Answering Affirmative Tag Questions

- Have students work in pairs.
- Student A should look at page 251 in the Student Book. Student B should look at page 259.
- Set a time limit of five minutes.
- Move around the room to monitor and provide feedback.
- Review the answers as a class.

4 Role-Play

- Read the directions for the activity. Have students work in pairs to role-play each of the situations. When they have finished, they can change partners and practice them again.
- Ask for volunteers to role-play their conversations for the class.

ANSWER KEY

Student A:
a) You don't smoke, do you?
b) There's no homework tonight, is there?
c) It isn't raining, is it?
d) You don't have children (grandchildren, sisters, brothers), do you?

Student B:
a) You don't eat meat, do you?
b) There's no test tomorrow, is there?
c) You don't have a computer (cell phone), do you?
d) Milk isn't good for adults, is it?

> **REPRODUCIBLE** **Expansion Activity**
>
> - The aim of this activity is to practice the language of offering and responding to congratulations and sympathy.
> - Please see Black Line Master "Congratulations and Sympathy" on page BLM 29 of this Teacher's Manual. Photocopy enough so you have one strip for each student. (There are 15 strips on the page.)
> - Cut the copies into strips so that you have one strip for each student.
> - Have students walk around the room and say their sentence to each person they meet. The other students must respond with an expression of congratulations or sympathy. The first student will then respond appropriately.
> - Set a time limit of ten minutes.
> - At the end, select individual students to read out their sentence and choose another student in the class to respond.

PART 4 Real-World Task: Making Wedding Plans

Student Book pages 238–240

- Read the information about Katsu and Sandra and look at the pictures. Ask students to predict what kind of wedding these people might want to have.

Culture Note

Read the information in the Culture Note. Ask students to describe their idea of a typical U.S. wedding. Compare with weddings in other cultures if appropriate.

Before You Listen

1 Comparing Wedding Preferences

- Read the chart and check comprehension of any new vocabulary.
- Have students complete the chart individually and compare answers in groups.

Listen

Best Practice

Cultivating Critical Thinking

This is an example of an activity that requires students to solve a problem collaboratively. Each group of students has a different set of information. They will need to share their information in order to complete the task. This involves comparing, evaluating, and synthesizing information.

2 Taking Notes on Wedding Preferences

- You may want to do this activity in a computer lab, or use two audio players in two separate rooms.
- Explain that students will divide into two groups and each group will listen to a different recording.
- Nominate one person in each group to be in charge of starting, stopping, and replaying the recording.

- Set a time limit of ten minutes.
- As they listen, they will try to complete the chart.
- Bring the groups back together.

AUDIOSCRIPT

Katsu

Consultant: OK, Katsu, to get started, why don't you look at this list for the wedding ceremony, and let me just ask you first of all if there are any items that you have really strong feelings about, like you absolutely must do this or you absolutely refuse to do that...

Katsu: Hmm... Well, I really don't want a religious service. I think a big, traditional American service would be very strange for my parents. So I'd prefer to get married outdoors, in a garden or something, and have a justice of the peace perform the service.

Consultant: OK. Have you and Sandra discussed a date?

Katsu: Not an exact date but we agree that we'd like to do it in April or May.

Consultant: Got it. What else?

Katsu: I'd like it small, just our families and close friends. And informal. I don't want to wear a tuxedo, and I don't want bridesmaids and all those extra people. I think it would be nice if each of us walked in with our parents and that's it. I really want to honor my parents at my wedding.

Consultant: OK, Katsu, obviously you know that Sandra's family is Christian and they've been in America for generations. So let me ask you, is there anything from that tradition that you really like and would want to include in your ceremony?

Katsu: Let's see... Well I'm sure Sandra will want to wear a white dress and that's fine. And, um, well, I don't like organ music, but maybe we could have a flute and a violin, something soft like that.

Consultant: And what about Japanese culture? Is there something you'd like to include from that?

Katsu: Wow. That's a hard question. I've never been to a traditional Japanese wedding. But I know that in Japan purple is, like, the color of love, so maybe Sandra could carry purple flowers.

<u>Sandra</u>

Consultant: OK, Sandra, to start off, I'm going to ask you the same question I asked Katsu. Look at this list of items in a typical wedding ceremony and tell me if there's anything you feel very strongly about.

Sandra: Well, I've always dreamed of having a big traditional wedding, you know, in a church, with an organ playing, and bridesmaids and groomsmen, and a beautiful white dress. But that was before I met Katsu. His family isn't Christian, you know, and my family's not super religious either, so maybe we could have a garden wedding instead of a church. But I'd like my family's minister to perform the service, and I definitely want my father to walk me down the aisle, and I want my little cousin to be our flower girl. I guess the most important thing is to be able to include everybody. My family is huge, and I want to invite them all.

Consultant: So you want to wear a white dress.

Sandra: Of course.

Consultant: And what about Katsu?

Sandra: He hates anything formal. It's fine if he wears a suit.

Consultant: OK, Sandra. Tell me, do you like the color purple?

Sandra: Purple? At a wedding?

Consultant: Katsu suggested you could carry purple flowers. He says that in Japanese culture purple is the color of love.

Sandra: Hmmm... purple. That could work. I love irises, and maybe the bridesmaids' dresses could be violet.

Consultant: That sounds like a wonderful idea. What about music?

Sandra: Well, if we're outdoors, then we can't have an organ, can we; so, hmmm, how about something soft like classical guitar or flute?

PART 4

Student Book page 241

After You Listen

3 **Discussion**

- Help students find a partner from the other group.
- In pairs, students will try to complete the chart by asking their partner for information.
- Compare answers as a class.

ANSWER KEY

	Sandra	Katsu
Location	garden	outside, in a garden
Date/time of year	(no exact time is mentioned, but it's probably warm weather because Sandra says "...if we're outdoors then...")	April or May
Type of service/ceremony (e.g., religious, traditional, modern)	religious, family minister	not religious, justice of the peace
Number of guests (approx.)	all the family	close friends and parents
Attendants (bridesmaids, groomsmen, etc.)	flower girl, bridesmaids	none
Role of parents/grandparents	walk down aisle with father	walk in with parents
Clothing	Sandra: white dress Katsu: suit bridesmaids: violet dresses	Sandra: white dress and purple flowers Katsu: no tuxedo
Music	classical guitar or flute	flute and violin, soft music
Colors	white, violet	white and purple
Other details	Irises sake-sharing ceremony	-----------------

Student Book pages 242–243

Talk It Over

4 Role-Play

- Have students work in groups to role-play planning a wedding.
- Then they will role-play a conversation among Katsu, Sandra, and the wedding planner.
- They should come to an agreement about all the details of the wedding ceremony.

Expansion Activity

- The aim of this activity is to practice affirmative tag questions and answers.
- Have students work individually to write down the details of their ideal birthday party. You may suggest the following categories: People/ Place/ Food/ Music/ Activities.
- Then students will work in pairs to plan a birthday party. Have them ask and answer affirmative tag questions.

  Example:
  Your friends will give you lots of presents, won't they?

- After five minutes, invite volunteers to summarize the details of their party to the class.

Self-Assessment Log

- The purpose of the log is to help the students reflect on their learning.
- Read the directions aloud and have students check vocabulary that they learned in the chapter and are prepared to use.
- Have students check the strategies they understand.
- Put students in small groups. Ask students to find the information or an activity related to each strategy in the chapter.
- Tell students to find definitions in the chapter, or look in their dictionaries.

Name _____ Date _____

Chapter 1 Part 1: Class Survey

Why do you want to study English?
What subject do you want to major in or did you major in and why?
What kind of job or career do you have or want in the future?
What do you like to do in your free time?
How do you study English outside of class?
What other courses have you signed up for?
What is the most difficult thing about learning English?
What is the most difficult thing about going to college?
What is the easiest thing about learning English?
What skills do you most need to improve in your English?

Name _____ Date _____  BLM 2

Chapter 1 Part 2: What is Plagiarism?

PART 1: Form groups of four students. Each person in the group will choose one of the questions below. Each person will research information about the question and share it with the group.

1. What is the definition of plagiarism? Give one example of what is plagiarism and one example of what is *not* plagiarism. Why is it important?	2. Find three different categories of plagiarism.
3. Find three strategies for avoiding plagiarism.	4. Describe three possible consequences of academic plagiarism.

PART 2: In your groups, describe one example of plagiarism (real or imaginary) and discuss how you would respond to it if you were a teacher.

Example of plagiarism: (e.g., copying from a textbook)

_____

Teacher's response:

_____

Name _____ Date _____  BLM 3

Chapter 1 Part 3: Would You Like to...?

1. Check the activities below that you like to do. Add three activities.
2. Choose four things you want to do next week and write them in your calendar.
3. Invite other students to go with you and write their names in your calendar.

☐ go to a movie ☐ go shopping in the mall ☐ play racquetball
☐ have dinner at my home ☐ go to a music concert ☐ go roller skating
☐ have lunch at a restaurant ☐ go to a party ☐ _____
☐ visit a museum ☐ go dancing ☐ _____
☐ go to the zoo ☐ watch a baseball game ☐ _____

	Morning	Afternoon	Evening
Monday			
Tuesday			
Wednesday			
Thursday			
Friday			
Saturday			
Sunday			

Chapter 2 Part 1: Looking for a Place to Live

You are looking for a place to live.
You want a room in a house that is clean, quiet, and near school.

You are looking for a place to live.
You want a large room in a house with a garden because you have a very nice friendly dog.

You are looking for a place to live.
You want a place where you can practice guitar and drums because you are in a rock group.

You are looking for a place to live.
You want a large room in a house with other students. You need parking for your car.

You are looking for a place to live.
You want a room in a house that has a large kitchen because you love cooking and you like to invite your friends for dinner.

You are looking for a roommate.
You have a small room in a house near the school. No pets. No noise. No parking.

You are looking for a roommate.
You have a large room in a house near the school. Large garden. No parking.

You are looking for a roommate.
You have a small room in your house. There are three musicians living there. No parking. No neighbors close by.

You are looking for a roommate.
You have a large room in your house. There are three other students. Parking is available.

You are looking for a roommate.
You have a small room in a house with a large kitchen. No pets. No parking. No noise after 10 P.M.

Name _____ Date _____   BLM 5

Chapter 2 Part 2: Safety on Campus

PART 1: Form groups of four students and have each student choose one of the issues below. Each member of the group will research safety tips about the issue. Write the information in the mind map below.

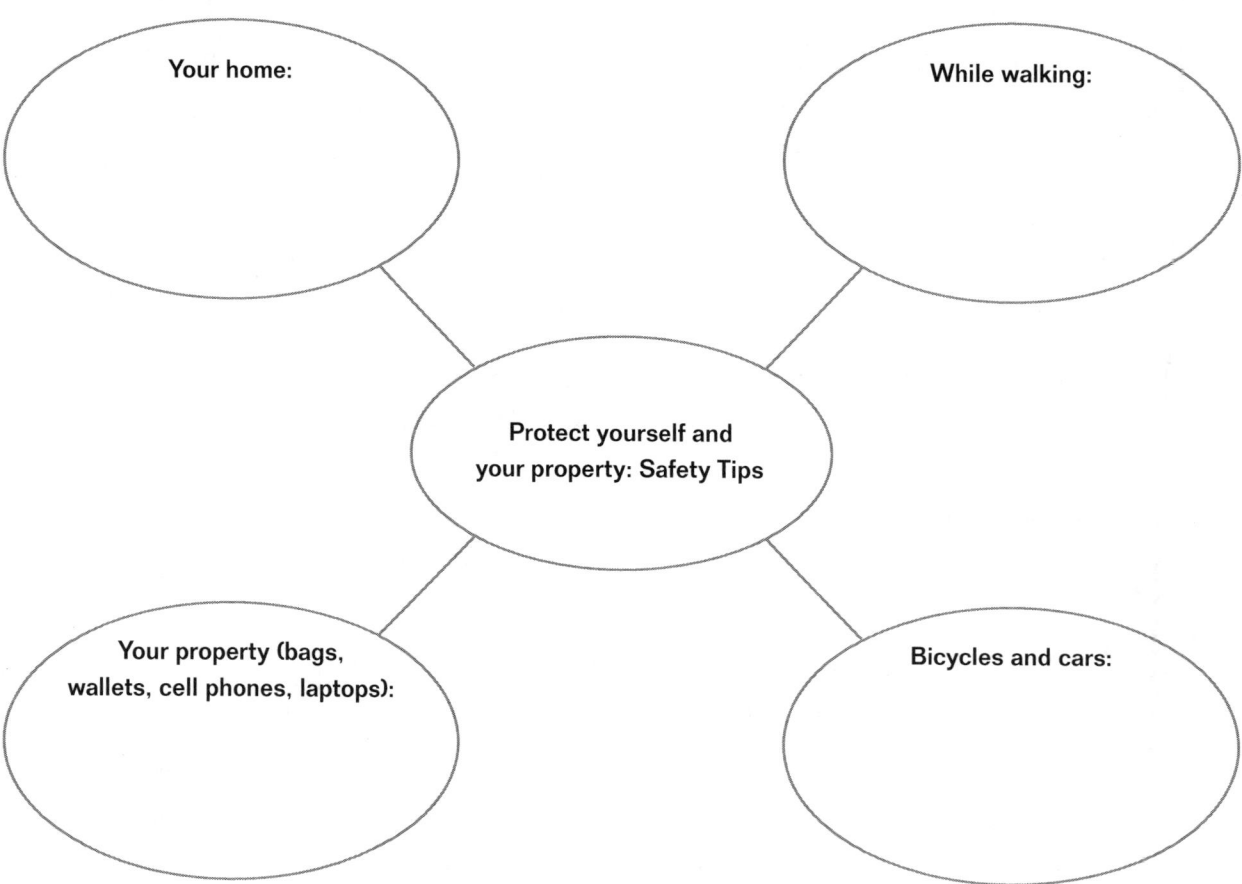

PART 2: Share your information with the group. As you listen to other group members, write the information in the mind map above.

Name _____ Date _____  BLM 6

Chapter 2 Part 3: Can You Fix It?

PART 1: Read the list of problems in the box. Discuss them with your group. Who would you call to fix each problem? Write each problem in a box in the chart.

broken window	broken shower curtain	lights don't work
dripping faucet	broken front door	no electricity
broken toilet	mice	cockroaches
leaking water pipe	bugs in the food	refrigerator doesn't work
microwave doesn't work	broken closet door	shower doesn't work

Plumber	Electrician

Carpetner	Exterminator

Fix it yourself

PART 2: Role-play a conversation with your landlord complaining about one of the problems.

Interactions 2 Listening / Speaking

Name _____ Date _____ BLM 7

Chapter 3 Part 1: Lend or Borrow?

DIRECTIONS Half of the class will be A and the other half will be B. Take this paper and a pencil. Stand up and move around the classroom. Group A students ask classmates to lend them each of the things in Table A. Group B students are able to lend each of the things in Table B only one time. When you borrow or lend an item write the student's name in the chart. Use lend or borrow in your requests.

EXAMPLE: **A:** Excuse me. Can you do me a favor? Could you lend me your cell phone, please? (or Can I borrow your cell phone, please?)

B. Yes, of course. / No, I'm sorry. I lent it to (student's name).

TABLE A:

Items you want to borrow	Student's Name
textbook	
jacket	
cell phone	
pen	
tablet	
dictionary	

TABLE B

Items you can lend	Student's Name
cell phone	
pen	
tablet	
dictionary	
textbook	
jacket	

Try to lend and borrow all the items on your lists. Then switch roles—group A will be group B and group B will be group A.

Name _____ Date _____  BLM 8

Chapter 3 Part 2: Famous Entrepreneurs

PART 1: Form groups of four students and choose one of the famous entrepreneurs listed below. Each member of the group will research information about this entrepreneur and then share it with the group.

Steve Jobs (computers)   Debbie Fields (cookies)
Sam Walton (supermarkets)   Mary Kay Ash (cosmetics)

1. Name:

   Innovation:

   Background:

   Secret of success:

2. Name:

   Innovation:

   Background:

   Secret of success:

3. Name:

   Innovation:

   Background:

   Secret of success:

4. Name:

   Innovation:

   Background:

   Secret of success:

PART 2: In your groups, take a vote on which entrepreneur you admire the most and why. Report the results to the class.

Entrepreneur I admire the most: _____

Reason: _____

Name _____ Date _____

Chapter 3 Part 3: Group Survey

Everybody in this group has a bank account.
Number of students: Yes _____ No _____

Most people in this group have a savings account.
Number of students: Yes _____ No _____

Almost everyone in this group has a credit card.
Number of students: Yes _____ No _____

Some people in this group pay their bills online.
Number of students: Yes _____ No _____

No one in this group dislikes using an ATM.
Number of students: Yes _____ No _____

Most people in this group have bought something online.
Number of students: Yes _____ No _____

Most people in this group use a debit card when they go shopping.
Number of students: Yes _____ No _____

Everyone in this group pays their bills by check.
Number of students: Yes _____ No _____

Most people in this group keep a record of their checks each month.
Number of students: Yes _____ No _____

No one in this group has a safety deposit box.
Number of students: Yes _____ No _____

Name _____ Date _____  BLM 10

Chapter 3 Part 4: Balancing Your Checkbook

STUDENT A

No.	Date	Description	Payment	Deposit	Balance
					598.12
150	5/21	Phone			480.06
151	5/21		60.17		419.89
152	5/23	Auto payment	160.00		
153	5/26	Groceries			79.75
	5/30	Deposit		625.00	704.75
154	6/02		219.45		
155	6/03	Credit card payment			70.30
	6/05	Deposit			386.30
156	6/08	Groceries			236.13
157	6/09		15.00		236.13

STUDENT B

No.	Date	Description	Payment	Deposit	Balance
					598.12
150	5/21		118.06		480.06
151	5/21	Gas	60.17		
152	5/23	Auto payment			259.89
153	5/26		180.14		79.75
	5/30	Deposit			
154	6/02	House insurance			485.30
155	6/03		415.00		
	6/05	Deposit		316.00	386.30
156	6/08	Groceries	150.17		236.13
157	6/09	Doctor			

Chapter 4 Part 1: Saying You're Sorry

You borrowed your friend's dictionary and left it on the train.
You promised to meet your friend in the library after school yesterday, but you forgot and went home.
You borrowed ten dollars from your friend and said you would pay it back today, but you can't.
You can't go to your friend's birthday party because you have a date with your girlfriend or boyfriend.
Your friend gave you a very nice coffee mug for your birthday, and you broke it.
You promised to take your friend to a baseball game on Saturday, but now you can't go.
You borrowed your friend's cell phone and got it wet.
You promised to buy your friend some potato chips in the coffee shop, but you forgot.
You borrowed your friend's bicycle and crashed it. It's a little damaged.
You didn't have time to help your friend study for an exam, and she failed.

Name _____ Date _____  BLM 12

Chapter 4 Part 2: Researching Your Career

PART 1: Form groups of four students. Each student will choose a different job and write the job title in the #1 position in the chart below. Use the Internet to complete the information about your job.

PART 2: Go back to your groups and share your information. Listen, ask questions, and take notes on the three other jobs researched by your group.

Job	Training and qualifications needed	Possible places of employment	Websites
#1:			
#2:			
#3:			
#4:			

PART 3: Discuss your opinions about these four jobs. Which job do you think a) needs the most training and qualifications b) is most in demand c) is the most stressful?

Interactions 2 Listening / Speaking

Chapter 4 Part 4: Tag Questions

DIRECTIONS: Complete the questions with the appropriate tag.

1. This homework is for tomorrow, _____?
2. They are coming to lunch with us, _____?
3. We are going to have a break soon, _____?
4. You live near the school, _____?
5. He has a car, _____?
6. You were absent yesterday, _____?
7. The teacher gave you an A, _____?
8. She took her college exam last week, _____?
9. You'll help me with my homework, _____?
10. We'll finish early today, _____?
11. I got the best grade on the quiz, _____?
12. You have to work late tonight, _____?
13. They study very hard, _____?
14. You're worried about the test, _____?
15. Our teacher's very strict, _____?
16. You know how to drive, _____?
17. She takes the bus to school, _____?
18. We have to finish this activity at home, _____?

Name _____ Date _____

Chapter 5 Part 1: Can You Do Me a Favor?

PART 1: Take this paper and a pencil. Walk around the classroom. Ask classmates to do each of these favors for you. Your classmates will refuse with an excuse. (The excuse can be creative or unusual.) Write the student's name and his or her excuse in the chart.

Example
Student A: Can you do me a favor?
Student B: Sure, what do you need?
Student A: Would you mind looking after my cat this weekend?
Student B: Sorry but I'm allergic to cats.

Favor	Student's Name	Excuse
1. look after my cat this weekend		
2. help me fix my computer		
3. give me a lift to the airport tomorrow morning		
4. help me take boxes to my car		
5. lend me your phone		
6. lend me $20		
7. help me with some gardening this weekend		
8. do some shopping for me tonight		
9. get me a sandwich from the coffee shop		
10. lend me your English dictionary		

PART 2: When you have finished, sit down with a partner and compare answers. Who had the most creative excuse?

Interactions 2 Listening / Speaking

Name _____ Date _____ BLM 15

Chapter 5 Part 2: Starting a Workplace Daycare Center

PART 1: Form groups of four students and have each student choose one of the roles below. Each member of the group will research information to support the opinions of his or her role.

Role 1: Working mother

You are a working mother. You want to return to work because you are well qualified and you enjoy your job. But childcare is very expensive and unreliable. You want to start a daycare center in your company. Research the advantages for the company and present your arguments.

Role 2: Company manager

You are under a lot of pressure from the company director to maintain profits in your company. Research the reasons why it would not be cost-effective to start a daycare center in your company and present your arguments.

Role 3: Workplace child care company representative

You have a lot of experience providing daycare facilities to companies. Research the kinds of services you could offer and reasons why the company should use your services and present your arguments.

Role 4: Employee representative

Many of your co-workers are against workplace daycare because it will cost too much and may reduce other benefits or salaries. Research possible alternatives to providing workplace daycare and present your arguments.

PART 2: After researching the information for your role, go back to your group. Role-play a company discussion about starting a workplace daycare center. Take notes of the arguments in the chart below.

Arguments in favor	Arguments against

PART 3: Present your final decision to the class and explain the reasons.

Interactions 2 Listening / Speaking

Name _____ Date _____  BLM 16

Chapter 5 Part 3: Questionnaire

DIRECTIONS: Read the sentences and check Agree or Disagree, giving your own opinion. Then work in groups. Try to agree on your responses.

What do you think....?
1. Mothers should stay home to look after their children until they go to school. My opinion: _____ Agree _____ Disagree Group opinion: _____ Agree _____ Disagree
2. Fathers should stay home from work to look after their children. My opinion: _____ Agree _____ Disagree Group opinion: _____ Agree _____ Disagree
3. All companies should have free child care facilities for their workers. My opinion: _____ Agree _____ Disagree Group opinion: _____ Agree _____ Disagree
4. Parents should get paid by the government for looking after their children. My opinion: _____ Agree _____ Disagree Group opinion: _____ Agree _____ Disagree
5. Stay-at-home parents should be paid for doing housework. My opinion: _____ Agree _____ Disagree Group opinion: _____ Agree _____ Disagree
6. Families should have no more than two children. My opinion: _____ Agree _____ Disagree Group opinion: _____ Agree _____ Disagree
7. Elderly parents should be looked after at home by their children. My opinion: _____ Agree _____ Disagree Group opinion: _____ Agree _____ Disagree
8. Elderly people should live in retirement homes. My opinion: _____ Agree _____ Disagree Group opinion: _____ Agree _____ Disagree

Interactions 2 Listening / Speaking

Name _____ Date _____  BLM 17

Chapter 6 Part 1: Interrupting Politely

In what way is communicating by email better than by phone?	Why are text messages popular?	What are some dangers of Internet communication for children?	What is most annoying about text messages?
How are cell phones different from landline phones?	Why do people like to have blogs?	What are some possible negative effects of email?	What is the best thing about emails?
Why do people write letters less than they did in the past?	Which do you prefer, email or telephone?	How can the Internet help you with your studies?	How can the Internet help you to stay in touch with other people?
What is one way of cutting down on emails?	What is most annoying about cell phones?	What is most useful about cell phones?	What do you think will be the next major development in communication technology?

Name _____ Date _____  BLM 18

Chapter 6 Part 2: Naming Practices

PART 1: Form groups of four students. Each student will choose one of the countries below and write the country in the chart under Country #1. Use the Internet to complete the information about naming practices in that country.

PART 2: Go back to your groups and share your information. Take notes on the other countries researched by your group. Write your notes in the chart.

PART 3: Summarize the differences and similarities in the naming practices of all four countries.

Choose a country:

| Spain | Vietnam | Iceland | Nigeria |

	System for choosing names	Examples of names
Country #1:		
Country #2:		
Country #3:		
Country #4:		

Interactions 2 Listening / Speaking

Name _____ Date _____

Chapter 7 Part 1: Do You Agree?

DIRECTIONS: Read and complete each sentence, giving your opinion and a reason for your opinion. Some sentences have phrases in parentheses. Choose the positive or negative in each sentence, depending on your opinion.

1. Languages are (are not) difficult to learn because…

2. It is easier to learn another language if…

3. The best way to learn a language is….

4. Misunderstandings usually happen when…

5. We need (don't need) different languages in the world because…

6. You need (don't need) to know about grammar because…

7. Learning in a group is helpful (unhelpful) because…

8. Children should (should not) learn a second or third language because…

9. American English is…

10. British English is…

Name _____ Date _____  BLM 20

Chapter 7 Part 2: Varieties of English

PART 1: Translate the words and expressions into standard American English.

PART 2: Check your answers by researching them on the Internet.

PART 3: Add some more examples for each category.

Canadian English
Vocabulary
  chesterfield _____
  runners _____
Expressions
  Hang up your skates. _____
  Is that skookum? _____
Additional examples:
  _____
  _____
  _____
  _____
  _____

Australian English
Vocabulary
  barbie _____
  esky _____
Expressions
  Good day. _____
  I'm feeling crook. _____
Additional examples:
  _____
  _____
  _____
  _____
  _____

British English
Vocabulary
  queue _____
  chips _____
Expressions
  I'm over the moon. _____
  He's at sixes and sevens. _____
Additional examples:
  _____
  _____
  _____
  _____
  _____

Name _____ Date _____  BLM 21

Chapter 7 Part 4: Spelling Bee

DIRECTIONS: Take turns reading each word aloud to your partner. Your partner will spell the word aloud. Give one point for each correct answer.

STUDENT A

- accommodation _____
- independent _____
- separate _____
- disappointed _____
- business _____
- apparent _____
- believe _____
- misspell _____
- license _____
- occasionally _____

DIRECTIONS: Take turns reading each word aloud to your partner. Your partner will spell the word aloud. Give one point for each correct answer.

STUDENT B

- neighbor _____
- accidentally _____
- changeable _____
- pronunciation _____
- questionnaire _____
- argument _____
- guarantee _____
- height _____
- jewelry _____
- weather _____

Name _____ Date _____  BLM 22.1

Chapter 8 Part 1: What Kind of Person Are You?

DIRECTIONS: Find out if your partner likes or dislikes the following.

STUDENT A

Do you like to…	I love it.	It's OK.	I can't stand it.
1. …have long conversations on the phone?			
2. …talk to other people about your problems?			
3. …invite all your friends on your birthday?			
4. …go to parties and meet new people?			
5. …cook for family and friends?			
6. …go out with a group of friends?			
7. …be busy all day?			
8. …have a job where you can meet lots of people?			
9. …meet your friends every lunch break?			
10. …go out with your friends every night?			

Scoring system:
   I love it. = 3 points
   It's OK. = 2 points
   I can't stand it. = 1 point

Score:
   20–30: You are very sociable and outgoing. You love meeting people and talking.
   10–20: You are sometimes sociable, but you like to have your privacy, too.
   1–10: You are shy and quiet. You like to have a few close friends who understand you.

Name _____ Date _____  BLM 22.2

Chapter 8 Part 1: What Kind of Person Are You?

DIRECTIONS: Find out if your partner likes or dislikes the following.

STUDENT B

Do you like to…	I love it.	It's OK.	I can't stand it.
1. …read a book when you want to relax?			
2. …think quietly on your own when you have a problem?			
3. …celebrate your birthday alone?			
4. …go to parties where you know everyone?			
5. …read a book or a magazine on your lunch break?			
6. …go out with just one or two good friends?			
7. …be alone for a part of every day?			
8. …have a job where you can concentrate and not talk?			
9. …have coffee by yourself in a coffee shop?			
10. …stay home most nights and go out only once a week?			

Scoring system:
I love it. = 3 points
It's OK. = 2 points
I can't stand it. = 1 point

Score:
20–30: You are very sociable and outgoing. You love meeting people and talking.
10–20: You are sometimes sociable, but you like to have your privacy, too.
1–10: You are shy and quiet. You like to have a few close friends who understand you.

Name _____   Date _____    BLM 23

Chapter 8 Part 2: What Do You Mean?

DIRECTIONS: Complete the following sentences with appropriate paraphrases:

1. Most jobs nowadays require some computer skills. In other words, there are very few jobs that _____.

2. Two-thirds of all teenagers in the U.S. have a cell phone. To put it another way, _____.

3. If you want to get the latest music downloads, you have to go online. What I mean is _____.

4. More people tend to watch movies at home online nowadays. That is to say, fewer people _____.

5. Higher gas prices mean that people are buying smaller cars. In other words, people aren't _____.

6. There has been an increase in demand for sport vacations in distant locations. In other words, _____.

7. Consumers are becoming more concerned about the salt and sugar content in their food. What I mean is _____.

8. Online shopping is a way for busy people to save time. To put this another way, _____.

9. Many people now use their tablets to watch movies and listen to music. That is to say, they don't _____.

10. Nowadays you can get news instantly on the Internet, I mean, you don't have to _____.

Interactions 2 Listening / Speaking   CHAPTER 8   BLM 23

Name _____ Date _____  BLM 24

Chapter 8 Part 4: Fads and Fashions

DIRECTIONS:

1. Choose one of the topics in the box below. Decide if you approve or disapprove.

2. Work with your group to fill out the chart. Write your reasons why each of the people in the chart might or might not approve of it.

3. Choose one of the roles and discuss your topic.

Topic choices

New! Cell phones for children aged 5–7!	Home Tattoo Kit. Painless. Easy to use!	Diet foods for teenagers. Delicious and low-calorie!	Car TVs, and computers. Entertainment for your car!

Group topic: _____

	Reasons for approving	Reasons for disapproving
Parents		
Police/Doctors		
Teachers:		
Sales representatives		

BLM 24 CHAPTER 8 Interactions 2 Listening / Speaking

Name _____ Date _____  BLM 25

Chapter 9 Part 3: That's Amazing!

STEP 1: Work in groups of three students. Fill in the diagram with information about your skills and abilities. In the space where all three circles overlap, write the skills that all three of you have. In the space where only two circles overlap, write the skills that two of you have. In the remaining spaces, write the skills that only one person has.

STEP 2: Share your information with other groups and tell them the most amazing, interesting, or surprising things that you found out about your group.

STEP 3: Based on the shared abilities in your group, what kind of enterprise or adventure would you be best at? Think of a name for your new enterprise.

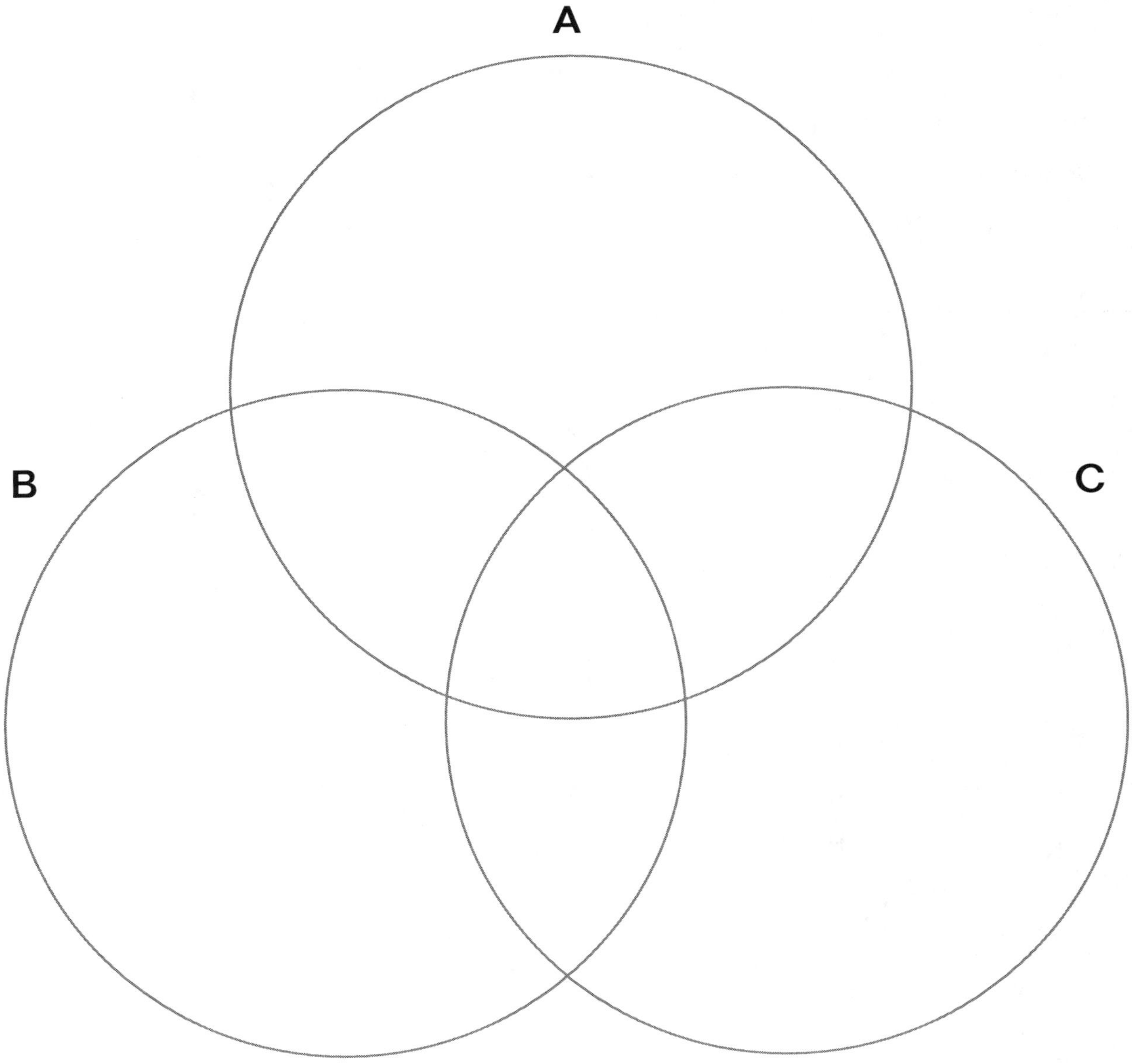

A

B   **C**

Interactions 2 Listening / Speaking   CHAPTER 9   BLM 25

Chapter 9 Part 4: Inventions and Discoveries

penicillin	the Internet	DNA	the theory of gravity
electricity	the home computer	the printing press	the telescope
the telephone	television	the steam engine	Wild card: Choose your own invention or discovery!
gunpowder	chocolate	home video cassette recorder	Wild card: Choose your own invention or discovery!
paper	sewing machine	the automobile	Wild card: Choose your own invention or discovery!

Name _____ Date _____  BLM 27

Chapter 10 Part 1: May I Help You?

I'm having a birthday party on Saturday, and my apartment is a mess.
I have a bad backache, and I can't go out.
My parents are coming this weekend, and my car has broken down.
I've invited 20 people to dinner at my house for my sister's birthday.
I have to go away this weekend, and I can't find anyone to look after my cat.
I don't know what to buy for my parents' anniversary.
I have to work overtime this weekend, and I don't have time to shop for groceries.
I can't find anything to wear for my best friend's wedding.
I have to finish my assignment by tomorrow morning, but my computer is broken.
I don't understand my homework assignment.

Name _____ Date _____   BLM 28

Chapter 10, Part 2: Ceremonies Around the World

PART 1: Choose one of the ceremonies from the list below.

PART 2: Choose four countries that have different traditions for this ceremony.

PART 3: Fill out as much of the chart as you can. Use the Internet to research additional information.

PART 4: Share your information with your group.

| birthday | wedding | graduation | coming of age | birth | death |

Name of Cermony: _____

	Activities	Clothing (choose one main item)	Food (choose one main item)	Symbolic meaning of ceremony
Country 1				
Country 2				
Country 3				
Country 4				

Name _____ Date _____ BLM 29

Chapter 10 Part 3: Congratulations and Sympathy

I broke my ankle last weekend when I went skiing.
My cat died yesterday.
I just passed my driver's test.
I won $500 in the lottery.
My uncle's funeral is tomorrow.
I just got a new job.
I passed my college examination.
I won a scholarship for college.
My best friend got injured in a car accident.
I got fired from my job.
I just got promoted.
My bicycle was stolen.
I'm going to graduate tomorrow.
I have just gotten engaged to be married.
I'm getting married on Sunday.

Interactions 2 Listening / Speaking

Name _____ Date _____ Score _____

CHAPTER 1 Test — Interactions 2 Listening/Speaking

SECTION I Listening to a Conversation Listen to the conversation. Then choose the best answer to each question. *(4 points each)*

1. Where are the two people?
   - A in a bookstore
   - B in a library
   - C on a college campus

2. Which building does the man want to find?
   - A art museum
   - B gym
   - C music building

3. Where is the building?
   - A at Willow Street and Alumni Street
   - B at the intersection of Willow Street and College Avenue
   - C between Willow Street and Alumni Street

4. Which of these is true?
   - A The woman asks the man to walk with him.
   - B The woman asks the man if he wants to walk with her.
   - C The man asks the woman if he can walk with her.

5. When Yumi says, "Oh, really?" what feeling does she express?
   - A boredom
   - B interest
   - C shyness

SECTION II Listening to a Lecture Listen to the lecture. Then choose the best answer to each question. Listen to the Lecture again. *(4 points each)*

1. The lecture is about four types of _____.
   - A colleges
   - B classes
   - C subjects

2. What can you practice in the small group classes?
   - A speaking
   - B business
   - C computer skills

3. What do you do in the language lab class?
   - A work with a teacher
   - B work in a group
   - C work individually

T1 CHAPTER 1 TEST

CHAPTER 1 **Test**   Interactions 2 Listening/Speaking

4. What is the maximum individual study you can sign up for?
   - Ⓐ up to three hours a week
   - Ⓑ up to two hours a week
   - Ⓒ up to one hour a week

5. What is the most popular type of class?
   - Ⓐ small group
   - Ⓑ language lab
   - Ⓒ individual study

SECTION III **New Words** Use the words in the box to complete the activities below. *(4 points each)*

cite	fill out	paraphrase	rush	term paper
dormitory	major	plagiarism	syllabus	unique

Fill in the blanks with words from the box.

1. Reading assignments, quizzes, and exams are all part of the course _____.
2. When you write a research paper, it is important to _____ the sources of your information.
3. Kenji wants to live in a _____ on campus.
4. You sometimes have to research and write a _____ in order to get a grade.
5. When you register for courses, you have to _____ some forms with personal information.

Find words from the box with the same meaning as the words in italics.

6. Joanne's *specialty* is computer design. _____
7. To *put it in other words*, I am very happy at this university. _____
8. My French professor has a very *unusual* way of teaching. _____
9. *Copying someone else's words without giving the source* is not tolerated at U.S. universities. _____
10. We will be late for class if we don't *hurry*. _____

CHAPTER 1   Test   Interactions 2 Listening/Speaking

SECTION IV Using Language Use the five expressions in the box to complete the conversation.
(4 points each)

| can't | thanks | wondering |
| sure | what did you say | |

Lianne: Hi, Pete. I was _____1_____ if you want to see a movie tonight.

Pete: Sorry. _____2_____? Can you repeat that?

Lianne: Do you want to go see a movie tonight?

Pete: I'd like to, but I _____3_____. But _____4_____ for asking. How about Friday night?

Lianne: _____5_____! Friday night is good.

TOTAL _____ /100 pts.

Name _____ Date _____ Score _____

CHAPTER 2 Test — Interactions 2 Listening/Speaking

SECTION I Listening to a Conversation Listen to the conversation. Then choose the best answer to each question. *(4 points each)*

1. Who is Ken talking to?
   - A) a roommate
   - B) a friend
   - C) a house-owner

2. Ken wants to know about _____.
   - A) the rent
   - B) the location
   - C) the rent and the location

3. How many students are living in the house now?
   - A) one student
   - B) two students
   - C) three students

4. Ken is moving because _____.
   - A) he has a cat
   - B) he needs somewhere quieter
   - C) he needs to be alone

5. What does *Do you mind pets?* mean?
   - A) Do you like pets?
   - B) Do you allow pets?
   - C) Do you have pets?

SECTION II Listening to a Talk Listen to the talk. Then choose the best answer to each question. Listen to the talk again. *(4 points each)*

1. The talk is about _____ type(s) of security on campus.
   - A) one
   - B) three
   - C) five

2. Which of these should you *not* do?
   - A) loan your key
   - B) lock your door
   - C) leave your room

3. Where should you *not* walk at night?
   - A) in dark areas
   - B) well-lighted areas
   - C) near phones

CHAPTER 2 TEST T4

CHAPTER 2 Test — Interactions 2 Listening/Speaking

4. What should you do *before* you go out?
   - (A) carry a cell phone
   - (B) have your key ready
   - (C) tell friends where you are going

5. How can you prevent theft of your property?
   - (A) study in the library
   - (B) watch your property carefully
   - (C) take a self-defense class

SECTION III New Words Use the words in the box to complete Activities 1 and 2 below. *(4 points each)*

alarm	break in	can't miss it	come by	device
lifts a finger	prevent	slob	timer	valuables

1. Fill in the blanks with words from the box.

1. A _____ can be used to turn your lights on and off automatically.
2. My roommate never cleans up his room. He's a real _____.
3. If you leave the window of your home open, it's easy for someone to _____.
4. It's a good idea to have a locking _____ on the steering wheel of your car.
5. A car _____ makes a lot of noise, but it does not usually help to prevent car theft.

2. Find words from the box with the same meaning as the words in italics.

6. You should not leave *expensive things* in your car. _____
7. Neighborhood Watch tries to *stop* crime in the neighborhood. _____
8. My house is on the corner. You *will find it easily*. _____
9. My roommate never *helps* with the housework. _____
10. Why don't you *visit* us after school tomorrow? _____

CHAPTER 2 Test   Interactions 2 Listening/Speaking

SECTION IV Using Language Use the five expressions below to complete the dialog.
(4 points each)

| I'd love | sure | thanks |
| were you | would you | |

Lianne: Hi, Pete. _____1 planning to go to the movies tonight?

Pete: I'm not sure…

Lianne: Well, _____2 like to go?

Pete: _____3, but I have my midterm next week, and I have to study…

Lianne: You can study tomorrow, can't you?

Pete: Well, that's true. OK, _____4 to go. Thanks for inviting me.

Lianne: _____5. I'm glad you can come.

TOTAL _____ /100 pts.

Name _____ Date _____ Score _____

CHAPTER 3 Test — Interactions 2 Listening/Speaking

SECTION I Listening to a Conversation Listen to the conversation. Then choose the best answer to each question. *(4 points each)*

1. What does the customer want to do?
   - Ⓐ apply for a credit card
   - Ⓑ borrow some money
   - Ⓒ pay back a loan

2. What does the bank clerk advise the customer to do?
   - Ⓐ apply for new credit card
   - Ⓑ talk to another bank
   - Ⓒ speak to a loan specialist

3. The bank clerk suggests that a different type of loan would be _____.
   - Ⓐ cheaper
   - Ⓑ faster
   - Ⓒ easier

4. What is the interest on Elsa's credit card?
   - Ⓐ 8%
   - Ⓑ 18%
   - Ⓒ 80%

5. What kind of loan is Elsa interested in?
   - Ⓐ a personal loan
   - Ⓑ a car loan
   - Ⓒ a home improvement loan

SECTION II Listening to a Lecture Listen to the lecture. Then choose the best answer to each question. Listen to the lecture again. *(4 points each)*

1. The lecture is about four types of _____.
   - Ⓐ products and services
   - Ⓑ new inventions
   - Ⓒ entrepreneurial ideas

2. The idea of a home computer _____.
   - Ⓐ was a new way of doing business
   - Ⓑ created a new product
   - Ⓒ solved a problem

3. In what way was Anita Roddick's chain of stores a new idea?
   - Ⓐ She invented a new type of cosmetic.
   - Ⓑ She specialized in natural cosmetics.
   - Ⓒ She has 2,000 stores around the world.

CHAPTER 3 Test — Interactions 2 Listening/Speaking

4. Henry Ford's idea of the assembly line is an example of _____.
   - (A) a new method of production
   - (B) a new product or service
   - (C) an improvement of an existing product

5. In what way was Jeff Bezos' company a new idea?
   - (A) It was a new way of selling books.
   - (B) It is a multimillion-dollar business.
   - (C) It sells books to customers directly.

SECTION III New Words Use the words in the box to complete the paragraph below.
(4 points each)

| balance | borrow | budget | capital | checking |
| earn | interest | lend | risks | statement |

Most people have a _____ account at a bank where they can take out money by
                        1
using a check or a debit card. Whenever you write a check or make a deposit, you should keep
a record of it. Then it will be easier for you to _____ your checkbook. The bank
                                                         2
usually sends you a _____ at the end of every month with details of your account.
                          3
If you want to make sure that you do not spend more than you _____, you should
                                                                        4
try to keep to a _____. It's better not to _____ too much money on
                       5   6
your credit card because the rate of _____ is usually very high. Banks sometimes
                                              7
_____ money to people who want to start their own business, but entrepreneurs also
      8
need to raise _____ by getting other people to invest. They need to be ready to take
                    9
_____ because they might make a profit, or they might lose everything.
      10

CHAPTER 3 Test

Interactions 2 Listening/Speaking

SECTION IV Using Language Complete the conversation with the phrases from the box.
(4 points each)

| I suggest that you | you recommend | should I do |
| can you give me | think about it | |

Monica: How did it go with your Dad on the phone?

Billy: Oh it's the same story. He says I have to stick to a budget and he won't lend me any money.

What _____1_____?

Monica: I'm not sure. Have you tried asking your Mom?

Billy: Well, she always agrees with Dad. _____2_____ any other advice? I'm really broke.

What do _____3_____?

Monica: I can lend you some money for this week, but _____4_____ try and get a part-time job that pays more than that computer store.

Billy: Thanks, I'll _____5_____.

TOTAL _____ /100 pts.

Name _____ Date _____ Score _____

CHAPTER 4 Test   Interactions 2 Listening/Speaking

SECTION I Listening to a Conversation Listen to the conversation. Then choose the best answer to each question. *(4 points each)*

1. Who is Andrew talking to?
    - (A) a friend
    - (B) a co-worker
    - (C) a manager
2. What kind of job does Andrew want?
    - (A) a computer programmer
    - (B) a computer analyst
    - (C) a computer salesperson
3. How much work experience does Andrew have?
    - (A) a lot
    - (B) a little
    - (C) none
4. What does Andrew do in his spare time?
    - (A) He plays on computers.
    - (B) He spends money on computers.
    - (C) He learns about computers.
5. What did the manager assume about Andrew's education?
    - (A) He doesn't have a college degree.
    - (B) He already has a college degree.
    - (C) He is going to have a college degree.

SECTION II Listening to a Lecture Listen to the lecture. Then choose the best answer to each question. Listen to the lecture again. *(4 points each)*

1. What is the main topic of this lecture?
    - (A) how technology has changed
    - (B) how technology has changed us
    - (C) how technology has changed our work
2. One effect has been the trend in people working from home. What does *trend* mean in this sentence?
    - (A) ability
    - (B) increase
    - (C) advantage
3. What is one effect of working from home?
    - (A) It's difficult to separate work and home life.
    - (B) It's difficult to have time for family life.
    - (C) We have to work all the time.

CHAPTER 4 TEST   **T10**

CHAPTER 4 Test   Interactions 2 Listening/Speaking

4. Why are workers losing interpersonal skills?
   - (A) because they always use email
   - (B) because they don't like talking
   - (C) because they waste time

5. Why have jobs moved to other countries?
   - (A) because people don't have skills in the U.S.
   - (B) because there aren't enough workers in the U.S.
   - (C) because salaries are lower in other countries

SECTION III New Words Use the words in the box to complete the sentences below. *(4 points each)*

automation	competition	complain	labor	manufacturing
market	part-time	salary	service	support

1. Jobs where people make things like cars or clothes are known as _____ jobs.
2. Jobs where people do things like cook food or drive a taxi are known as _____ jobs.
3. If you work for a company and they pay you every month, that is your _____.
4. I was not satisfied with the food in the restaurant, so I called the manager to _____.
5. I work 12 hours a week, so it is only a _____ job.
6. Jon helps _____ his parents so he gives them some money every month.
7. The money employers pay workers is their _____ costs.
8. _____ is causing some companies to cut jobs and increase the number of robots.
9. There are many more computer- and health-related jobs in the job _____ today.
10. It is difficult for U.S. companies to fight _____ from other countries where salaries are lower.

CHAPTER 4 Test   Interactions 2 Listening/Speaking

SECTION IV Using Language Complete the conversation with words from the box. *(4 points each)*

didn't	aren't	doesn't
haven't	don't	

Peter: You've been working in the library for quite some time, _____(1)_____ you?

Chen: Yes, for about eight years.

Peter: You had some experience before, _____(2)_____ you?

Chen: Yes, I worked in the public library for two years before this.

Peter: And you like this job, _____(3)_____ you?

Chen: It's interesting and I like helping people. Your sister works in a library, _____(4)_____ she?

Peter: Yes, and she loves it.

Chen: I think you're planning to apply for the new librarian's job, _____(5)_____ you?

Peter: How did you guess?

TOTAL _____ /100 pts.

Name _____ Date _____ Score _____

CHAPTER 5 | Test   Interactions 2 Listening/Speaking

SECTION I Listening to a Conversation Listen to the conversation. Then choose the best answer to each question. *(4 points each)*

1. Sandra is a _____.
   - A homemaker
   - B single mother
   - C teenager

2. Where is Sandra living now?
   - A with her parents
   - B by herself
   - C with friends

3. What is Sandra looking for?
   - A a babysitter
   - B a job
   - C an apartment

4. Which sentence is true?
   - A Sandra has a new job.
   - B Sandra went back to her old job.
   - C Sandra doesn't have a job.

5. Who is Sandra speaking to?
   - A a co-worker
   - B her mother
   - C a friend

SECTION II Listening to a Lecture Listen to the lecture. Choose the best answer to each question. Listen to the lecture again. *(4 points each)*

1. What is the main topic of this lecture?
   - A people getting older
   - B workers getting older
   - C retirement

2. How many babies were born during the baby boom?
   - A 19 million
   - B 46 million
   - C 76 million

3. Who are the baby boomers?
   - A people born between 1946 and 1964
   - B people born 19 years ago
   - C people born in 1978

CHAPTER 5 Test   Interactions 2 Listening/Speaking

4. The percentage of workers aged 45 and older will increase _____.
   - Ⓐ from 25 to 44 percent
   - Ⓑ from 33 to 40 percent
   - Ⓒ from 38.7 to 40.7 percent

5. What will happen because of changes in pensions?
   - Ⓐ Pensions will go up.
   - Ⓑ People will not be able to retire.
   - Ⓒ People will retire later.

SECTION III New Words Use the words in the box to complete the paragraph below. (4 points each)

bring up	check up on	cost of living	daycare	flexible
homemakers	maternity	old-fashioned	opportunity	run out

Many mothers need to work because the ___1___ is very high. It is very difficult for a mother to ___2___ a child and go out to work at the same time. Companies have to give new mothers 12 weeks of ___3___ leave. When they ___4___ of leave, they have to make some difficult decisions. Some companies offer ___5___ centers, where mothers can ___6___ their children at any time of the day. But most companies prefer to offer more ___7___ working hours, or the ___8___ to work from home. Some mothers decide to stay home when they have young children. They choose to be ___9___ — doing the shopping, cooking, and housework for the family, but this work is usually unpaid and some people think it is ___10___.

CHAPTER 5   Test   Interactions 2 Listening/Speaking

SECTION IV Using Language Complete the conversation with the words and phrases from the box.
(4 points each)

| would you | let me | do |
| I'd like | do you need | |

Miguel: Cheri, can you _____(1)_____ me a big favor?

Cheri: Yes, of course. What _____(2)_____?

Miguel: _____(3)_____ mind looking after my little sister while I go to the baseball game on Saturday?

Cheri: Well, _____(4)_____ to help you, but I'm kind of busy this weekend, you know...

Miguel: I don't often ask you for a favor. Please?

Cheri: OK. _____(5)_____ think about it.

Miguel: Thanks.

TOTAL _____ /100 pts.

Name _____ Date _____ Score _____

CHAPTER 6 Test Interactions 2 Listening/Speaking

SECTION I Listening to a Conversation Listen to the conversation. Then choose the best answer to each question. *(4 points each)*

1. What is Gina's job?
   - Ⓐ a student
   - Ⓑ a teacher
   - Ⓒ a computer programmer

2. What is Gina's problem?
   - Ⓐ She doesn't like emails.
   - Ⓑ She doesn't have time to answer all her emails.
   - Ⓒ She doesn't know how to use email.

3. What advice does Mike give?
   - Ⓐ Answer all emails immediately.
   - Ⓑ Only answer important emails.
   - Ⓒ Answer important emails first.

4. What is Mike's advice about a website?
   - Ⓐ Answer emails on a website.
   - Ⓑ Write emails to a website.
   - Ⓒ Post messages on a website.

5. Which sentence is true?
   - Ⓐ Kendra interrupts Gina and Mike because Gina received a phone call.
   - Ⓑ Mike interrupts Gina because Gina received a phone call.
   - Ⓒ Mike interrupts Gina and Kendra because Kendra received a phone call.

SECTION II Listening to a Lecture Listen to the lecture. Choose the best answer to each question. Listen to the lecture again. *(4 points each)*

1. What is the main topic of this lecture?
   - Ⓐ rules of politeness in different cultures
   - Ⓑ ways of shaking hands
   - Ⓒ how to solve misunderstandings

2. What is most important when Americans meet?
   - Ⓐ to be friendly
   - Ⓑ to offer help
   - Ⓒ to use first names

3. What is most important when Japanese meet?
   - Ⓐ to make eye contact
   - Ⓑ to ask each other for help
   - Ⓒ to offer help

CHAPTER 6 Test — Interactions 2 Listening/Speaking

4. What message is communicated by avoiding eye contact in American culture?
   - (A) politeness
   - (B) insincerity
   - (C) friendliness

5. What can we learn from this comparison?
   - (A) that Americans are not polite
   - (B) that Japanese are more polite
   - (C) that rules of politeness can cause misunderstandings

SECTION III New Words Look at the list of words below. Use the words to complete the sentences. *(4 points each)*

| catch up on | deadline | gestures | interrupt | stay in touch |
| convenient | feedback | hug | offended | unintentionally |

1. Our English teacher says it's ok to _____ her if we don't understand something. But we do it politely!

2. _____ can have different meanings in different cultures, and this can cause misunderstandings.

3. In Latin cultures, it is not unusual for strangers to _____ each other on a happy occasion.

4. Many people use Facebook to _____ with friends.

5. I _____ on my homework—and my sleep!—on the weekend.

6. I have an important _____ this week. I must submit my presentation by Friday.

7. If you point your foot at someone in Egypt, a person might feel _____.

8. Sue received very positive _____ from Professor Jones about her term paper.

9. It is important to know about nonverbal communication in other cultures to avoid offending someone _____.

10. In today's globalized world, having a tablet or smartphone makes communication very _____.

CHAPTER 6 Test

Interactions 2 Listening/Speaking

SECTION IV **Using Language** Match the sentences that have the same meanings. *(4 points each)*

1. _____ May I interrupt?
2. _____ Are there any disadvantages?
3. _____ Could you repeat that?
4. _____ Are there any good points?
5. _____ Are they different?

a. Are there any drawbacks?
b. Can you say that again?
c. Are they the opposite?
d. Can I say something?
e. Are there any advantages?

TOTAL ____ /100 pts.

Name _____ Date _____ Score _____

CHAPTER 7 Test Interactions 2 Listening/Speaking

SECTION I Listening to a Conversation Listen to the conversation. Choose the best answer to each question. *(4 points each)*

1. What is the main topic of the conversation?
    - A telephones
    - B telephone messages
    - C automated phone systems
2. What doesn't Jenny like?
    - A phoning
    - B leaving messages
    - C waiting
3. Why does Stan disagree with Jenny about the job?
    - A He thinks it's a boring job.
    - B He prefers to speak to a real person.
    - C He thinks it saves time.
4. Which is true at the end of the conversation?
    - A Jenny contradicts Stan.
    - B Stan contradicts Jenny.
    - C Jenny and Stan agree.
5. What does *aha* mean?
    - A What does that mean?
    - B I understand.
    - C I'm not sure. Let me think.

SECTION II Listening to a Lecture Listen to the lecture. Choose the best answer to each question. Listen to the lecture again. *(4 points each)*

1. What is the main topic of this lecture?
    - A mistakes in English
    - B grammar and vocabulary
    - C spoken and written English
2. Which three categories are mentioned in the lecture?
    - A pronunciation, spelling, and grammar
    - B intonation, vocabulary, and mistakes
    - C medium of communication, vocabulary, and grammar
3. What can you use to convey mood in written English?
    - A stress
    - B punctuation
    - C intonation

CHAPTER 7 Test Interactions 2 Listening/Speaking

4. Which is not used in formal written English?
- (A) slang
- (B) pronouns
- (C) stress

5. Which sentence is true?
- (A) People often notice mistakes in spoken English.
- (B) People don't often notice mistakes in written English.
- (C) People often make mistakes in spoken English.

SECTION III New Words Use the words in the box to complete the paragraph. *(4 points each)*

| catch on | dialect | friendliness | friendship | identical |
| majority | noticeable | two-faced | unique | whereas |

When you move to a new culture, it is sometimes difficult to understand differences in communication. Every culture has its own _____1_____ way of interacting, and it usually takes a while to _____2_____. In the U.S., for example, people are often impressed by everyone's _____3_____ when they first meet, but true _____4_____ takes some time to build up. When someone says *How are you?*, it's just a greeting like *hello* or *hi*. They do not usually want to know about your health or your mood, but this does not mean they are _____5_____. Misunderstandings can also arise between speakers of English because of differences in _____6_____. British and American English have a few _____7_____ differences in pronunciation and vocabulary. For example, Americans use the word *elevator* _____8_____ British speakers use the word *lift*. But the _____9_____ of English speakers have no trouble understanding each other, and in general, the grammar and vocabulary of these language varieties are almost _____10_____.

CHAPTER 7 Test — Interactions 2 Listening/Speaking

SECTION IV Using Language Match the interjections such as *uh-huh* and *uh-oh* with their meanings. *(4 points each)*

1. _____ A: Is this seat free?
   B: Uh-huh.
2. _____ A: Be careful with that coffee!
   B: Oops!
3. _____ A: Did you remember about the test today?
   B: Uh-oh.
4. _____ A: There's a problem with your intermodular protocol regulator.
   B: Huh?
5. _____ A: Do you know where the key to the store room is?
   B: Hmm…

a. What does that mean?
b. I dropped something.
c. I'm not sure. Let me think.
d. I forgot something.
e. Yes.

TOTAL _____ /100 pts.

Name _____ Date _____ Score _____

CHAPTER 8 Test Interactions 2 Listening/Speaking

SECTION I Listening to a Conversation Listen to the conversation. Then choose the best answer to each question. *(4 points each)*

1. What is the conversation is about?
   - Ⓐ birthdays
   - Ⓑ travel
   - Ⓒ food
2. What does Maria think of Mexican food?
   - Ⓐ She loves it.
   - Ⓑ She doesn't mind it.
   - Ⓒ She hates it.
3. What does Joe think of spicy food?
   - Ⓐ He likes it.
   - Ⓑ He doesn't like it.
   - Ⓒ He doesn't hate it.
4. What does Joe think of Indian food?
   - Ⓐ He likes it.
   - Ⓑ He doesn't mind it.
   - Ⓒ He hates it.
5. Which statement is true about Joe?
   - Ⓐ He doesn't like to try new food.
   - Ⓑ He likes to try new food.
   - Ⓒ He is not interested in food.

SECTION II Listening to an Interview Listen to the interview. Choose the best answer to each question. Listen to the interview again. *(4 points each)*

1. What is the main topic of this interview?
   - Ⓐ food
   - Ⓑ fashion
   - Ⓒ music
2. What is an example of a natural material?
   - Ⓐ wool
   - Ⓑ nylon
   - Ⓒ polyester
3. What does *spread the message* mean?
   - Ⓐ make more money
   - Ⓑ make the issue popular
   - Ⓒ save the environment

CHAPTER 8 Test

Interactions 2 Listening/Speaking

4. What is *vintage clothing*?
   - Ⓐ last year's fashion
   - Ⓑ environmental fashion
   - Ⓒ fashion from the 50s and 60s

5. What does Marietta hope to do by combining old and new?
   - Ⓐ make people keep their clothing for longer
   - Ⓑ make people buy more clothing
   - Ⓒ make people throw their clothing away

SECTION III New Words Use the words in the box to complete each sentence. *(4 points each)*

confident	conflict	diverse	income	loyal
optimistic	phenomenon	significant	see eye to eye	tolerant

1. There are more than 70 million people in Generation Y. That is a very _____ number.
2. They come from a variety of ethnic backgrounds. They are _____.
3. They are sure about their ability to succeed. They are _____.
4. They are very positive about the future. They are _____.
5. They accept a wide variety of different opinions. They are _____.
6. They don't stay with one brand or product. They aren't _____ to one type of product.
7. They have different values than their parents. There is sometimes a _____ between their values and those of the older generation.
8. They sometime disagree with their parents. They don't always _____ with their parents.
9. They spend money at the mall. They like to spend a lot of their _____ on fashion, fast food, movies, CDs, electronics, and concert tickets.
10. This generation of young people with these characteristics is found in many countries around the world. It is an international _____.

CHAPTER 8 Test — Interactions 2 Listening/Speaking

SECTION IV Using Language Fill in the blanks with words from the box below. *(4 points each)*

| for | agains | in favor |
| approve | disapprove | |

Janet: Are you _____ of laws that forbid smoking?
                       1

Dan: I _____ of smoking in public spaces or at work, but I think people can do
              2
what they like at home. What do you think?

Janet: I'm _____ smoking. It's really bad for your health.
                  3

Dan: Would you _____ of anti-smoking laws then?
                          4

Janet: Yes, I'm _____ a total ban.
                        5

TOTAL ____ /100 pts.

Name _____ Date _____ Score _____

CHAPTER 9 Test   Interactions 2 Listening/Speaking

SECTION I Listening to a Conversation Listen to the conversation. Then choose the best answer to each question. *(4 points each)*

1. What is the main topic of the conversation?
   - A heart problems
   - B medical advances
   - C new medicines

2. Why did the girl need a second heart operation?
   - A because her new heart didn't work
   - B because her old heart didn't work
   - C because she needed another heart

3. When Jane says *That's so weird.* what does she mean?
   - A It's good.
   - B It's not true.
   - C It's strange.

4. When Jane says, "*Unbelievable!*" What does she mean?
   - A I don't believe you.
   - B It's hard to believe.
   - C It isn't true.

5. Why is the story amazing?
   - A because the girl's original heart got better
   - B because the girl was born with two hearts
   - C because the girl had a new heart

SECTION II Listening to a Lecture Listen to the lecture. Choose the best answer to each question. Listen to the lecture again. *(4 points each)*

1. What is the main topic of this lecture?
   - A theories about life on Mars
   - B exploration of Mars
   - C reasons for exploring space

2. According to the lecture, which of these is a fact?
   - A People want to travel to other planets.
   - B People want to know if there is life on other planets.
   - C People have found evidence of life on other planets.

3. Which of these was true in the 19th century?
   - A They thought there was water on Mars.
   - B They found evidence of water on Mars.
   - C They found evidence of life on Mars.

CHAPTER 9 Test
Interactions 2 Listening/Speaking

4. Which of these is true about the meteorite from Mars?
   - (A) There was evidence of life.
   - (B) There was no evidence of life.
   - (C) There was disagreement about the evidence of life.

5. How can scientists get more evidence of life on Mars?
   - (A) by studying rocks that are similar to the ones they found on Earth
   - (B) by getting rocks from Mars where life may have survived the longest
   - (C) by collecting older rocks from Mars

SECTION III New Words Look at the list of words below. Use the words to complete the paragraph. *(4 points each)*

appliances	display	essential	installs	potential
convenient	efficient	impact	leave on	utility bill

Ken works for an energy company. The company has a product that helps people lower their energy usage and, therefore, the price of their _____1_____. The company _____2_____ a device in your home. It monitors your _____3_____, such as your refrigerator, and your lights. The device has a _____4_____ on the front that shows exactly how much electricity you are using. This makes it very easy and _____5_____ to think about your habits and to change them so that you use less energy. The device also shows you which appliances are using a lot of electricity, that is, the ones that are not energy-_____6_____.

The company also gives you advice about how to use less energy, such as the piece of advice we all know—do not _____7_____ the lights when you go out of a room!

In today's world, it is _____8_____ that we conserve energy. The device from Ken's company has great _____9_____. If everyone uses this device, it can have a big _____10_____ on energy usage.

CHAPTER 9 Test Interactions 2 Listening/Speaking

SECTION IV Using Language Use the five expressions below to complete the dialog.
(4 points each)

| believe it or not | really | I'm shocked |
| that's a great story | I can't believe it | |

Mike: I read an amazing news story today.

Mary: Oh, _____1_____? Tell me about it! I'm always interested in amazing stories.

Mike: Well, _____2_____, it was about a woman who left $5 million to her pet cat when she died.

Mary: _____3_____!

Mike: You are? I was too, but it's true!

Mary: _____4_____!

Mike: I couldn't believe it either. But what's more, she said in her will that if the cat dies, she wants them to make a clone of the cat and the money will go to the clone.

Mary: Oh, now _____5_____!

Mike: Yes, it is, isn't it?

TOTAL ____ /100 pts.

Name _____ Date _____ Score _____

CHAPTER 10 Test — Interactions 2 Listening/Speaking

SECTION I Listening to a Conversation Listen to the conversation. Then choose the best answer to each question. *(4 points each)*

1. What is this conversation about?
   - A) a wedding
   - B) a baby shower
   - C) a birthday

2. Which sentence is true?
   - A) Mike invites Tina to a party.
   - B) Tina invites Mike to a party.
   - C) Mike and Tina are both hosting a party.

3. Which offer from Mike does Tina decline?
   - A) to bring some food and drinks
   - B) to bring some music
   - C) to bring some ice cream

4. Which offer from Mike does Tina accept?
   - A) to bring some drinks
   - B) to bring some cake
   - C) to bring some ice cream

5. Which sentence is true?
   - A) Mike is Tina's boyfriend.
   - B) Mike is Tina's brother.
   - C) Mike is Tina's friend.

SECTION II Listening to a Lecture Listen to the lecture. Choose the best answer to each question. Listen to the lecture again. *(4 points each)*

1. What is the general topic of this talk?
   - A) weddings and divorces
   - B) weddings in the U.S.
   - C) hiring a wedding planner

2. What is the main idea of this talk?
   - A) Large weddings are better than small weddings.
   - B) Couples should hire a wedding consultant.
   - C) Big weddings are important.

3. Which of these is a digression from the main topic?
   - A) Weddings are very popular.
   - B) People who get married again have big weddings.
   - C) The divorce rate for first marriages is 50 percent.

CHAPTER 10 TEST   T28

CHAPTER 10 Test

Interactions 2 Listening/Speaking

4. Which of these is a digression from the main topic?
   - (A) the advantages of a big wedding
   - (B) the advantages of having a wedding planner
   - (C) the problems of bringing families together

5. What are the disadvantages of a big wedding?
   - (A) Families can disagree.
   - (B) Families have to cooperate.
   - (C) Families can get to know each other.

SECTION III New Words Use the words from the box to complete the paragraph. *(4 points each)*

hosted	involve	mother-to-be	pour	pray
priest	purify	shower	sin	symbolize

Many ceremonies around the world _____1_____ the use of water. In Thailand, the custom is to _____2_____ over other people at the start of the New Year. This is meant to _____3_____ washing away of bad luck. In some Islamic countries, people wash their faces with water to _____4_____ themselves before they _____5_____. In the Christian religion, a _____6_____ sprinkles water on the baby's head. This is meant to wash away _____7_____. Another custom connected with new babies is a baby _____8_____. This has nothing to do with water. It is a kind of party for the _____9_____, which is usually _____10_____ by her girlfriends.

SECTION IV Using Language Complete the tag questions with the correct verbs. *(4 points each)*

1. You aren't 21 yet, _____ you?
2. You won't forget my birthday, _____ you?
3. You don't want to stay late, _____ you?
4. You didn't phone me yesterday, _____ you?
5. You can't help me with my homework, _____ you?

TOTAL _____/100 pts.

CHAPTER Test Answer Key — Interactions 2 Listening/Speaking

Chapter 1 Test Answer Key

Section I Listening to a Conversation
1. c 2. a 3. a 4. c 5. b

Section II Listening to a Lecture
1. b 2. a 3. c 4. a 5. c

Section III New Words
1. syllabus 2. cite 3. dormitory 4. term paper
5. fill out 6. major 7. paraphrase 8. unique
9. plagiarism 10. rush

Section IV Using Language
1. wondering 2. What did you say 3. can't
4. thanks 5. Sure

Chapter 2 Test Answer Key

Section I Listening to a Conversation
1. c 2. c 3. a 4. b 5. b

Section II Listening to a Talk
1. b 2. a 3. a 4. c 5. b

Section III New Words
1. timer 2. slob 3. break in 4. device
5. alarm 6. valuables 7. prevent 8. can't miss it
9. lifts a finger 10. come by

Section IV Using Language
1. Were you 2. would you 3. Thanks 4. I'd love
5. Sure

Chapter 3 Test Answer Key

Section I Listening to a Conversation
1. b 2. c 3. a 4. b 5. c

Section II Listening to a Lecture
1. c 2. b 3. b 4. a 5. a

Section III New Words
1. checking 2. balance 3. statement 4. earn
5. budget 6. borrow 7. interest 8. lend
9. capital 10. risks

Section IV Using Language
1 should I do 2. Can you give me 3. you recommend
4. I suggest that you 5. think about it

Chapter 4 Test Answer Key

Section I Listening to a Conversation
1. c 2. b 3. c 4. c 5. b

Section II Listening to a Lecture
1. c 2. b 3. a 4. a 5. c

Section III New Words
1. manufacturing 2. service 3. salary 4. complain
5. part-time 6. support 7. labor 8. Automation
9. market 10. competition

Section IV Using Language
1 haven't 2. didn't 3. don't 4. doesn't 5. aren't

Chapter 5 Test Answer Key

Section I Listening to a Conversation
1. b 2. a 3. c 4. b 5. a

Section II Listening to a Lecture
1. b 2. c 3. a 4. b 5. c

Section III New Words
1. cost of living 2. bring up 3. maternity 4. run out
5. daycare 6. check up on 7. flexible
8. opportunity 9. homemakers 10. old-fashioned

Section IV Using Language
1. do 2. do you need 3. Would you
4. I'd like 5. Let me

Chapter 6 Test Answer Key

Section I Listening to a Conversation
1. b 2. b 3. c 4. c 5. a

Section II Listening to a Lecture
1. a 2. a 3. b 4. b 5. c

Section III New Words
1. interrupt 2. Gestures 3. hug 4. stay in touch
5. catch up on 6. deadline 7. offended
8. feedback 9. unintentionally 10. convenient

Section IV Using Language
1. d 2. a 3. b 4. e 5. c

Chapter 7 Test Answer Key

Section I Listening to a Conversation
1. c 2. c 3. a 4. c 5. b

Section II Listening to a Lecture
1. c 2. c 3. b 4. a 5. c

Section III New Words
1. unique 2. catch on 3. friendliness 4. friendship
5. two-faced 6. dialect 7. noticeable 8. whereas
9. majority 10. identical

Section IV Using Language
1. e 2. b 3. d 4. a 5. c

Chapter 8 Test Answer Key

Section I Listening to a Conversation
1. c 2. a 3. b 4. c 5. a

Section II Listening to an Interview
1. b 2. a 3. b 4. c 5. a

Section III New Words
1. significant 2. diverse 3. confident 4. optimistic
5. tolerant 6. loyal 7. conflict 8. see eye to eye
9. income 10. phenomenon

Section IV Using Language
1. in favor 2. disapprove 3. against 4. approve
5. for

Chapter 9 Test Answer Key

Section I Listening to a Conversation
1. b 2. a 3. c 4. b 5. a

Section II Listening to a Lecture
1. a 2. b 3. a 4. c 5. b

Section III New Words
1. utility bill 2. installs 3. appliances 4. display
5. convenient 6. efficient 7. leave on 8. essential
9. potential 10. impact

Section IV Using Language
1. really 2. believe it or not 3. I'm shocked
4. I can't believe it 5. that's a great story

Chapter 10 Test Answer Key

Section I Listening to a Conversation
1. c 2. b 3. a 4. c 5. c

Section II Listening to a Lecture
1. b 2. c 3. c 4. b 5. a

Section III New Words
1. involve 2. pour 3. symbolize 4. purify
5. pray 6. priest 7. sin 8. shower
9. mother-to-be 10. hosted

Section IV Using Language
1. are 2. will 3. do 4. did 5. can

CHAPTER Test Audioscripts — Interactions 2 Listening/Speaking

Chapter 1 Test Audioscripts

Section I Listening to a Conversation

Francisco: Excuse me.

Yumi: Yes?

Francisco: Could you tell me where the art museum is?

Yumi: Yes, of course. It's on Willow Street, across from the gym and next to the music building. It's at the intersection of Willow Street and Alumni Street. I'm walking that way, too.

Francisco: Could I walk with you?

Yumi: Yes, of course. Are you an art student?

Francisco: Yes, I am.

Yumi: Oh really? I'm majoring in business. It's my second year. How long have you been here?

Francisco: About two weeks. I'm still finding my way around.

Yumi: Well, here we are. It was nice to meet you.

Francisco: Yes, see you again.

Section II Listening to a Lecture

Good morning everyone, my name is Nancy Anderson, and I'm the director of the Study Support Center. OK. This morning I want to give you a general introduction to the kind of study support we offer here. After that, we'll have time for some questions before taking a break for coffee. OK?

First, I want to tell you about the different types of classes we have available here in the Center. There are four main types of classes: small group classes, language lab, computer lab, and individual study.

Small group classes usually have five to eight students. They meet with a teacher once a week to practice speaking and communication skills. Groups are usually divided according to their major: business or law, for example. Language lab classes are for practicing pronunciation and listening skills. You can sign up for language lab classes at any time. There's no teacher, but a teaching assistant will help you find the right program, which you can work through at your own speed. Computer lab classes are in the library. You don't need to sign up. But look at the schedule for times of classes when a teaching assistant can help you with the basics of using computers and the Internet. Finally, you can meet with an individual tutor in our support center to get advice on any problems you're having with your studies. You can meet for one hour up to three times a week. But sign up early, the schedule gets filled up very quickly, especially around exam time!

We hope that you will use our support center, and we'll do our best to help you make the most of your learning experience here with us.

OK, that's it for now. Before we take a break, I'll try to answer some of your questions, and when we come back after the break, we'll talk about some of the course requirements. Now, are there any questions? Yes....

Student: Could you tell me...

Chapter 2 Test Audioscripts

Section I Listening to a Conversation

Ken: Hello. May I speak to Mrs. Hansen, please?

Mrs. Hansen: Yes, speaking.

Ken: Hi Mrs. Hansen. My name is Ken, and I'm calling about the room for rent.

Mrs. Hansen: Yes, what would you like to know?

Ken: Could you tell me how much the rent is?

Mrs. Hansen: It's $400 a month.

Ken: I see. And how far is it from campus?

Mrs. Hansen: It's very near, I'd say about ten minutes' walk. Are you a student?

Ken: Yes, I am. I need somewhere quiet because the dorm is too noisy.

Mrs. Hansen: We only have one other student here and she's very quiet.

Ken: And do you mind pets, because I want to bring my cat with me.

Mrs. Hansen: I'm sorry, but we don't allow pets.

Ken: OK. Thanks anyway. Good-bye.

Section II Listening to a Talk

Hello everyone. My name is Pat Sanders, and I'm in charge of college campus security. I'm here to give you a few tips on how to stay safe and how to keep your property safe while you are on campus.

First of all, let's talk about safety in the dormitories. The most important thing is never to loan your keys or ID card to anyone. This is against college regulations. Lock your door when you are sleeping or when you leave the room. If you see anyone suspicious, call campus security.

Next, let's talk about security while you are walking around the campus. Avoid walking alone at night. You should tell other friends where you are going and what time you will be there. Try to walk only in well-lighted areas and know where the emergency telephones are on your route. Have your key ready before you get to the door. Take your cell phone and also carry a personal alarm with you. It may be a good idea to take self-defense classes. If someone approaches you, the best defense is to scream, sound an alarm (if you have one), and run to the nearest emergency phone.

OK, now let's move on and talk about how you can prevent theft of your property. By property, I mean your bags, wallets, cell phones, or laptops. You may think you are safe when you're studying in the library or in the cafeteria. But these are all places where thieves look for opportunities to steal. The main thing is never to leave your backpacks or laptops out of your sight. It also helps to label all your valuable items—that includes textbooks—with your name. It is a good idea to keep a list of the make, model, and serial number of valuable property such as laptop computers.

Following these tips will help to make you more safety-aware and will help to protect you and your property. Remember, we're here to help you. So report any crime or any suspicious activity to us immediately. But following these few simple safety procedures could help to save your property and even your life.

Chapter 3 Test Audioscripts

Section I Listening to a Conversation

Bank clerk: Good morning. International Bank. How can I help you?

Elsa: Can you tell me how much I can borrow on my credit card?

Bank clerk: OK, can you give me your name, please?

Elsa: Jansen. J-a-n-s-e-n. My first name is Elsa.

Bank clerk: For security purposes, can you give me the last four digits of your social security number, please?

Elsa: Yes, of course. It's 1234.

Bank clerk: Just a moment, let me look up your records. OK, here we are... yes, you have credit up to $2,000. If you need more than that, you should speak to one of our customer loan specialists.

Elsa: Yes, I think I might need more than that. I want to do some remodeling on my kitchen, and it will cost about $3,000.

Bank clerk: In that case, I advise you to choose one of our other loan options. The interest on your credit card is about 18 percent, but if you take out a personal loan or a home improvement loan, you can borrow the same amount for a much better rate, as low as 8 percent.

Elsa: OK. How do I find out about a home improvement loan?

Bank clerk: Just a moment, I'll put you through to our loan specialist.

Section II Listening to a Lecture

Let's think about a key part of the entrepreneurial process: Coming up with a new idea! It's easy to think of problems in our daily lives. Your car won't start in the morning. Or your alarm clock doesn't wake you up! But have you ever tried to come up with an idea for something completely new and different to try and solve any of these problems? A new idea for a product or a service? It's quite difficult, isn't it?

Well, the good news is that you don't have to come up with a totally new invention in order to be an entrepreneur. Today, I'm going to talk about four different types of entrepreneurial ideas.

First, a small proportion of entrepreneurs actually do come up with ideas for totally new inventions. An example of this is the concept of the home computer, which was chiefly developed in the 70s by entrepreneur Steve Jobs of Apple Computers. This product created a whole new market for something that had not existed before. Now, we can hardly imagine our lives without a home computer.

Many new ideas, however, are actually refinements of existing ideas, or specializations for specific segments of the market. Anita Roddick's chain of cosmetic stores, for example, sells to customers who are interested in environmental issues and want cosmetics made from natural ingredients. Founded in 1976, her company now has almost 2,000 stores around the world.

Another type of innovation is to improve production methods. Henry Ford, for example, invented the assembly line for the production of cars. He didn't invent cars, but he came up with an idea for increasing the speed and decreasing the cost of production, which made cars more affordable for consumers.

And finally, an entrepreneur can develop new ways of doing business to sell existing products. A good example of this is Jeff Bezos of Amazon.com, who was one of the first to use the Internet to sell to customers directly online. Though selling books was not a new idea, selling books via the Internet was a new idea at the time. Nowadays, online selling is a multimillion-dollar business.

Chapter 4 Test Audioscripts

Section I Listening to a Conversation

Manager: Please come in and take a seat.
Applicant: Thank you.
Manager: Now Andrew, what can you tell me about your job experience?
Applicant: Well, I don't have any job experience yet... but I'm very eager to learn.
Manager: OK. So, why are you interested in being a computer analyst?
Applicant: I like solving problems and fixing things. I spend all my spare time learning about computers. I know all about the latest technology.
Manager: Do you think you can work well on a team?
Applicant: Yes, I like working with people.
Manager: And you have a college degree, don't you?
Applicant: Not yet. I hope to graduate this year.

Section II Listening to a Lecture

We all know that we're using more and more technology in our daily lives. Most jobs nowadays require some computer skills and there are many benefits to using technology. Just think of all the jobs that had to be done by hand in the past—processing checks in a bank, for example—and which are now done electronically in a fraction of the time and with fewer mistakes.

The question I want to discuss today is: how have our work lives changed as a result of using more technology?

One effect has been the trend in people working from home. This is an advantage for people who live far away from their office, or who have small children to look after. On the other hand, it is more difficult for them to separate work and home life. Cell phones, pagers, faxes, and email can reach us at any time of the day at home. This can have a negative effect on family and personal relationships. Working from home also means that jobs can be more easily transferred to other parts of the country or to other countries. When you buy insurance, for example, there is no need for the sales representatives to be in your town or city. They can be in Florida, in Texas, or in India. So another effect has been an increase in the number of technology jobs which have moved to countries where salaries are lower.

What about the effects on our job skills? Most people would agree that computers help us to communicate faster and more efficiently. Are there negative effects, too?

Student: We don't talk to each other?

That's right. Because of technology, we don't have to meet our customers or co-workers in person. The downside is that people are losing their face-to-face interpersonal skills. Even in offices, team meetings and informal conversations are often replaced by email messages and conference calls. Some companies even discourage workers from wasting too much time talking!

So, while it is easy to see the benefits of technology, we should not forget there may also be some drawbacks.

Chapter 5 Test Audioscripts

Section I Listening to a Conversation

Sandra: Hi, Jenny.

Jenny: Hey Sandra, how's it going?

Sandra: Fantastic. It's great being back at my old job.

Jenny: It's good to have you back. Did you find an apartment yet?

Sandra: No, I'm still living with my parents...

Jenny: How's that going?

Sandra: It's great because my mother can take care of Timmy during the day. He's still only two years old. On the other hand, it kind of feels like I'm a teenager again.

Jenny: What will you do about Timmy when you find your own place?

Sandra: I guess I'll have to find a babysitter during the day. Too bad our company doesn't offer any workplace child care.

Jenny: Yes, maybe we should try to start one. I'll ask the manager about it at the next meeting.

Section II Listening to a Lecture

Today I'm going to talk to you about the aging labor force in the U.S. and the impact on the U.S. economy. The main reason that a large percentage of the labor force is getting older is because of the large increase in the number of babies born in the U.S. just after the Second World War. This was known as the "baby boom." It began in 1946 and continued through 1964. During those 19 years, 76 million people were born in the U.S. People who were born during the baby boom are all now approaching retirement age... all at the same time.

In 1978, when baby-boomers were aged 15 to 32, they made up approximately 45 percent of the labor force. Now, as baby-boomers are starting to age, the percentage of workers aged 45 and older is starting to increase. In 1998, it was 33 percent of the labor force and in 2008, it will be up to 40 percent. At the same time, workers aged 25 to 44 will decrease from 51 percent to 44 percent. As a result, the average age of the labor force will rise from 38.7 years old in 1998 to 40.7 years old in 2008.

What does this mean in terms of impact on the economy? Naturally, if all the baby-boomers suddenly retired at the same time, there would be a problem. Who would pay their retirement or social security? Who would take over their jobs? Well, that's not going to happen. First, the retirement age is going to go up. Over the last 20 years, the age of retirement has remained fairly stable. But—for a number of different reasons— the retirement age will start to increase. Between 2000 and 2022, the normal retirement age will rise from 65 to 67. A second factor is that company pensions no longer provide the same type of benefits for retirement. Workers nowadays have to work longer to get a pension they can live on. These are just two factors which will result in workers staying in the workforce longer.

Chapter 6 Test Audioscripts

Section I Listening to a Conversation

Mike: How many emails do you typically get in a day, Gina?

Gina: Well... that's hard to say... maybe 20 or 25?

Mike: And do you answer them all?

Gina: I answer the urgent ones, like the ones from students who don't understand their assignments, but I don't manage to answer them all, and I generally have to catch up on the weekend. Do you have any tips?

Mike:	What you're doing is a good idea. Choose the most important ones and answer those first.
Gina:	OK.
Mike:	But it's also a good idea not to answer emails immediately, because very often people come up with the solution by themselves, or they send a second email soon after the first one with a different question. Or another idea is to post general messages on your website, then instead of writing emails, you can just send the website link....
Gina:	That's true, I had several emails the....
Kendra:	Excuse me for interrupting you Gina, there's a student on the phone who urgently needs to speak with you.
Gina:	Thanks, Kendra. I'll come right over. Uh-oh it's probably someone who sent me an email, and I haven't answered it yet! See you later, Mike!

Section II Listening to a Lecture

Today I'm going to talk about greetings in different cultures. And in particular about greetings in more formal work and business settings. Now of course, we all know some of the basic differences in greetings customs, for example, that handshakes are more common in North American and European contexts, while bowing is more common in some Asian cultures, particularly in Japan. But there are also some other differences in rules of politeness that can cause misunderstandings.

In North America, it is usual to shake hands when you first meet someone. When you shake hands, it should be accompanied by eye contact, a smile, and a friendly greeting such as How are you? or I'm glad to meet you. In this situation, it is polite to ask someone to call you by your first name. The aim is to look and sound sincere and friendly, and to try to decrease social distance by establishing an equal relationship.

In Japan, it is common to bow when first meeting someone. It is polite to avoid eye contact by looking down. The greeting is usually accompanied by a phrase asking for the other person's help, for example, by using the phrase, doozo yoroshiku o negai shimasu which may be translated as "I hope you will be able to help me." The appropriate response is "I ask for your help, too." The aim is to establish a relationship of mutual dependence where everyone helps each other.

Now if a Japanese person were to shake hands with an American and tried to translate his or her cultural 'rules' what would happen?

First of all, avoiding eye contact would not show politeness, as intended, it would show distance and perhaps insincerity. Secondly, asking for someone's help when first meeting him or her would sound like you were asking for a favor, which is a little strange when you don't know the person. The American might think he or she was really being asked for help, which could be difficult.

On the other hand, what if an American person were to shake hands with a Japanese person and tried to translate his or her own cultural rules? What would happen? By trying to decrease social distance by eye contact, first names, or a friendly informal tone, that person would seem less polite. Second, when he or she hears someone asking for help, the American person may respond by offering help, which could also sound impolite.

To summarize, each person, while doing their best to be polite according to their own cultural rules, would sound impolite and insincere to the other person. And they've only got as far as the greeting!

Chapter 7 Test Audioscripts

Section I Listening to a Conversation

Stan:	What's the matter, Jenny?
Jenny:	I was trying to get through to my bank. I really dislike those automated phone messages you get all the time.
Stan:	You mean the ones where you have to listen and choose a number and press the right key?
Jenny:	Yes... usually there's a list of choices and at the end you just get another automated message. It's so frustrating...I prefer to speak to a real person.

Stan:	I know it's frustrating sometimes, but I think it's a good idea. Just think how boring it is for people to answer the same questions all day long.
Jenny:	That's true, but my question usually doesn't fit into any of the categories!
Stan:	So what happens?
Jenny:	They just put me on hold and I usually have to wait a long time…and…
Stan:	Aha! So you just don't like waiting, is that it?
Jenny:	Yes, I suppose you're right.

Section II Listening to a Lecture

My topic for today's lecture is differences between spoken and written English. And I'm going to group these differences under three main categories. These categories are: the medium of communication, grammar, and vocabulary.

So first of all, quite obviously, the main difference between written and spoken English is the medium of communication. Speaking and writing are two quite different ways of transmitting meanings. In spoken language, we can use stress and intonation to add meaning to our words. What about written language? Well, in writing you have to use punctuation—a question mark instead of a questioning intonation, for example. Or you can add words that convey mood, such as certainty or uncertainty. For example, in speech you might say It isn't true! but you might write It is certainly not true!, using an exclamation mark for emphasis.

The second category is vocabulary. If you are writing a note or a short email to your friend, then you might use some slang expressions or contractions. But in more formal written English, you should avoid slang and contractions such as isn't or doesn't. There is more frequent use of pronouns in spoken English. When you are speaking to someone, it is often quite clear from the surrounding context what you mean when you say It's fine. But when you're writing, you need to be more specific and say if it means the weather, your work, the food… or something completely different.

The third category is grammar. In spoken English, people often use incomplete sentences. They stop and start and interrupt each other, and leave sentences unfinished. You might find mistakes in verb agreement, for example, because people change their mind in the middle of a sentence. In written English, however, especially formal written English such as business letters or academic essays, you have to use complete sentences, and mistakes in grammar are much more noticeable—so you have to be more careful!

Chapter 8 Test Audioscripts

Section I Listening to a Conversation

Joe:	How was your birthday meal last night?
Maria:	Fantastic! I'm crazy about Mexican food! How about you?
Joe:	No, I don't care for spicy food.
Maria:	How about Indian? There's a new Indian restaurant in town. It looks really awesome. Do you want to go there on Saturday?
Joe:	Oh, no. I can't stand curry.
Maria:	OK. How do you feel about Thai food?
Joe:	I've never tried it, but how about just having steak and fries?
Maria:	Why do you always want to eat the same thing?

Section II Listening to an Interview

Host:	And today I'd like to welcome, Marietta Delfontini, the famous fashion designer who is going to tell us about her new line of environmentally-friendly fashion. Marietta, thank you for joining us today.
Marietta:	My pleasure.
Host	To begin, could you tell us the meaning of the term environmentally-friendly fashion?
Marietta:	Sure. Environmentally-friendly fashion refers to clothing that has been created in a way that is sensitive to the environment. In other words, it is made from natural materials, such as cotton or wool. It doesn't use nylon or polyester, for example, which are made from chemicals. And it uses natural materials that have not been

Host: produced using chemical insecticides or pesticides, I mean they are all produced organically.

Host: I see. And do you think there is a demand for this kind of fashion nowadays?

Marietta: Absolutely! Young people nowadays are very aware of environmental concerns. And they want to have fashion that responds to those concerns. Our new line will not only help to save the environment, but people who wear it will spread the message about environmentally-friendly fashion.

Host: In other words, by wearing your fashion, people will make the issue more popular?

Marietta: That's it exactly!

Host: There must be some things that aren't organic, buttons for example?

Marietta: Yes, that's true. We do make buttons from wood or from glass, but for those elements which cannot be made from organic materials, we re-use decorative accessories from vintage clothing, that is clothing from the 50s or 60s. It is contemporary clothing with a vintage twist.

Host: How is that good for the environment?

Marietta: Well, we think people are too quick to throw their clothing away. So we'd like to see more fashion that combines old and new to create an exciting modern look. I mean we're encouraging people to use their clothing for a longer time.

Host: Thanks very much, Marietta. We look forward to seeing your new collection.

Marietta: Thank you.

Chapter 9 Test Audioscripts

Section I Listening to a Conversation

Sally: There was an amazing story in the news today.

Jane: Oh yeah? What was it?

Sally: Well, it was about a little girl who had a heart transplant when she was just two years old.

Jane: You mean they gave her a new heart?

Sally: That's right. Believe it or not, they left her own heart inside her and just added the new one.

Jane: So she had two hearts?

Sally: Exactly.

Jane: That's so weird.

Sally: Well, now she's 12 years old and she's had some problems with the new heart so they took out the new heart and reattached the original one, which was still inside her. The most amazing thing is that the old heart had gotten better and now it works perfectly.

Jane: Unbelievable!

Section II Listening to a Lecture

It is a well-known fact that people have been searching for signs of life on other planets for many hundreds of years. Are we alone in the universe? Or are there other civilizations out there just waiting to be discovered? Only in the last few decades has it become physically possible for us to visit other planets. And today, I'm going to talk about some theories concerning life on one of our nearest neighbors—the planet Mars. How likely is it that there is life on Mars?

The belief that there may be life on Mars became popular in the 19th century when an Italian astronomer named Giovanni Schiaparelli observed lines on the surface of the planet which he called canali. This was mistakenly translated into English as canals and other astronomers thought that they might be evidence of the presence of water which would mean that life was possible.

Nowadays, with the use of much more powerful and accurate telescopes, it has been proven that these so-called canals do not exist, or in some cases, are dried-up water channels. But, although there may have been water on Mars in the past, there is no evidence of any water on the planet today.

Another source of evidence for life on Mars was the discovery of a meteorite, a piece of rock from Mars, which was found in Alaska in 1996. When scientists studied this meteorite, they found evidence of single-cell biological organisms in the rock. However, this evidence was contradicted by other scientists who say that there is no proof that this rock was ever in temperatures suitable for water, and that, therefore, it is impossible to say whether these organisms were ever alive.

The exploration of Mars in 2003 made the exciting discovery of evidence that there has been water on Mars in the past. So now the question is: How can scientists find out whether life has ever existed on Mars? Well, the obvious answer is that they'll have to get more samples of rocks. But, they'll need to get rocks from a site that will provide a good source of evidence. One possibility might be a dried-up lake, for example, where life may have existed even after life on other parts of the planet had disappeared. Another possibility is to obtain rock samples from the polar ice caps of Mars which have a temperature of minus 95 degrees Fahrenheit (that's minus 70 degrees Centigrade). Because of the lower temperatures, micro-organisms would be preserved for a much longer time and could still possibly be found.

These are some of the exciting questions being asked in the study and exploration of life on Mars. And the answers to these questions could tell us a lot about our universe and our world. Now what kind of questions do you have?

Chapter 10 Test Audioscripts

Section I Listening to a Conversation

Tina: Mike, are you busy on Saturday?

Mike: Why, what's happening?

Tina: It's my 21st birthday, and I'm having a small party. Can you come?

Mike: I'd love to. What would you like me to bring? Food, drinks?

Tina: No, that's OK, thanks, I think we'll have enough.

Mike: How about music? I have some really good dance music.

Tina: Oh sure, that would be great.

Mike: Are you doing something special, since it's your 21st?

Tina: Well, I think my sister's making a cake, and my boyfriend's bringing the drinks.

Mike: Could I bring some ice cream then?

Tina: OK, if you wouldn't mind.

Section II Listening to a Lecture

Host: As part of our course on the sociology of weddings, we're going to hear from an expert on the topic of weddings. I'd like to introduce our guest speaker today, Annette Cook. Annette is a professional wedding consultant. Today she is going to talk to us about weddings in the U.S.

Speaker: Thank you, Professor Jackson. And thanks for inviting me. Good afternoon everyone.

Well, the topic of weddings is a pretty broad topic and I thought I would try to narrow this down by focusing on the type of wedding that I'm typically involved in, and that is the big formal wedding. Why is it so important? I mean, why do people spend so much time and money planning a big wedding?

Almost five million Americans get married each year. And by the way, this number includes not only people who are marrying for the first time, but also people who are getting married a second, third, or fourth time. You may not know that the divorce rate for first marriages is about 50 percent, and there is a strong trend for divorced persons to have just as big or even a bigger celebration for their second (and even third and fourth) weddings. But to get back to the topic, why are big weddings so popular?

Of course, the main reason couples have a wedding celebration is to enjoy themselves and celebrate the start of their married life. But a wedding also has a symbolic meaning. It is a symbol of the couple's commitment to the relationship. Weddings are important for families, too. In our mobile and fragmented society, such family occasions are increasingly rare. Bringing families together, however, can also bring problems, of course, such as when there are family members who don't get along, or families of different religions or ethnic backgrounds who have different ideas about what the wedding should be like.

Before I forget, let me just mention that this is the time when a wedding planner can be very helpful. An experienced wedding planner can help to solve practical problems in a way that keeps everyone happy. Anyway, to get back to the topic… where was I? Oh yes… you can look at large weddings as a way for the two families to cooperate and get to know each other, and this will help provide a support network for the couple in their later lives.

Name _____ Date _____ Score _____

PLACEMENT Test   INTERACTIONS/MOSAIC Listening/Speaking

DIRECTIONS: Read these directions before listening to the recorded test.

There are four sections in this test, each with a different type of listening and questions. There are a total of fifty questions to answer. You will hear the test questions only once; they will not be repeated.

SECTIONS:

1. Ten question items – after you hear each question, choose the best response. (questions 1–10)
2. Ten statement items – after you hear each statement, select the best conclusion. (questions 11–20)
3. Ten short conversations – after each conversation there is one question to answer. (questions 21–30)
4. Four longer selections – after each longer listening selection, there are five questions to answer about the listening. (questions 31–50)

SECTION 1 Listen to the question and choose the best response. *(2 points each)*

Example   (You hear:) Where's your sister gone?
(You read:)
(A) to Canada
(B) without her friends
(C) because she was late
(D) yesterday
Choice "a" is the best answer.

1. (A) tomorrow
   (B) to visit his sister
   (C) just this morning
   (D) the train

2. (A) Yes, I must go there.
   (B) About five hundred dollars
   (C) I'll have a good time.
   (D) A few days

3. (A) He's been once.
   (B) She's been there for three months.
   (C) No, she's still there.
   (D) She was there as a child.

4. (A) It's not very fair.
   (B) It takes an hour.
   (C) It's two dollars.
   (D) It's not very far from here.

PLACEMENT Test
Listening/Speaking

5. (A) Yes, they can.
   (B) The bus stops near the theatre.
   (C) There is no way we could make it in time.
   (D) It's too bad we missed the eight o'clock show.

6. (A) It's a little too casual.
   (B) Yes, the pants fit.
   (C) They have three different sizes.
   (D) It's a bit tight.

7. (A) They prefer going to the movies.
   (B) I haven't really thought about it.
   (C) I have no references.
   (D) It's either black or white.

8. (A) I would be pleased if she finds a job that she enjoys.
   (B) My mother hopes she will go on to college.
   (C) I took her on a trip last year.
   (D) I want my legs to stop hurting.

9. (A) Yes, the doctor told me to start drinking it more often.
   (B) Yes, I needed something to eat.
   (C) No, I still drink milk every day.
   (D) Sorry, I don't have time.

10. (A) I'm sorry I was late.
    (B) I couldn't have come earlier.
    (C) Would you like me to come back in a while?
    (D) Sorry we left so late.

SECTION 2 Listen to each statement and then choose the best conclusion. *(2 points each)*

11. (A) Peter's lawyer likes his mother.
    (B) Peter likes his mother.
    (C) Peter is a liar.
    (D) Peter's mother is a lawyer.

12. (A) The flight arrived at 2:30.
    (B) The flight took off at 2:30.
    (C) The flight will arrive in an hour and a half.
    (D) The flight arrived at 1:30.

13. (A) Sixty students went on the sailing trip.
    (B) No students went on the sailing trip.
    (C) Only a few students arrived to go on the sailing trip.
    (D) Nobody signed up for the sailing trip.

14. (A) Judy has to plan something for her birthday.
    (B) Someone gave Judy flowers on her birthday.
    (C) Judy intends to do something special on her birthday.
    (D) Judy bought some plants as a gift.

15. (A) Peter is a fair player.
    (B) The match was relatively short.
    (C) Peter won the match.
    (D) Steve hit the ball fast.

16. (A) Mary was losing her eyesight.
    (B) John won the argument with Mary.
    (C) Mary forgot why she and John were arguing.
    (D) Mary and John argued because it was very hot.

17. (A) Gary preferred Robert to Peter.
    (B) Gary preferred Peter to Robert.
    (C) Robert liked Peter better than Gary.
    (D) Peter liked Gary better than Robert.

18. (A) It's time to plant things in the garden.
    (B) Soon it will be warm enough to start planting seeds.
    (C) You ought to visit the garden at the sea.
    (D) You should be considerate of the garden.

19. (A) The dinner was very good in general.
    (B) Dinner was at a restaurant.
    (C) Everyone thought the dinner was very good.
    (D) Dinner was very good every night.

20. (A) John's brother lives near the club.
    (B) John's brother owns the club.
    (C) John has never invited his brother to the club.
    (D) John's brother has never invited John to the club.

PLACEMENT Test — Listening/Speaking

SECTION 3: Listen to each conversation. Answer the question you hear after each conversation. *(2 points each)*

21. (A) It hasn't rained for many years.
    (B) It has rained an unusual amount this year.
    (C) It hasn't rained much here.
    (D) It hasn't rained this year.

22. (A) He thought the restaurant could have been better.
    (B) He agreed with the woman.
    (C) He thoroughly enjoyed the restaurant.
    (D) It was impossible for the restaurant to be nice.

23. (A) The wind hurt the man's house.
    (B) The wind hurt the woman's son.
    (C) Paint in the woman's basement was ruined.
    (D) Flood water damaged artwork in the woman's house.

24. (A) The man's brother is not strong enough to lift things.
    (B) The man's brother is not making any effort to find work.
    (C) The brother is unlucky.
    (D) The woman is surprised the man's brother is still not working.

25. (A) It's not unusual for him to play in hot weather.
    (B) At an earlier time in his life, he played tennis in such weather.
    (C) Playing tennis in hot weather uses up his energy.
    (D) He's concerned about playing in the heat.

26. (A) It's contradictory.
    (B) She doesn't agree.
    (C) She wants the man to look at the ducks.
    (D) She's angry.

27. (A) He's not planning to purchase anything.
    (B) He doesn't need to get anything at this store.
    (C) He doesn't agree about the prices.
    (D) He doesn't like to buy cheap things.

PLACEMENT Test Listening/Speaking

28.
- (A) The city nearly burned down.
- (B) The mayor was rescued from a burning building.
- (C) The mayor was hurt and moved.
- (D) The mayor was criticized and left his job.

29.
- (A) He thinks she should buy a large pizza.
- (B) He thinks she should ask for extra mushrooms and cheese.
- (C) He likes the mushroom and cheese pizza best.
- (D) He thinks the pizzas are too big.

30.
- (A) The judge was very sure about handling the case.
- (B) The judge gave the man a severe punishment.
- (C) The judge was difficult to understand.
- (D) The judge couldn't decide the theif's punishment.

SECTION 4 Listen to each longer selection and answer the five questions for the selection. Listen to the first selection. Then answer questions 31–35. *(2 points each)*

31. What do you think T-A-L-K is?
- (A) a radio station
- (B) a TV station
- (C) an animal rescue service
- (D) a movie studio

32. What animals are missing?
- (A) one dog and two cats
- (B) two dogs and one cat
- (C) two dogs and two cats
- (D) one dog and one cat

33. Which of the animals were taken from a backyard?
- (A) None of the animals
- (B) All of the animals
- (C) Oxen the German Shepherd
- (D) Winston the wire-haired terrier

PLACEMENT Test — Listening/Speaking

34. Who had a seeing-eye dog?

- (A) Mr. Wilson
- (B) Mrs. Lincoln
- (C) Mrs. Thompson
- (D) Oxen

35. What are the listeners supposed to do if they find one of the pets?

- (A) Call the T-A-L-K phone line.
- (B) Call the police station.
- (C) Call the local animal shelter.
- (D) Wait a week to call.

DIRECTIONS: The following selection is a lecture in two parts. Listen to Part 1 and answer questions 36–40. *(2 points each)*

36. In what situation does this talk probably take place?

- (A) nutrition class
- (B) business or marketing class
- (C) supermarket training
- (D) a one-day seminar

37. According to the speaker, what is true about product placement?

- (A) It's only important in supermarkets.
- (B) The concept is hardly used in the United States.
- (C) Children are not affected by it.
- (D) It's an extremely important selling tool.

38. The speaker said that children often "pester their parents" in a supermarket. What does *pester* mean?

- (A) nagging and begging
- (B) petting or touching
- (C) wanting candy
- (D) grabbing food

39. What's the speaker's focus?

- (A) product placement outside of the United States
- (B) product placement both in and out of the United States
- (C) product placement in the United States
- (D) products you shouldn't buy

40. What specific examples did the speaker use?

    A) Candy was the only example.

    B) Candy was one of the examples.

    C) The examples were taken directly from the textbook.

    D) The examples would be on the test.

DIRECTIONS: Listen to Part 2 of the lecture and answer questions 41–45. *(2 points each)*

41. What products did the speaker talk about?

    A) expensive products

    B) headache medicine

    C) tropical shampoo

    D) shampoo for oily hair

42. What did the speaker say about U.S. stores?

    A) All U.S. stores follow the same process for placing items on shelves.

    B) Most U.S. stores place pricey items at eye level.

    C) Many U.S. stores place inexpensive items at eye level.

    D) No U.S. stores place items at eye level.

43. What position was stated by the speaker?

    A) Inexpensive items are better than expensive ones.

    B) Expensive items are better than inexpensive ones.

    C) He didn't endorse inexpensive items or expensive ones.

    D) He doesn't like candy or shampoo.

44. What did the speaker tell the participants?

    A) They didn't have any homework.

    B) They had to get ready for a test.

    C) They had to do some research.

    D) They had to finish an assignment in class.

45. When does the class probably meet?

    A) Tuesday and Thursday nights

    B) Tuesday nights

    C) Tuesday mornings

    D) every other week

PLACEMENT Test — Listening/Speaking

DIRECTIONS: The following selection is a lecture. Listen to the lecture and answer questions 46–50. *(2 points each)*

46. What best describes folk wisdom?
- A) American folklore
- B) jokes
- C) sayings that give advice about life
- D) different means of expressing oneself

47. Which expression of folk wisdom is *not* mentioned?
- A) myths
- B) fairy tales
- C) songs
- D) poetry

48. What will the speaker probably focus on in the lecture?
- A) humorous sayings
- B) legends
- C) songs of joy and sorrow
- D) famous American Presidents

49. What source of folk wisdom will be used in the talk?
- A) Abraham Lincoln
- B) Mark Twain and Benjamin Franklin
- C) students in this class
- D) All of the above

50. Which is not mentioned about Ben Franklin?
- A) He loved to eat and drink.
- B) People admired his wit.
- C) He took the bitter medicine.
- D) He told others not to overdo things.

PLACEMENT Test Answer Key — Listening/Speaking

Interactions/Mosaic Listening/Speaking Placement Test Answer Key

Section 1

1. c   2. d   3. d   4. c   5. c
6. d   7. b   8. a   9. a   10. c

Section 2

11. d   12. a   13. c   14. c   15. b
16. c   17. b   18. a   19. a   20. d

Section 3

21. b   22. c   23. d   24. b   25. a
26. a   27. c   28. d   29. c   30. b

Section 4

31. a   32. b   33. d   34. a   35. a
36. b   37. d   38. a   39. c   40. a
41. a   42. b   43. c   44. c   45. b
46. c   47. d   48. a   49. d   50. c

SCORING FOR INTERACTIONS/MOSAIC LISTENING/SPEAKING PLACEMENT TEST

Score	Placement
0–27	Interactions Access
28–46	Interactions 1
47–65	Interactions 2
66–84	Mosaic 1
85–100	Mosaic 2

This is a rough guide. Teachers should use their judgment in placing students and selecting texts.

Listening/Speaking Placement Test Audioscripts

Narrator:	Number 1. When did Steve get in?
Narrator:	Number 2. How much time will you have to spend in Boston?
Narrator:	Number 3. Has she ever been there before?
Narrator:	Number 4. How much is the subway fare?
Narrator:	Number 5. Should we try to get to the eight o'clock movie?
Narrator:	Number 6. Do you think that this jacket fits?
Narrator:	Number 7. What are your preferences in art?
Narrator:	Number 8. What are your hopes for your niece?
Narrator:	Number 9. On the way home from the doctor, did you stop for some milk?
Narrator:	Number 10. Couldn't you have arrived an hour later?
Narrator:	Number 11. Peter is a lawyer like his mother.
Narrator:	Number 12. Mary's flight was due at one, but it was delayed an hour and a half.
Narrator:	Number 13. Sixty students signed up for the sailing trip, but most of them failed to show up.
Narrator:	Number 14. Judy's got big plans for her birthday.
Narrator:	Number 15. Peter was beaten fairly quickly by Steve in the tennis match.
Narrator:	Number 16. In the heat of the argument, Mary lost sight of her original disagreement with John.
Narrator:	Number 17. Although Gary liked his uncle Robert, he was fonder of his cousin Peter.
Narrator:	Number 18. Considering the season, you really should plant the seeds in the garden before the frost.
Narrator:	Number 19. On the whole, the dinner was great.
Narrator:	Number 20. John's never been invited to the club by his brother.
Narrator:	Number 21.
Man:	The weather has been so hot this summer…
Woman:	And we haven't had rain like this in years.
Narrator:	What does the woman mean?
Narrator:	Number 22.
Woman:	The restaurant wasn't very good in my opinion.
Man:	I thought it couldn't have been nicer.
Narrator:	What does the man mean?
Narrator:	Number 23.
Man:	The storm sounded like it would blow the roof off my house.
Woman:	Wasn't it terrible? The flood in our basement ruined my son's paintings.
Narrator:	What did the storm do?
Narrator:	Number 24.
Man:	My brother is having a lot of trouble finding a job.
Woman:	What a surprise. I haven't seen him lift a finger.
Narrator:	What does the woman mean?
Narrator:	Number 25.
Woman:	Your serve. Whew. It's gotten very hot.
Man:	I know, but I'm used to playing tennis in weather like this.
Narrator:	What does the man mean?
Narrator:	Number 26.
Man:	The less I try to whack the ball, the farther it goes.
Woman:	Hmm, that's quite a paradox!
Narrator:	What does the woman mean?
Narrator:	Number 27.
Woman:	Richard told me about this store. He said they have the lowest prices in town.
Man:	You think? I don't necessarily buy that.
Narrator:	What does the man mean?

PLACEMENT Test Audioscripts — Listening/Speaking

Narrator:	Number 28.
Man:	Did you hear that city hall almost burned down?
Woman:	Right, and then the Mayor was removed under fire.
Narrator:	What does the woman mean?
Narrator:	Number 29.
Woman:	How's the pizza here?
Man:	Good, by and large, especially the mushroom and cheese.
Narrator:	What does the man mean?
Narrator:	Number 30.
Woman:	That young man got 20 years for stealing a bicycle.
Man:	Hmm. The judge sure handed down a hard sentence.
Narrator:	What does the man mean?
Female Announcer:	This is the T-A-L-K "Lost Pet Watch." Tonight we are telling you about three missing pets.
	Blacky is a black-and-white kitten, six months old, who ran away from her owner, Mrs. Lincoln. Her house is next to the high school.
Male Announcer:	And then, Oxen, a large German Shepherd, is a guide dog for John Wilson who's been blind since birth. Mr. Wilson cannot get around without his dog. Oxen was last seen running through the Green Acres neighborhood. He's wearing a black collar and has a big scar over his left eye.
	Also, Winston, a wire-haired terrier, was taken from Mrs. Thompson's back yard. Winston is a prize-winning purebred worth about $3,000.
Female Announcer:	If you have any information, please call our studio at 1-800-PET-HELP. The police station no longer handles missing animal reports. The animal shelter's phone is broken and won't be repaired for a week.
	Stay tuned for news here at 103.7.
Narrator:	Part 1.
Male Professor:	This evening I am going to talk about product placement. Product placement is probably one of the most important concepts I will cover this semester. In the United States special care is taken when placing items in different parts of the supermarket. For example, candy is generally placed next to the cashier or check-out counter. This is because customers are often likely to grab a candy bar while waiting in line. Children, who are waiting in line with their parents, often pester their parents to buy candy for them. Another example has to do with the placement of expensive products.
	Oh – Let me turn that off…
Narrator:	Part 2.
Male Professor:	Now where was I… Right —
	Well, many stores in the U.S., not all, will place expensive products at eye level. Imported shampoos, for example, are placed at a level where they are clearly visible and people can easily reach for them. Please note that I am not supporting or endorsing cheap items over expensive ones. Before we end this evening, I want to talk about your next assignment.
	Though you might not think of it as homework, I expect each of you to go to a large supermarket before next Tuesday to see where the over-the-counter medicine is placed. I look forward to hearing about your findings in a week.

PLACEMENT Test Audioscripts — Listening/Speaking

Narrator: The final selection.

Female Professor: Hello, class. Today we're going to be talking about folk wisdom.

Every culture has many sayings that give advice about life. These sayings are part of what is commonly called "folk wisdom." Of course, folk wisdom is also expressed in other ways, such as myths, fairy tales, legends, and songs. Often, however, folk wisdom is shared in the form of short sayings about the best ways to approach life's joys and sorrows.

Today, we'll look at some of the humorous sayings of three famous Americans: Benjamin Franklin, Abraham Lincoln, and Mark Twain. Then I'll ask you to share some examples of folk wisdom from your own communities.

One characteristic of American folk wisdom is its humor. Humor makes the bitter medicine of life easier to swallow.

Ben Franklin was the first of many Americans to be admired for his humorous folk wisdom. Franklin himself loved to have fun. He liked to eat a lot, drink a lot, and be merry, but he always told others to practice moderation.